HALLOWED BE THY NAME

HALLOWED BE THY NAME

The Starr System of Numerology

SECOND EDITION

Dyan Starr

Exact Rush Multimedia Publishing
Exact Rush, LLC.
353 W. Greensboro Ct.
Boise, ID 83706

Exact Rush Multimedia Publishing and the Exact Rush logo
are trademarks of Exact Rush, LLC.

Second Edition: 2025
Copyright © Dyan Starr, 2024

Cover Design: Exact Rush, LLC.
Cover Image © Exact Rush, LLC.

All rights reserved. No part of this publication may be reproduced or transmitted in any form or by any means, electronic or mechanical, including photocopying, recording, or any information storage or retrieval system, without prior permission in writing from the publishers.

Exact Rush, LLC. does not have control over, or responsibility for, any third-party websites referred to or in this book. All internet addresses given in this book were correct at the time of going to press. The author and publisher regret any inconvenience caused if addresses have changed or sites have ceased to exist, but can accept no responsibility for any such changes.

Library of Congress Control Number: 2025907130

ISBN: 979-8-9898235-4-3

*To Cassy, Dillon, Audrey, and Amari,
my constant source of unconditional love.*

Contents

PART ONE: The Starr System   11

What Is Numerology?	13
The Roots of Numerology	15
The History of Numbers	17
The Geometry of Numbers	19
The History of Zero	21
The History of Tarot	23
The Alphabetic Lexicon of Numerology	25
Your Frequency Chart	37
Your Guide to Tarot Numbers 1-78	40
Guidelines	43
Heart Number	48
Personality Number	53
Destiny Number	58
A Brief Guide to Understanding Karma	64
Practice	67
Your Spiritual Path	69
Pinnacles	72
Challenges	81
Polarity	84
Personal Year	89
Personal Month	94
Personal Day	98
Putting It All Together	101
Compatibility	104
The Quickie	107
The Ultimate Cure for Road Rage	109

PART TWO: The Delineations — 111

Section One: The Major Arcana — 113

1: The Magician — 115
2: The High Priestess — 119
3: The Empress — 125
4: The Emperor — 129
5: The Hierophant — 133
6: The Lovers — 137
7: The Chariot — 141
8: Strength — 146
9: The Hermit — 150
10: The Wheel of Fortune — 154
11: Justice — 158
12: The Hanged Man — 162
13: Death — 166
14: Temperance — 170
15: The Devil — 174
16: The Tower — 178
17: The Star — 183
18: The Moon — 188
19: The Sun — 192
20: Judgment — 196
21: The World — 199
22: The Fool — 203

Section Two: The Wands — 207

23: King of Wands — 208
24: Queen of Wands — 211
25: Knight of Wands — 214
26: Page of Wands — 217
27: Ace of Wands — 220

28: Two of Wands	223
29: Three of Wands	226
30: Four of Wands	229
31: Five of Wands	232
32: Six of Wands	236
33: Seven of Wands	239
34: Eight of Wands	242
35: Nine of Wands	245
36: Ten of Wands	248
Section Three: The Cups	251
37: King of Cups	252
38: Queen of Cups	254
39: Knight of Cups	257
40: Page of Cups	260
41: Ace of Cups	263
42: Two of Cups	266
43: Three of Cups	269
44: Four of Cups	272
45: Five of Cups	275
46: Six of Cups	278
47: Seven of Cups	281
48: Eight of Cups	284
49: Nine of Cups	287
50: Ten of Cups	290
Section Four: The Swords	293
51: King of Swords	294
52: Queen of Swords	297
53: Knight of Swords	300
54: Page of Swords	303
55: Ace of Swords	306

56: Two of Swords   309
57: Three of Swords   313
58: Four of Swords   316
59: Five of Swords   319
60: Six of Swords   322
61: Seven of Swords   325
62: Eight of Swords   328
63: Nine of Swords   331
64: Ten of Swords   334

Section Five: The Pentacles   337

65: King of Pentacles   338
66: Queen of Pentacles   341
67: Knight of Pentacles   344
68: Page of Pentacles   346
69: Ace of Pentacles   349
70: Two of Pentacles   352
71: Three of Pentacles   355
72: Four of Pentacles   358
73: Five of Pentacles   361
74: Six of Pentacles   364
75: Seven of Pentacles   367
76: Eight of Pentacles   370
77: Nine of Pentacles   372
78: Ten of Pentacles   374

About the Author   377

PART ONE:
The Starr System

What Is Numerology?

Everything, every name, every birthdate, has an energy, a unique frequency. We quantify this frequency using numbers. In essence, numerology is the translation of names, birthdates, and words into numbers. Each number, you see, holds its own specific meaning and position within your unique chart.

Why do names matter so much? From the perspective of numerology, the name given at birth – specifically the name on your birth certificate – establishes the blueprint for your life. This is your soul contract, your spiritual itinerary for this earthly journey. When you change your name, it doesn't negate your previous name; instead, it adds a new chapter, a different route on your life map.

When you translate your birthdate, you reveal the spiritual path you've chosen for this lifetime. You easily see your aspirations, the four major life schools or "pinnacles" you've selected, and how your energy ebbs and flows with each passing day, month, and year.

Mathematics provide us with insights into realms as varied as black holes, quantum physics, and artificial intelligence. Yet, some find it hard to accept numerology as a legitimate tool for self-discovery – even though its calculations are rooted in basic mathematical principles. Pythagoras, revered as the "Father of Numbers," once stated that we are all "manifestations of diversity in a unified continuum."

The significance of numbers is startlingly precise. Change just one digit in a phone number, and you're connected to a completely different person. Each of us has chosen our own unique experiences for specific lessons about love, forgiveness, and gratitude. Barbara Colgan, a true humanitarian, summarized it best: "You have three jobs here in this lifetime: Unconditional love, forgiveness, and gratitude. And that's it!"

As you explore this book and construct your own Starr chart, the meanings of the numbers remain constant; what changes is their placement within your chart. Leonardo da Vinci said, "One can have no smaller or greater mastery than mastery of oneself." If we are investing the effort to be born, why not mine this life for all its worth, challenging ourselves at the deepest levels?

The Roots of Numerology

The tapestry of numerology is as ancient as it is enigmatic. Its beginnings are shrouded in the mists of history, a spectral figure floating through time. Long before Pythagoras, the mathematician who formalized its principles, this esoteric art thrived in the civilizations of Egypt, Babylon, and China.

According to Britannica.com, Pythagoras, born around 570 BCE in Samos, Greece, was a philosopher and mathematician. Crucially, he was the founder of the Pythagorean Brotherhood – a fraternity that combined religious beliefs with groundbreaking principles, leaving an indelible mark on Western philosophy and mathematics. Pythagoras was, in a very real sense, the Father of Numerology.

While documented origins are sparse, our understanding of numerology is deepened by Manly P. Hall's *The Secret Teachings of All Ages*. It narrates a tale of Pythagoras' parents, Mnesarchus and Parthenis, consulting the Oracle of Delphi for guidance. The oracle foretold the birth of a son, exceptional in wisdom and beauty, destined to profoundly impact humanity. So impactful was this prophecy that Mnesarchus changed his wife's name to Pythasis, in tribute to the Pythian priestess.

Pythagoras himself declared that, "...number is the ruler of forms and ideas and the cause of gods and daemons." But, following the First Council of Nicaea in 325 A.D., numerology faced a grim chapter. Classified as civil violations, numerology and other mystical arts were denounced by the Roman Empire as devilish. Yet, it survived. The Christian science of Gematria flourished, because early biblical texts were written in Greek and Hebrew, languages where letters had numerical values. Priests like Dorotheus of Gaza kept numerology alive within the confines of Christianity, examining "sacred numbers" through a theological lens.

In literature, Sir Thomas Browne's 1658 discourse, "The Garden of Cyrus," reveals how numerology, specifically the number five, is woven into the arts and nature. Ganeshspeaks.com elaborates that even in modernity, the Chaldean System, rooted in ancient Babylon and Egypt, reverberates through our understanding of numbers and life. China, Rome, and Japan, too, offer evidence that this fascination with numerology is as ancient as it is universal.

So, as we trace the footprints of numerology across civilizations and centuries, one realization stands paramount: The essence of numbers is, perhaps, as old as human curiosity itself.

The History of Numbers

In *The Universal History of Numbers*, Georges Ifrah exclaims that numbers are not mere abstractions; they are drenched in the very essence of human storytelling. They serve as vessels for myths and legends, marking the shared cultural heritage of our species.

Youtube's SciShow delves into the mesmerizing tale of Abu Abdullah Muhammad ibn Musa al-Khawarizmi, colloquially known as al-Khawarizmi. Born around 780 AD in what is contemporary Uzbekistan, he is the linchpin in the narrative of modern arithmetic. His first significant role was as an instructor at Baghdad's House of Wisdom, one of antiquity's grandest academies. Here, al-Khawarizmi found that Ptolemy's celestial calculations were flawed. Driven by meticulous rigor, he revised them in a seminal work, "The Face of the Earth," which included charts to track lunar phases and planetary movements. These calculations were so accurate that centuries later they found their way into Latin and Chinese texts, making rounds globally.

But al-Khawarizmi's ultimate passion was mathematics. Eagerly accepting a mandate from Muslim leaders, he composed an accessible guide for the public, aptly named, *The Compendious Book on Calculation by Completion and Balancing*. This text showcased elementary calculations vital for trade and measurements. During his research, al-Khawarizmi stumbled upon ancient Indian manuscripts on numerals. His exposition on Hindu mathematics proved revolutionary. Centuries later, an English monk found his text, translated it, and thus, al-Khawarizmi morphed into "algorithme," simplifying math and numerology far beyond the convoluted Roman numerals.

In a curious turn of events, Florence, Italy, in 1299, outlawed Arabic numerals. The reason? They were deceptively simple to alter – a mere stroke could change a '6' into an '8'. Interestingly, these so-called "Arabic" numbers were, in truth, of Hindu origin.

The Geometry of Numbers

Imagine a single dot – like the period that ends this sentence. It embodies One, The Magician, a universe teeming with limitless potential and possibility. It heralds the inception of life cycles, both corporeal and spiritual, laying the groundwork for the ego to emerge.

Introduce a second dot, and you now have a line – a symbolic journey between two points. This line encapsulates the duality in our world: good and evil, power and force, light and dark, the profound yin and yang balance teetering on this thin string of existence.

Introduce a third dot, and you've created a triangle. This sacred geometry sings hymns of harmony, creativity, and fertility. It stands as a beacon of holy trinity – Father, Son, and Holy Spirit – and represents a communion of energies that fosters wishes and dreams.

Add a fourth dot, and the shape transcends into the third dimension – a pyramid. Four represents not just a number, but a framework. Herein lies the cornerstone of law, justice, and order. The four elements – earth, air, water, and fire – coalesce to manifest a world with windows into the future and doorways into alternate dimensions.

With five dots, a pentagon emerges. This shape can signify both sanctuary and subversion: it's a home, a church, and also an emblem found in the underbelly of secret societies. It is the balance of five virtues against five vices, the physical manifestation of our freedom and dexterity expressed through fingers and toes.

Move to six dots and the Star of David forms, its intersecting triangles whispering the ancient hermetic principle: "As above, so below." According to Britannica, the number six is considered "perfect," as it equals both the sum and the product of its divisors – 1, 2, and 3.

Reach seven, and you harmoniously blend the square's materialism with the triangle's spirituality. This number has long captivated minds, from Pythagorean musings to medieval education systems. Seven distinct notes make up a musical scale, culminating in the celestial eighth note – the octave.

Speaking of eight, it's a cube in a symbolic dance with another square. It represents mastery over the physical realm, echoing ancient Babylonian myth where the eighth realm was a paradise where gods resided.

Finally, nine – a triad of trinities. It's the culmination of earthly experiences distilled into the nectar of wisdom. Here, the gnostic reaches an impersonal life, detached, yet deeply insightful.

The History of Zero

The distance between zero and one is infinite. Zero is Nothing-ness, a void, and yet from it comes all of creation. In numerology, zero represents God, Divine protection, ten times the number immediately to its left. Every time we see the number zero, there is always divine protection associated with it. Zero represents infinity. It is cyclical. We can write it repeatedly without lifting the pen. This also represents our opportunity to incarnate and reincarnate, as many times as it takes. There is no beginning and no end in the zero. Zero represents the alpha and the omega.

Robert Kaplan stated in *The Nothing That Is: A Natural History of Zero*, "If you look at zero you see nothing; but look through it and you will see the world."

"Seek ye first the kingdom of heaven and all will be given unto you."

I had thought the earliest known recording of zero dated from the 9th century because that's where zero was engraved in a small temple in central India. Zero was used as a place holder for the purpose of knowing how much soil and how many roses or flowers needed to be planted. But then Y*outube*, "When Zero Was First Discovered, Science Museum," the Bakhshali Manuscript gives a new answer. It originates in India. According to Marcus du Sautoy, professor of mathematics at Oxford University:

> One of the things zero gave rise to was the ability for the common person to do mathematics. Before we had an idea of zero, calculations were done on an abacus. It was hard to record what was happening, and it meant that

mathematics was in the power of the authorities, those who could do math. Suddenly with zero, we were able to record what was happening and it sort of democratized mathematics…And why this Bakhshali manuscript is so important is this seems to be the first place we see this idea of zero beginning to be born.

The zero first started as a dot, then it later opened up. The Bakhshali manuscript was finally carbon dated. And the age of the manuscript is third to fourth century.

The following excerpt is, to date, the best example of the meaning of zero, as zero is said to represent nothing, the void, starting out as a mere placeholder: From *The Book of Five Rings* by Miyamoto Musashi, "What is called the spirit of the void is where there is nothing. It is not included in man's knowledge. Of course, the void is nothingness. By knowing things that exist, you can know that which does not exist. That is the void... In the void is virtue, and no evil. Wisdom has existence, principle has existence, the Way has existence, spirit is nothingness."

The History of Tarot

Tarot cards – every flip of the card, a glimpse into an unfathomable universe. The enigma begins with their murky origins. Manly P. Hall, in his seminal work, *The Secret Teachings of All Ages*, illuminates the debate swirling around their advent. Were they smuggled into Europe from the mystic East by the Knights Templar? Did they arrive courtesy of wandering Gypsies, their futures as nebulous as the cards they dealt?

Many speculate that the Tarot's arcane symbols were part of a concealed wisdom acquired by the Templars from either the Saracens or Syria's flourishing mystical sects. To dodge persecution, these chivalric warriors smuggled these pictorial leaves into Europe, masking their esoteric essence behind the facade of a gambling pastime. Mrs. John King Van Rensselaer supports this narrative, affirming that returning warriors, infatuated by Oriental mysticism, carried these cards as cultural souvenirs.

Then come the Gypsies, the nomadic guardians of the Tarot's ancient Egyptian roots. Samuel Roberts, in his remarkable tome *The Gypsies*, offers ample evidence for this. This wandering tribe, described in English laws of Henry VIII's era as an "outlandish people," preserved the remnants of the Serapeum in Alexandria. This hidden knowledge manifested as the Book of Enoch or Thoth, morphing over time into the Tarot deck we know today. Their perpetual pilgrimage across the Earth makes them living vessels of arcane wisdom, their heritage shrouded in magic and enigma.

The etymology of the word 'Tarot' itself is swathed in mystery. Count de Gebelin posits it originates from two Egyptian words: "Tar," meaning 'road,' and "Ro," meaning 'royal.'

Hence, the Tarot serves as the "royal road to wisdom."

Mitch Horowitz, a modern historian, provides a contrasting lens. He traces the earliest known Tarot decks to 15th century Northern Italy where they featured as whimsical items in a game, a precursor to modern bridge. These early decks adorned with emblems of hope, death, and empresses then migrated to Southern France. By the early 1500s, Marseilles emerged as a hub of Tarot production.

Eliphas Lévi, a pivotal figure born Alphonse Louis Constant, added another layer of complexity in 1854. With his book *The Doctrine and Ritual of High Magic*, he cemented the Tarot's association with Hebrew alphabets, Kabbalah, and celestial bodies – integrating it into the complex cosmogony of the occult.

The Tarot, then, is more than a deck of cards; it's an evolving tapestry of philosophy, mysticism, and divine understanding – continuously enriched by cultures and interpretations, each adding threads to this intricate weave.

The Alphabetic Lexicon of Numerology

The chart below serves as your foundational guide for translating every letter of the alphabet into its numeric counterpart:

1	2	3	4	5	6	7	8	9
A	B	C	D	E	F	G	H	I
J	K	L	M	N	O	P	Q	R
S	T	U	V	W	X	Y	Z	

Unpacking the Columns

The first letter of your name has great significance as well as the first vowel of your name. Check out the following for a brief breakdown of each letter:

Column 1: A, J, S - Think independence, inventor, new, possibilities, the beginning of the cycle of incarnation and reincarnation, birth, starting. For Yes, press one. Innovative. The challenge aspects of the 1 column are arrogance, bossiness, inability to be motivated.

'A' is very focused, closed off from above with much to accomplish. It represents the Alpha and the Omega, the beginning and the end. The line straight across the A represents a bridge connecting the earthly realm to the spiritual realms. 'A' is related to the Akashic records. From Wisdomtavern.com, "According to esoteric school, the first letter that God designed was 'A,' meaning Aleph in Hebrew and Alif in Arabic. It is necessary to breathe out (F) when we pronounce its sound. Thus, it represents the breath of God. Aleph is both life and breath. The letter A represents 'ruach' in Hebrew, 'prana' in Sanskrit, 'pneuma' in Greek, and 'spiritus' in Latin. Aleph symbolizes the oxhead and its astrological sign is Taurus, which is the symbol of physical reproduction. The oxhead is a symbolic representation of the uterus with the horns being the fallopian tubes. Altogether, the letter A represents physical reproduction." Many alphabets begin with the letter 'A.'

'J' represents justice, joy, Jupiter, journey. Being rounded and open at the bottom, 'J' always likes to see all sides before passing any judgment. From Hiddensignificance.com, "The letter 'J' originates from the Hebrew script. It was originally called 'Yod,' which means 'hand.' In ancient times, people believed that the hand was an extension of one's will and power. Consequently, the Yod symbolizes the divine connection between humanity and God. In medieval Europe, the letter 'J' evolved into its modern form. The upper part of the letter is reminiscent of the cross, while the lower part represents the womb or earthly realm where creation takes place. This duality further highlights the spiritual significance of the letter 'J.' In Christian tradition, the letter 'J' symbolizes Jesus Christ. As a personal savior, Jesus extends his hand to humanity, offering salvation and a connection to God. The lower part of the letter 'J' represents the human realm where Christ's sacrifice took place to reconcile humans with their Creator.

Note the S is twisted showing an intriguing journey that is not a straight line, but having some fascinating twists and turns along the way. Being the 19th letter of the alphabet, or The Sun, it represents the element of fire along with the stars.

From WisdomTavern.com, "According to esoteric Egyptian teachings, the letter 'S' is spiritually symbolic of the sacred serpents (asps) of Isis. As Isis is the 'double-wise' goddess, she is usually depicted with 2 serpents on both sides, representing the duality principle of nature. Resurrect Isis said that the serpent 'hisses' to produce sound 's.' Therefore, Isis's name comes from the double 'hiss' sound of the serpent. This can explain why when we add 'S' after a noun in English, it becomes 'two or more' nouns. This concept resembles the 'double- wisdom' of Isis."

Column 2: B, K, T - the microcosm, the world of the unseen, Press 2 for No, listen, the mystical, unseen, intuitive, duality, poetic, artistic, quiet, the spirit realm. Virgin. Look but don't touch. The challenging aspects of the 2 column are moodiness and painful shyness.

Note the 'B' as being closed off, being a collector, such as a honeybee literally collecting and redistributing pollen in order to make honey, or Elizabeth Barret Browning collecting words and creating her classic poetry. 'B' represents breast, birth, body. It is the nurturing mother breastfeeding her baby. 'B' gives birth to that which is sacred and secret. Blood holds secrets and DNA.

'K' being the 11th letter of the alphabet represents light, the mystical, kinetics, kinesiology, kindness, the ability and knowledge to scientifically evaluate the world of the unseen and translate the spiritual realm into usable information. 'K' represents the Kundalini energy, the coiled serpent achieving transformation. In old Semitic scripts, 'K' represented hand derived from the word "Kaph." Kung- fu, karma, king and koi fish all represent the energy of the 'K.'

'T' is the cross, the reminder to lay our burdens down, let go. The 20th letter of the alphabet, this represents secrets, that which was long thought dead comes back to life again. Crossroads, big life decisions, maintaining balance, truth, Tarot, caduceus. In science, the letter 'T' is often used as a variable to represent temperature or the passage of time. Writing, words, and diplomacy are part of 'T,' or Thoth, the Egyptian god of writing, knowledge, and the moon. He was also the patron of scribes and the inventor of hieroglyphs.

Column 3: C, L, U - Almost spelling "Clue," harmonizing, blending, fertile, seen and heard, socializing, communicating, artistic, creative, fashion, beauty, triple threat - Father, Son and Holy Spirit. The challenging aspects of the 3 column are tendency to be a shopaholic, a gossip.

'C' being the third letter of the alphabet or The Empress, representing the curve of the pregnant empress's belly, nurturing, pregnancy, fertility, the crescent moon and cycles. The 'C' holds and nurtures, then gives birth with divine timing in all things. 'C' communicates and is very creative, curvy. Cosmic consciousness. 'C' loves beauty, the arts, fine food and wine, culinary cuisine.

'L' is love, loyalty, law. The 12th letter of the alphabet, or The Hanged Man, being of service through love. The shape of 'L' is open and listens, leads by example. Around 1800 BC, a hook- shaped letter called "El" emerged in ancient Semitic inscriptions. "El" means "God."

'U,' the 21st letter of the alphabet, 21 being The World, goes deep, underground, holding. It is deeply emotional, spiritual, unique. In Vaishnavism, it symbolizes the soul's dependency on the Lord. Biblically, 'U' stands for unleavened. The 'U' explores the depths and the unseen, sharing only that which stands the test of light. The depth of this mystical letter is seen in its shape. It resembles a tuning fork. It represents unity, united. In physics it denotes the sign of potential energy.

Column 4: D, M, V - Reflects the DMV: laws, rules, and regulation, system, structure, order, military, discipline, budget, athletic. The challenging aspects of the 4 column are stubbornness, slow to change, obstinate, bossy, mean, and overbearing.

'D' is thought to have originated as a picture of a door, and is derived from the Semitic letter daleth. 'D' represents stability, practicality, hard work, and structure. It is the fourth letter of the alphabet, or The Emperor, who is married to our Empress (3). The Emperor sticks to a budget, has been to school and values justice, order, logic, discipline, exercise, outdoors, law. It represents death (transformation), destiny, duality, divine wisdom, and the door to higher consciousness, as well as domination.

'M' is mother, the 13th letter of the alphabet representing the Christ consciousness and is capable of climbing the highest heights while at the same time being grounded and firmly planted in Mother Earth. The letter 'M' comes from the Egyptian Hieroglyph for water, waters of wisdom, the Torah. The Romans used the 'M' to represent the number 1000. Our current 'M' started out as the Egyptian hicroglyph for "owl." 'M' represents strength, stability, strong work ethic, symmetry, new beginnings as well as mountains, challenges and obstacles, the balance between sacred masculine and feminine energies within you, part of the sacred sound of Om.

Column 5: E, N, W - Rearrange them to spell "NEW," emblematic of the five energy, sensuality, sexuality, jack-of-all trades, dexterous, master of one's lower self. The challenging aspect of the 5 column is addiction, food, sex, gambling, drugs, jack-of-all trades, yet master of none.

'E' represents eternity and everlasting life, endurance, earth, emotions and ethics, expansion, enlightenment. Being the fifth letter of the alphabet, it represents man mastering his lower self. From TempleStudy.com: Learn how the letter 'E' may have started as a picture sign of a man with arms upraised, meaning " joy" or "rejoice" in Egyptian and Semitic writing. 'E' energy is mentally quick, witty, sharp and represents the all seeing eye.

'N' is straight up and sharply angled. Nourishment, new, renewal and transformation, need to verify and experience. 'N' is unapologetically open from above as well as open from below and seeks first sensuality, duality, then masters the self and seeks the spiritual. With sharp angles, there can be sudden and sharp ascent or descent depending on free will. 'N' seeks knowledge. The Angel of Temperance vibrates to 14 which takes anger and rage, puts it in the holy fire of transformation and elevates the emotions to their highest form of compassion.

'W' has very high and steep walls to climb, such as overcoming an addiction. 'W' is the 23rd letter of the alphabet, King of Wands, which is divine protection. Wet and water, witch, werewolves, wisdom, wanting, world, world wide web, war, war of the worlds, wish, whale. The energy of 'W' is expansive, all encompassing. When the journey is steep and seemingly impossible to climb, the 'W' finds a way by connecting with the wisdom of the world, or cosmic consciousness.

Column 6: F, O, X - An easy mnemonic, as in the sly Fox, commitment, family, long- term goals, pillar of the community. Each of these letters, F, O, X, is a pillar of the community, nurturing, supporting. At its worst, it's bondage, energy vampire, controlling.

'F,' flamboyant, father, finesse, flow, family, fertility, faith, fair, forgiveness, freedom, female, fortune. 'F' is the 6th letter of the alphabet, The Lovers, feather of Maat, the Egyptian goddess and her feather of truth. From HiddenSignificance.com: The letter 'F' is often associated with transformation, as it resembles a butterfly in flight or an upward-facing triangle, representing the ascension of consciousness and self-awareness. In many cultures, the butterfly symbolizes metamorphosis and the ability to break free from one's past, much like the letter 'F' encourages us to let go of limiting beliefs and patterns that no longer serve us. In alchemy, the letter 'F' is often used as a symbol for fire or the element of transformation. Fire was believed to purify and refine substances, much like our thoughts and emotions can be refined through spiritual practice and self-awareness. The letter 'F' is also associated with the planet Mars, which represents energy, drive, and ambition.

'O' is the 15th letter of the alphabet and is completely closed in perfectly within itself. It holds and nurtures. As the 15th letter or The Devil, 'O' seeks to discern if the relationship we hold near and dear is loving and supporting or if we are held in bondage and servitude. 'O' sees into the void. Optimist, occult, overt, Om, oxygen, oracle, owl, omnipotence. From Etymonline.com: 'O,' the fifteenth letter of the alphabet, originated from a Phoenician symbol for "eye" and became a vowel in Greek. Our eyes have an 'O' shape. It's what we say in an exclamation of pain, or curiosity. 'O' is a pillar of the community, nurturing, supporting. At its worst, it's bondage, energy vampire, controlling.

'X' is open from above and below, or reaching the highest heights and at the same time being tempted from the lowest depths, eventually finding balance in the center. The historic figure who resonates most with the letter 'X' is Malcolm X who strayed in his marriage and was fiercely protective of his family, both characteristics of 'X.' 'X' marks the spot. Or being done in relationship referring to an ex. The cross of St. Andrew. From WisdomOfTheSpirit.com: "The letter X holds deep spiritual significance, symbolizing transformation, choice, balance, and the gateway to higher consciousness. It represents the process of releasing the old and embracing change, the power of decision-making, the integration of opposites, and the connection between the physical and spiritual realms."

Column 7: G, P, Y - Close to spelling "Gypsy," an air of mystery, the realm of the spirit, silence, retreat, nature, water, the 7 Wonders of the World, psychic, quiet, spiritual wealth. This column needs alone time most to recharge away from people and loud noise. The column 7 challenges are dark moodiness, lethargy, pessimism, judgment, desire to disappear.

'G' is almost completely closed. The seventh letter of the alphabet, The Chariot in Tarot, the 'G' is secret and sacred as in the word God. 'G' requires water, quiet and alone time. Growth, guidance, grace, generosity, geometry, gnostic, Genesis, garden. 'G' is a silent letter at times, and holds secrets. From GnosticWarrior.com: Therefore, the letter 'G' in Freemasonry signifies Gnosis, Generation and the Grand Architect. Gnosis (Greek for knowledge) in its simplest form is "knowledge of thyself" or the Great Arcanum, Daath

(Da'ath - Hebrew for knowledge). Philo also refers to the "knowledge" (gnosis) and "wisdom" (sophia) of God. This fact we find in the biblical passage Proverbs 2.6; "The Lord gives wisdom (sophia), from his face come knowledge (gnosis) and understanding (sunesis). Generation (from the Latin generare, meaning "to beget"), also known as procreation in biological sciences, is the act of producing offspring. Hence, it is from the blood that Gnosis or knowledge is transmuted through the act of procreation that then passes the knowledge encrypted within our DNA to our offspring.

'P,' the 16th letter of the alphabet, or The Tower in Tarot, represents sudden illumination and the falling down or destruction of that which has not been based on a solid foundation. 'P' is present, provocative, peaceful, playful, paradise, philosophy, philanthropy, pain, punishment, can be pouty, pious, parasitic. Round at the top, 'P' holds knowledge and narrowly focuses that information straight down to the base, sharing some of its secrets while holding onto most of them. From Coloringfolder.com: Like in Edgar Allan Poe's seminal horror story "The Pit and the Pendulum," where the 'P' in Pit emphasizes the feeling of being trapped and helpless. Overall, the letter 'P' symbolizes a spectrum of emotions and ideas, both good and bad, making it a powerful tool in the hands of writers and communicators.

'Y' open from above while being narrowly focused at the base. Pythagoras himself wanted to experience the mystical energy frequency of the letter 'Y,' so he temporarily changed his name to Yavanacharya. 'Y' being the 25th letter of the alphabet, or Knight of Wands in Tarot, this represents much work to be done on the spiritual plane, sometimes difficulty making decisions, but always connected to the divine guidance from above. 'Y' is a fork and a definite decision to be made as to which direction one should go. You are highly intuitive, prone to feeling everyone's emotions and energy. 'Y' loves secrets, mystery, sacred spaces and places and lots of water.

Column 8: H, Q, Z - Think of Halo, Queen, Zebra: strength personified, strength of the physical realm, financial wealth, physical strength such as athletes, body builders, executives, master organizers. Think of 800 phone numbers for business. HQ stands for headquarters, the hub of business and planning. The negative aspects are brutality, hostility, bullying, emotional disconnect.

'H' is hero, horse, help, heaven, home, humility, humbleness, harmony, Horus, hate, head, honesty and healing. It is symmetrical, a ladder. The above is a mirror of the below, or As above, So below. As within, so without. This is decidedly karmic giving you the test of your own personal strength, maintaining the balance of being assertive without becoming aggressive. From Worldhistoryedu.com: In the Egyptian pantheon, the god Horus was a very formidable and important deity. It was believed that his realm of control was the sky and the sun. As a result, Horus was commonly referred to as "The One Far Above." The Greeks, on the other hand, called him Heru or Har - which means "the Distant One." In some cases, Horus was also venerated as the god of war, hunting, and kingship. Largely considered as the chief protector of the land of Egypt, he was depicted by ancient Egyptians as a stoic man with the head of a hawk (or sometimes a lion). He became known in some spheres as the hawk god of Egypt.

'Q' is most definitely the queen, question, query, quality, quiet, quest, quantum, Quran. 'Q' is the 17th letter of the alphabet, or The Star in Tarot, representing the journey of the wise men with three gifts to welcome Jesus. You follow your own star, chart your own path and you are not deterred. The tail of the 'Q' shows buried secrets or delving into the occult. You can be quite headstrong, very independent. The roundness of the 'Q' shows a journey that comes full circle while being firmly grounded in mother earth. 'Q' is the divine feminine.

'Z' is the 26th and last letter of the alphabet, imbued with tremendous physical strength with sharp angles that zigzag. Zenith, zeal, zen, zero. This is the culmination of a journey or battle that gifts its bearer with tremendous strength and the ability to change course suddenly. 'Z' is not just physically strong, it is also deeply connected to the High Priestess aligned with the spiritual realm. 'Z' takes decisive action in particular to protect loved ones and will take up a sword without hesitation to do so. Interesting fact about zebras is they can run sideways, as protection while being chased. 'Z' represents a lightning bolt and the god Zeus, the sky and thunder god in ancient Greek religion and mythology, who rules as king of the gods on Mount Olympus. 'Z' in your name brings much authority, responsibility. The lightning bolt represents 'Z' and brings sudden illumination and awareness.

Column 9: I, R - The humanitarian pillars of the table. Every time we say "I," such as "I am happy" or "I am sad," because of the 9 Hermit energy, we are connecting ourselves to the realm of cosmic consciousness where all things are possible, the realm of all of humanity and the impersonal life that we are here learning about and gaining wisdom from. The Omega. "Press 9 to end this call," endings, reflection, wisdom.

'I' is the 9th letter of the alphabet, or The Hermit. Every time you say "I," you are instantly connecting to the cosmic consciousness where all things are possible, the place of all wisdom, knowledge. 'I' can be followed by infinite possibility such as "I am hungry, I am happy, I want to be an astronaut," etc. 'I' is limitless potential with you as the master manifester. 'I' demands no less than your all. There is no halfway with 'I.' It is straight up and down, focused on the journey of The Hermit. This is the perfectly imperfect impersonal life, journey of the self. I am that I am. From WisdomTavern.com: In Egyptian mysticism, the letter 'I' represents the Djed, symbolizing the backbone of Osiris. It is our spinal column where if we raise the kundalini serpents from the base of our spine, we will " resurrect the dead," which are the inactivated chakras in our body.

'R' is the 18th letter of the alphabet and as such is ruled by The Moon. It takes any experience deeper. Just add "er" to an adjective and you get more of it, thus emphasizing the need for deeper connections. This is an emotional energy as the subconscious, ruled by the moon, comes alive at night and seeks to delve deep into the subconscious abyss, bravely embracing the outcome. 'R' resonates and harmonizes. The top of the 'R' is closed off from above, yet open from below showing the courage needed to experience the depths of the soul.

Memorizing this chart equips you to translate any word, phrase, or name into a numeric value. Each column tells a story, beckoning you into the transformative world of Numerology.

Your Frequency Chart

Unlocking the frequencies in Numerology isn't just a game of raw numbers; it's a nuanced dance between essence and expression. Understanding the base frequencies elevates your interpretation from rudimentary to nuanced.

As you study the Starr chart method, you will see why the tarot and numerology are made for each other, inextricably connected. In tarot we benefit from the 78 powerful represented archetypes. In utilizing these powerful archetypes in their rightful place in numerology, we take numerology to an entirely different level.

For example, take the number 1, The Magician, and compare this to its shared frequency numbers from the previous chapter: the experience of 1, The Magician, compared to the 10 of The Wheel of Fortune. Then, compare that to the 73, or Five of Pentacles. As Pythagoras said, "We are all manifestations of diversity in a unified continuum." Just as 1, 10, and 73 are also manifestations of diversity in the same frequency. Clearly, the 1 from The Magician knows all things are possible, as The Magician is able to create something out of nothing and is beginning his journey of creation, while the 10 Wheel of Fortune has gained momentum and wisdom and due partly to luck and a large part on skill and knowledge gained, is now in a much better position to invest wisely and has turned his life and luck around for the better.

Compare those both to the 73, Five of Pentacles, which says feeling totally bankrupt on every level such as poor health or accident, loss of money or funds frozen as in a divorce or corporate takeover, possibly emotional breakdown, yet through all of this promises the new beginning always present at its base of one, the profound opportunity to find one's greatest strength in the most challenging of circumstances; and, in fact, without all the turmoil, the ability to extend compassion to oneself then extend that same energy to others, would certainly not be present. Thus, it becomes obvious that in the classical traditional numerology, that I will always love as my first numerology teacher, we do not benefit at all when numbers continue to be reduced to their base frequency without even considering their profound and unique double-digit tarot archetype. It is then quite proper to ready not only the double-digit tarot archetype of each of your personal numbers, but its base single digit number as well.

With that in mind, here is the corresponding number for each of the 78 tarot archetypes:

Base Frequencies: The Major Arcana

Numbers 1-9 are the core, the so-called Major Arcana base numbers. These root frequencies inform and infuse every multi-digit number above 9. Take, for example, number 19, "The Sun." With basic arithmetic, we can reduce it: 1+9 equals 10, and 1+0 narrows it down to 1. So, "The Sun" shares the same vibrational frequency as 1, "The Magician." Whenever a number exceeds 9, explore its root base to gain a complete perspective.

Shared Frequency Lists by Base Number

Base 1: The Magician
- Numbers: 1, 10, 19, 28, 37, 46, 55, 64, 73

Base 2: The High Priestess
- Numbers: 2, 11, 20, 29, 38, 47, 56, 65, 74

Base 3: The Empress
- Numbers: 3, 12, 21, 30, 39, 48, 57, 66, 75

Base 4: The Emperor
- Numbers: 4, 13, 22, 31, 40, 49, 58, 67, 76

Base 5: The Hierophant
- Numbers: 5, 14, 23, 32, 41, 50, 59, 68, 77

Base 6: The Lovers
- Numbers: 6, 15, 24, 33, 42, 51, 60, 69, 78

Base 7: The Chariot
- Numbers: 7, 16, 25, 34, 43, 52, 61, 70

Base 8: Strength
- Numbers: 8, 17, 26, 35, 44, 53, 62, 71

Base 9: The Hermit
- Numbers: 9, 18, 27, 36, 45, 54, 63, 72

Keep this chart at your fingertips. When you encounter numbers, consider both the complex and the root, like a musician attentive to both melody and baseline. It will reveal the subtle frequencies in play – after all, in Numerology, resonance is everything.

Your Guide to Tarot Numbers 1-78

An essential tool for Tarot practitioners and enthusiasts alike, this chart lays down the numerical DNA for every Tarot card archetype, giving you a nuanced interpretative power.

Major Arcana: The Cosmic Blueprints

1. The Magician
2. The High Priestess
3. The Empress
4. The Emperor
5. The Hierophant
6. The Lovers
7. The Chariot
8. Strength
9. The Hermit
10. The Wheel of Fortune
11. Justice
12. The Hanged Man
13. Death
14. Temperance
15. The Devil
16. The Tower
17. The Star
18. The Moon
19. The Sun
20. Judgment
21. The World
22. The Fool

Minor Arcana: The Four Suits

Wands

Fire Element:
The Flame of Action

23. King of Wands
24. Queen of Wands
25. Knight of Wands
26. Page of Wands
27. Ace of Wands
28. Two of Wands
29. Three of Wands
30. Four of Wands
31. Five of Wands
32. Six of Wands
33. Seven of Wands
34. Eight of Wands
35. Nine of Wands
36. Ten of Wands

Cups

Water Element:
The Depth of Emotion

37. King of Cups
38. Queen of Cups
39. Knight of Cups
40. Page of Cups
41. Ace of Cups
42. Two of Cups
43. Three of Cups
44. Four of Cups
45. Five of Cups
46. Six of Cups
47. Seven of Cups
48. Eight of Cups
49. Nine of Cups
50. Ten of Cups

Swords	**Pentacles**
Air Element:	Earth Element:
The Clarity of Thought	The Substance of Life

51. King of Swords	65. King of Pentacles
52. Queen of Swords	66. Queen of Pentacles
53. Knight of Swords	67. Knight of Pentacles
54. Page of Swords	68. Page of Pentacles
55. Ace of Swords	69. Ace of Pentacles
56. Two of Swords	70. Two of Pentacles
57. Three of Swords	71. Three of Pentacles
58. Four of Swords	72. Four of Pentacles
59. Five of Swords	73. Five of Pentacles
60. Six of Swords	74. Six of Pentacles
61. Seven of Swords	75. Seven of Pentacles
62. Eight of Swords	76. Eight of Pentacles
63. Nine of Swords	77. Nine of Pentacles
64. Ten of Swords	78. Ten of Pentacles

Let this guide serve as a numerical compass for your Tarot journeys. Navigate the vast landscape of symbolic meanings, from cosmic lessons to elemental truths, each with their own numerical resonance. Whether it's the magical beginnings of The Magician or the earthly accomplishments of Ten of Pentacles, you'll find a deep well of knowledge in each number.

Guidelines

Every individual name encodes sacred contracts – unwritten agreements concerning our heart, destiny, and personality. For a nuanced reading, you must first analyze each name individually to obtain subtotals. Combine these subtotals to uncover the grand total, incorporating the first, middle, and last names.

Master numbers – 11, 22, 33, 44, 55, 66, 77, as well as 29, 38, 47, 56, 65, and 74, as each of these adds up to 11 – are double-edged swords. They embody both a challenge and a transformative opportunity. Depending on personal circumstances and free will, these numbers can manifest in their full challenge or as their base number. Take 22: it can be a challenging 22 or a foundational 4. Every master number, whether it be in your personal chart (heart, personality, destiny or spiritual path), or a temporary vibration (personal year, month, day, or pinnacle) always represents your own personal initiation into your Christ consciousness. Each of us has many of these opportunities throughout our lifetime and each occurrence provides us with the opportunity to expand our consciousness even further, every time. Nietzsche beautifully expresses this in his work from *Beyond Good and Evil*, "You must test yourself to see you are destined for independence and command and do it at the right time. You should not dodge your tests, though they may be the most dangerous game you could play and are tests that are taken in the end before no witness or judge but yourself." I would add a quote from my mom who said, "It is scary to listen to yourself, especially when yours is a lone voice; however, not to do so is even more scary."

Remember that we are all masters and no one escapes these profound opportunities. Whether these frequencies appear

temporarily in a pinnacle, year, month, or day, or show up in a subtotal or grand total of your heart, personality, destiny, or spiritual path number, always remember the following about master numbers: First, greater challenges; second, greater rewards; third, this is always a personal initiation to step even further into your own Christ consciousness;
fourth, it is always about love, forgiveness, and gratitude.

What if a name or phrase totals more than 78? Decompose the sum into its constituent numbers and consult the Tarot archetypes. For instance, with the number 185, analyze the 1 (The Magician), 8 (Strength), and 5 (The Hierophant). But also note the secondary sums – 18 (The Moon) and 85, which adds to 13 (Death). The grand total, 14, leads you to Temperance.

Your heart, personality, destiny, and spiritual path numbers, subtotals as well as grand totals are all your Personal Numbers as these numbers never change and are always the same calculation. Your pinnacles, personal years, personal months, and personal days are all temporary frequencies as there is a distinct start and stop date for these numbers.

Concerning spelling: every letter in a name or phrase alters its frequency. A misspelling isn't an error but a unique vibrational signature. If you've been spelling a word in a specific way, analyze that spelling to understand its unique energy and how it resonates with you. Remember, energy doesn't make mistakes.

As for titles and suffixes – Junior, Senior, Ms., Mrs., Dr. – they're not part of the core name and should be excluded from your calculations. The sole exception is nicknames, which offer insight into how others perceive you.

Always treat 'Y' as a vowel.

An important note in particular about the number 15, The Devil, as well as any other of the 78 delineations that appear to be a bit more challenging than other number delineations: This is a very powerful and wise archetype that does not represent the actual ruler of the underworld; rather it's a stunning opportunity to lift the veil of illusion and free ourselves from bondage, and hopelessness. When this shows up in the heart position (vowels), this individual will have a very profound opportunity with someone they likely have had one or more previous lifetimes with, to feel enslaved to the individual or to feel completely taken advantage of by them - Not as punishment, but, for whatever reason, I've noticed these individuals then have the best capacity for working in the areas of social work, social reform, helping others reclaim their humanity back.

If we see 15, the Devil as an individual's spiritual path number, they are here assisting all of us to break out of our own deceit, illusion, entrapment, or slavery. These people start or run homeless shelters or animal shelters, these people lead heroic rescue efforts to save others from cults. It is also possible these individuals run a cult as both the best and the worst of this frequency are both possible because of the divine law of free will. This is why the 15 gives us some of our most dynamic therapists or any profession dealing with the mind. No matter where this archetype shows up, it is always an incredible sign for the opportunity to free oneself and/or others from disillusionment and slavery. The same is also true of the numbers 45, Five of Cups, as well as 61, Seven of Swords, and 57, Three of Swords. Example, if 57, Three of Swords, is your spiritual path number, this does not ever mean you are doomed to a life of heartbreak, or that you must suffer more heartbreak than others; it means specifically that the heartbreak you experience activates the incredible gifts inherent in the 57. In a particular reading of a client, her spiritual path being 57, it turned out she was psychic (the 7 part of the 57) and had the incredible ability to separate emotions from fact. Because of this ability, she would be excellent assisting homicide detectives with her psychic abilities.

The reason behind every experience in life has to do with love, gratitude, or forgiveness. There is never an evil or dark purpose connected to anything we are here to learn. You chose your teachers. Remember, only love is real, all else is an illusion. This beautiful cyclic wheel some refer to as the mouse on the wheel is a Divine gift in that the wheel we run on is there for us for as long as we need it. You will see in the sections in this book on Personal year, personal month and personal day, the pattern of the numbers, the repeating that continues. Once we have received the gift from the lesson we chose for ourself, the next time we are in a similar cycle numerically, then we are in a position of teacher, having mastered the lesson.

Each tarot archetype has the potential for enlightenment or destruction because of the divine law of free will. Keep this in mind as you are studying your own chart as well as for anyone else's chart. As indicated above with regard to 15, the devil archetype, we see the divine purpose of this teacher as well. As you go through each of these archetypes, know that awareness, healing, gratitude and love are the purpose for every one of these.

In these guidelines, you'll find the roadmap to your numerological explorations. Each word, name, or phrase you choose to examine unfolds like a cosmic breadcrumb trail, leading you through the labyrinthine corridors of your destiny, heart, and spiritual path.

Heart Number

The Heart Number uncovers your natural passions and aptitudes, those extraordinary skills honed over multiple lifetimes. This innate prowess isn't just happenstance but the consequence of dedication across incarnations. Your closest circle might be privy to this quintessence of your being, while others may only see glimpses as it is mostly kept under lock and key. It takes about five lifetimes of study of the same subject to become an adept. See what your heart has been working on for lifetimes:

Sometimes your Heart Number shares territory with your Personality, Destiny, or Spiritual Path Number. When your Heart and Karma numbers coincide, it amplifies both your challenges and joys. Often seen in trailblazers and old souls, these numbers may summon mockery before they invite admiration, but they are indispensable to society.

If you're wondering how to calculate your Heart Number, it's derived from the vowels in your name. There are six vowels – A, E, I, O, U, Y. It is no coincidence that 6 is the Lovers, the heart being all about what we love. For illustration, let's consider "Lord Jesus Christ":

Heart Number Subtotals:

Always notate the heart number, vowels, above the word, name or phrase for visual clarity in this way:

$$\begin{array}{ccc} 6 & 5\,3 & 9 \\ \text{Lord} & \text{Jesus} & \text{Christ} \end{array}$$

Lord: 6 (The Lovers)
+
Jesus: 5+3=8 (Strength)
+
Christ: 9 (The Hermit)
=
Grand Total: 23 (King of Wands)

These subtotals shed light on the components of the grand Heart Number, revealing intricate details of each individual. The Tarot archetypes add another layer of understanding, making the reading both precise and multifaceted.

For example, the vowel O in "Lord" indicates the Lovers, encapsulating the essence of unconditional love. The vowels in "Jesus" resonate with the Strength card, pointing to mastery over the physical realm and the power of compassion. The "I" in "Christ" corresponds to the Hermit, a representation of an enlightened soul with hard-won wisdom. The grand total – King of Wands – embodies divine protection, a gift bestowed to all who seek it. Here's another example using the name "Roberta Joanne Schlender":

Heart Number Subtotals:

```
6 5 1    6 1 5      5 5
Roberta  Joanne  Schlender
```

Roberta: 6+5+1=12 (Hanged Man)
+
Joanne: 6+1+5=12 (Hanged Man)
+
Schlender: 5+5=10 (Wheel of Fortune)
=
Grand Total: 34 (Eight of Wands)

The pair of 12s in the first and middle names suggests expertise in two distinct areas nurtured over previous lifetimes. The Wheel of Fortune for the surname reflects a family of independent thinkers. These culminate in a Heart Number of 34, underlining a love for the non-mainstream and esoteric.

Understanding the subtotals illuminates how each contributes to the grand total of the Heart Number. These granular insights offer a multidimensional perspective into your being, like various threads weaving into the complex tapestry of your soul.

Your Heart Number: An Exercise

Intrigued by the arcane dance of numerology? The Heart Number is a profound cipher, offering glimpses into your emotional core and inner desires. Let's embark on this self-discovery. Ready your pen, a notepad, and a quiet space for contemplation.

Step 1: Your Full Name, Please

First, write your complete name as it appears on your birth certificate. Divide each part – first, middle, and last name – into separate sections. In this example, we'll use *Emily Rose Smith*, but encourage you to replace it with your own name and numerical values.

Step 2: Assign Values

Using a basic numerology chart, assign each letter a corresponding numerical value, noting the heart numbers directly above the name or phrase, and the personality numbers directly below:

Example:

```
5 9 7    6 5      9
Emily   Rose   Smith
  4 3    9 1   14 28
```

Step 3: Calculate Heart Number

To unearth your Heart Number, add together the vowels from each part of your name. This sum reveals your inner essence and emotional disposition.

Example:

Emily, 5+9+7 = 21, The World   Subtotal

Rose, 6+5   = 11, Justice   Subtotal

Smith, 9   = 9, The Hermit   Subtotal

21+11+9   = 41, Ace of Cups Grand Total

The subtotals are just as important as the grand totals because each experience of the sutotals supports the grand total.

Step 4: Grand Total Heart Number

Now, add together the subtotals to get the Grand Total Heart Number.

Example:

Grand Total Heart Number: 21 (Emily) + 11 (Rose) + 9 (Smith) = 41

Decoding Your Heart

With the Heart subtotals and grand total, read each of the numbers to decode the emotional facets of your life. 21 from Emily; 11 from Rose; 9 from Smith; and, 41 from the grand total. Do you notice any master numbers? What do these numbers suggest about your emotional vulnerabilities, passions, and instincts?

The Heart Number, like a backstage pass, grants you exclusive access to your inner self. A bit of arithmetic and introspection can reveal celestial wisdom. Now, it's your turn to decipher your own Heart Number and what it whispers about you.

Personality Number: A Subconscious Mask

Humility: I am God's gift to everyone in my life; everyone in my life is God's gift to me. We play or take on roles such as teacher/student or victim/perpetrator in all relationships in our lives. When we have played every role, then we have graduated.

The Personality Number is not just a numerical construct; it's a mask. This mask is the self you project to the world, revealing how people perceive you and the types of individuals you attract into your life. Calculated by adding up the numerical values of consonants in your name, it's a cipher for your social and interpersonal traits. Here are two examples:

The Case of Lord Jesus Christ

Let's consider the numbers beneath the iconic name "Lord Jesus Christ":

```
   6      5 3       9
  Lord   Jesus    Christ
  3 94   1 1 1    389 12
```

Lord: 3+9+4=16, represented by The Tower card
Jesus: 1+1+1=3, symbolized by The Empress card
Christ: 3+8+9+1+2=23, or the King of Wands

The Grand Total Personality Number: 42, captured in the Two of Cups.

The Tower, a card marked by disruptive transformation, might evoke the Crucifixion – an event of great intensity. The Empress, capturing a radiant and compelling orator, calls to mind Jesus' magnetic public persona. Meanwhile, the King of Wands represents divine protection, symbolizing Christ's role as a unifier of cultures and classes. The Grand Total, the Two of Cups, encapsulates Christ's essence of unconditional love.

Roberta Joanne Schlender: A Master of Trials

```
   6 5 1    61  5        5  5
   Roberta  Joanne    Schlender
   9 2 92   1   55     1383 54 9
```

Roberta: 9+2+9+2=22, embodied by The Fool card
Joanne: 1+5+5=11, reflected in the Justice card
Schlender: 1+3+8+3+5+4+9=33, mirrored in the Seven of Wands

Grand Total: 66, epitomized by the Queen of Pentacles.

Roberta's number sequence – 22, 11, 33 – are known as master numbers, each a trial in itself. She's had significant relationships with emotionally distant narcissists, and she, too, exhibited codependency. These relationships were classrooms; they taught her self-worth and assertiveness. The Grand Total, the Queen of Pentacles, manifests in her life quite literally. Roberta was a single mother and a court reporter for the LA County Superior Court for 27 years. Though she didn't particularly enjoy the profession, it provided a stable income.

Her Karma Number 7, subject for later discussion, implies her destiny was to be "seen, not heard."

Both cases show how Personality Numbers not only predict traits but sometimes foretell life experiences, sometimes down to the uncanniest details. It's not merely a game of numbers but a profound insight into one's existential DNA.

So, what's in your number?

An Interactive Exercise

Dive deeper into the narrative of your life by discovering your Personality Number. This particular cipher is a window into the social self you present to the world. Consider it your persona's unique fingerprint, revealing how others perceive you and the kind of people you attract.

Step 1: Your Full Name on Stage

Jot down your full name as it appears on your birth certificate, categorizing each part – first, middle, and last – into separate sections. In our exercise, we'll use *Emily Rose Smith* as our example. Like before, replace this generic name with your own name and corresponding numerical values.

Step 2: The Numeric Identity of Letters

Just like before, using a basic numerology chart, give each letter a corresponding number.

Example:

```
  5 9 7    6 5      9
  Emily    Rose    Smith
    4 3    9 1    14 28
```

Step 3: Unlocking the Personality Number

Now, for the Personality Number, focus only on the consonants. Add them together for each part of your name. The sum yields insights into your outward demeanor and the kinds of experiences and individuals you magnetize.

Example:

Emily, 4+3	= 7, The Chariot	Subtotal
Rose, 9+1	= 10, Wheel of Fortune	Subtotal
Smith, 1+4+2+8	= 15, Devil	Subtotal
7+10+15	= 32, Six of Wands	Grand Total

The Story Your Number Tells

With your Subtotals and Grand Total in hand, delve into the Tarot Archetypes or other numerology references to interpret the layers of your social self. Do you find master numbers? Whether or not you find them in your name, you are a master and you will experience the master number frequencies either from your name or your spiritual path number and most definitely in your temporary vibrations - i.e. a pinnacle of yours, a personal year, month, or day. No one escapes the beautiful and necessary self-mastery PhD of life. What secrets about your external persona do these digits unlock?

Your Personality Number is like the intriguing book cover that invites people to read your life's story. Now that you have the tools to calculate your own, what does your unique number reveal about you?

Destiny Number: The Blueprint of Our Life

The Destiny Number isn't just any ordinary digit, it's a guiding beacon. It represents your life's work – your purpose, your career, and what you leave behind after you depart from this world. Calculated by combining the Heart Number (vowels) and Personality Number (consonants), it offers clues that seem eerily precise in foretelling your professional journey.

The Archetypal Figure: Lord Jesus Christ

Destiny Subtotals:

```
   6      5 3     9
  Lord   Jesus  Christ
  3 94   1 1 1  389 12
```

Lord: 6+16 = 22, The Fool   Subtotal
Jesus: 8+3 = 11, Justice   Subtotal
Christ: 9+23 = 32, Six of Wands   Subtotal
            65, King of Pentacles
             Destiny Grand Total

The Grand Total Destiny Number?

65, symbolized by the King of Pentacles.

The destiny of Jesus is ripe with master numbers – 11 (Justice) and 22 (The Fool). Justice is the beacon of light and an emblem of karmic tests. Jesus offered humanity a path to self-trust by absorbing collective karma. The Fool epitomizes the timeless joy and work of a young journeyman, benefiting humanity eternally. The King of Pentacles, another King in Jesus's numerological profile, signifies a person of wealth and benevolence, much like a candle that continues to illuminate without ever depleting its own light. Different names may signify different energies, but the essence remains.

Roberta Joanne Schlender's Journey

Destiny Subtotals:

DESTINY:
Roberta,	12+22=34,	8 of Wands	Subtotal
Joanne,	12+11=23,	King of Wands	Subtotal
Schlender,	10+33=43,	3 of Cups	Subtotal

Grand Total   100

Her Grand Total Destiny Number?

An extraordinary 100.

Roberta's destiny number surpasses the Tarot's 78 archetypes, signaling an extraordinary journey. The individual digits – 1 and two 0s – indicate an interplay of divine protection and boundless potential. The Magician (1) heralds the onset of new possibilities; the zeros amplify this divine cushioning. This means Roberta is destined to walk an unconventional path. Numerology isn't just a subject; it's her soul's curriculum. Her mission? To revolutionize how we understand numbers and their influence over us.

Both these stories beckon you to ask: what role has destiny marked out for you? While numbers can be puzzling, sometimes it takes the amalgamation of Heart and Personality to truly unlock the enigma that is your life. Your destiny awaits – will you decipher its code?

Let's get you started on calculating your own Destiny Number. Grab a pen and a notepad, and set aside a quiet moment for this revealing exercise.

Step 1: Write Down Your Full Name

First, do your entire chart from your full name on your birth certificate. After you've done your chart for your full birth certificate name, then repeat the same process for any name changes. It is important to understand the birth certificate name first as the foundation that does not get replaced, but enhanced by new names. Example, for Emily Rose Smith, do her heart, personality and destiny number. Let's say she got married later. If her married name is now Emily Rose Jones, then use that name. Or maybe she dropped her middle name and only goes by Emily Jones, then calculate accordingly. Also, if you have a nickname, calculate that and you will know how others see you.

Write down your full name as it appears on your birth certificate. Separate each part of your name – first, middle, last – into different sections. For this exercise, we'll use the example name: *Alex John Doe*, but I invite you to replace the Names and Numerical values with your own.

Step 2: Assign Numerical Values

Utilizing the basic numerology chart from page 23, assign each letter in your name a corresponding numerical value.

Example:

```
 1 5    6      65
 Alex  John   Doe
 3 6   1 85   4
```

Step 3: Calculate Heart Number

Add together all the vowels in each part of your name to get your Heart Number. The sum will represent your inner world and emotional nature.

Example:

Alex, 1+5 = 6, The Lovers   Subtotal

John, 6   = 6, The Lovers   Subtotal

Doe, 6+5 = 11, Justice   Subtotal

6+6+11 = 23, King of Wands Grand Total

Step 4: Calculate Personality Number

For your Personality Number, you'll sum up the consonants in your name. This number will reflect how others perceive you.

Example:

Alex, 3+6   = 9, The Hermit   Subtotal
John, 1+8+5 = 14, Temperance   Subtotal
Doe, 4   = 4, The Emperor   Subtotal
_____

9+14+4   = 27, Ace of Wands Grand Total

Step 5: Determine Destiny Number

Finally, add your Heart and Personality Numbers for each name part, then sum those together to find your Grand Total Destiny Number.

Example:

Alex, 6+9 = 15, The Devil   Subtotal
John, 6+14 = 20, Judgment   Subtotal
Doe, 11+4 = 15, The Devil   Subtotal
_____

15+20+15 = 50, Ten of Cups   Grand Total

Grand Total Destiny Number:

15 (Alex) + 20 (John) + 15 (Doe) = 50

Note the 15, The Devil, showing up twice in the destiny subtotals underscoring an incredible career likely in social work or in assisting others in overcoming their own personal devils or addictions. See how that combines with 20, Judgment, which likely shows he must write books about the subject of addiction. Then, compare that to his grand total of 50, Ten of Cups, revealing success and freedom through the challenges learned from addiction/bondage, because of all the trials successfully navigated.

Decoding Your Destiny

Once you've calculated your Destiny Number, refer back to the Tarot Archetypes to glean insights into your life's work and journey. First, look up each of the subtotals, then the grand total, as these will reveal experiences that define your destiny. Can you identify any master numbers? Do you see more numbers from The Wands, or Cups, Swords or Pentacles in your chart? Does your destiny share the exact same or similar frequency number as your heart, personality or karma number? What do these numbers reveal about your career, your challenges, and your lasting legacy?

Unlocking your destiny might seem like a complex equation, but often the answers lie hidden in plain sight, waiting to be discovered. It's your turn – let the numbers speak. See the chapter "Putting It All Together."

A Brief Guide to Understanding Karma

> "Always assist a man in carrying his burden.
> Do not assist a man in putting down his burden."
> – Pythagoras

What is the simplest test to know if you have karma? Ask yourself: Are you breathing? If the answer is yes, you have karma. Even Jesus had karma – indeed, he embodied everyone's karma. So, what exactly is karma? One perspective sees it as the lessons we set for ourselves for growth and enlightenment. Another, rooted in Buddhism and Hinduism, understands it as the accumulated actions that influence our future existence. Simply put, karma guides our life's journey, orchestrated by a higher self, motivated by love and compassion.

Contrary to popular belief, karma isn't a form of punishment; it's a formative experience. Earth, with its low-vibrational third dimension, serves as an advanced course – a PhD program of sorts – where karma is expiated at accelerated rates.

When evaluating karma through the lens of numerology, we examine the energy frequencies encoded in a person's name. My interpretation of karma is any specific energy frequency experienced intensely, whether positive or negative. Understanding karma doesn't simplify life, but it enlightens us, and as we grow, our karma evolves. It transforms from burden to strength, echoing the Pythagorean wisdom of assisting others in carrying, not discarding, their burdens.

In numerology, missing numbers in your name reveal your karma. For instance, in a name lacking the letter H, Q, or Z, which corresponds to the number 8, issues like bullying or financial volatility may surface. These challenges aren't life sentences but growth opportunities. Wisdom acquired from conquering these trials empowers us for life.

Karma often leans towards the extreme – either an overwhelming intensity or a complete void of a specific energy. Here's how these imbalances manifest:

1. If your name has no A, J, or S – Self-Sufficiency Karma: This involves intense life lessons about standing alone and achieving independence. You may lack support in areas where autonomy is essential.

2. If your name has no B, K, or T – Voice and Femininity Karma: Here, your voice goes unheard or your creative and spiritual aspects are blocked. Alternatively, they may be so open that they overwhelm you. Immune system issues also fall under this category.

3. If your name has no C, L, or U – Self-Worth Karma: Struggles with self-esteem come to the forefront. You're either unable to express yourself or forcibly placed in the spotlight negatively. Fertility issues and being subject to gossip or scandal are other hallmarks.

4. If your name has no D, M, or V – Authority and Structure Karma: The lack of a strong foundation or support system is prevalent. This karma deals with issues around authority figures, discipline, and your body's structure – bones and spine. You're meant to rewrite laws and advocate for civil rights.

5. If your name has no E, N, or W – Sensuality Karma: This concerns the reclamation of physical joy or its excess, which can lead to addiction. Freedom is either restricted or overly abundant, and frequent changes of residence are common.

6. If your name has no F, O, or X – Relational Karma: This manifests as either extreme control or abandonment, especially in long-term relationships. This karma might even involve mother-child dynamics or force you to parent your own parents or siblings.

7. If your name has no G, P, or Y – Energy and Spirituality Karma: You may find yourself surrounded by energy vampires, feeling unheard or hypersensitive. Regaining your spirit becomes a significant focus.

8. If your name has no H, Q or Z – Boundaries and Wealth Karma: Issues with physical or financial boundaries manifest, along with struggles related to money and confrontations with bullies.

9. If your name has no I or R – Closure and Attachment Karma: Difficulty in completing tasks and grounding yourself is common. You may also find it hard to say goodbye to family and loved ones.

Look for any missing numbers in your name, then read more details in the delineation of numbers 1 through 9. Each has a karmic explanation. Consider this guide a map for navigating the roads of karmic destiny, offering you the opportunity to realign, recalibrate, and, perhaps, understand your life's path.

Practice

Now that you know how to calculcate any name or number, take it even further. Calculate nicknames you have or that you have for others. Do a Starr chart for your baby, your ex, your current love. Also intriguing, words and phrases. Here are a couple of words broken down:

   19
   Faith
   6 28

Heart 10, Wheel of Fortune
Personality 16, The Tower
Destiny 26, Page of Wands

The heart of Faith is 10, The Wheel of Fortune. This is an otherworldly number. One is The Magician, All things are possible, with zero being Divine Protection. This literally means I know I am God. This is the heart of Faith. The outer personality of Faith is 16, The Tower. This says, that which is built upon sand must come crashing down, or in other words, that which does not align with the 10 of the heart, I am God, is false, an illusion. Only that which truly comes from our alignment of knowing we are God is real, all else is an illusion. Then the destiny, 26, Page of Wands, being an 8 frequency means that which must be made manifest in this third dimension frequency of our earth plane. 26 is inheritance, responsibility, strength. The 2 of the 26 is The High Priestess, or the realm of the spirit, the unknown. When we call on faith, we are asking to be reminded that we are God(10), and asking that which does not align with this belief to be removed(16), so we can manifest(26) with the help of spirit(2) that which is true unconditional love(6).

575
Eye

Heart 17, The Star
Personality 0, Holy Spirit, Divine Protection
Destiny 17, The Star

In the word "eye," there are no consonants, no personality, just pure heart, as "eye" is just two vowels. Both the heart number and the destiny number are 17, The Star, thus intensifying both heart and destiny. Our eyes are literally stars, windows of our soul with no ego, mask, or personality to shield or protect as none is needed with the pure intensity of heart and destiny being exactly aligned. Zero (see the chapter History of Zero), we know gives Divine Protection and can take on all forms or remain formless.

Now play with some of your favorite words, phrases, sayings and see what you come up with.

Your Spiritual Path

The central theme of your life often unfolds in one simple sentence or paragraph, laying bare the spiritual lessons you've been destined to learn. These lessons aren't easy, but they are straightforward and deeply impactful. Among all the numerological digits that make you who you are, your spiritual path number holds the most sway. Unchanging and permanent – akin to your birth date – it leaves an indelible imprint on your life journey. Your spiritual path is that which you first experience, then you master, then you share with others. It represents the greatest challenges and obstacles of your life as well as the greatest joys and breakthroughs. Take note of any personal year, month, day or pinnacle that is either exactly the same number as your spiritual path or from the same frequency as these time periods bring your spiritual path challenges and gifts front and center in your life during these times. Also note if any of your name subtotals and/or grand totals are the exact same or similar frequency as your spiritual path as this aligns you further. And see what numbers are opposite to your spiritual path number to see where you challenge yourself.

Calculate Your Spiritual Path Number:

- *Month:* Keep the number of your birth month as is. October remains 10, November stays at 11, and December is a steadfast **12**.
- *Day:* The day you were born also stays as is. If it's the 31st, it stays **31**.
- *Year:* Add each digit in your birth year together. For example, 1967 becomes 1+9+6+7 = **23**.

Add the three numbers to reveal your spiritual path number.

An Example with December 31, 2004:

December (12) + 31 + (2+0+0+4 = 6)

12 + 31 + 6 = 49, representing the Nine of Cups Spiritual Path Number.

The Case of Roberta Joanne Schlender:

Born on August 5, 1967, her spiritual path number calculation is:

August (8) + 5 + (1+9+6+7 = 23)

13 + 23 = 36, representing the Ten of Wands Spiritual Path Number.

Roberta faced challenges that would test the limits of human endurance. Her Ten of Wands number revealed itself most poignantly on June 22, 1995. Her home swelled with the unexpected arrival of her niece, forcing her into motherhood overnight. As if scripted by fate, she assumed the role of caregiver, not just for her niece but also her ailing mother. Through family upheavals and legal battles over custody, Roberta felt the weight of responsibility. The Ten of Wands captured her essence: a person burdened yet uplifted by her challenges, coming full circle to a place of gratitude and understanding.

Interactive Exercise for You:

Grab a piece of paper, a calculator, and jot down your birth month, day, and year. Apply the formula:

Birth Month + Birth Day + (Sum of Birth Year digits)

What number did you get? This is your spiritual path number, a numerical value capturing the essence of your spiritual journey.

Much like Roberta, you will find that the spiritual path number's influence is both latent and pervasive. It emerges during life's most challenging and triumphant moments, guiding you toward an understanding of your very core. What's etched in your spiritual path number is not a prediction but a mirror – reflecting both the challenges you have co-created and the extraordinary human potential waiting to be unleashed.

Pinnacles

In every life journey, we encounter moments that can only be understood as pinnacles – those critical junctures that inform, disrupt, and most importantly, educate us. Pinnacles are the temporal classrooms that life enrolls us in, each tailored to impart a specific lesson. These are neither permanent fixtures nor arbitrary points; they have their own structure, their own rhythm. The pattern isn't mere coincidence – it can be calculated.

The Architecture of Pinnacles

We all have four pinnacles. The first and last span the longest, flanking the two shorter ones that last for nine years each. The climax of every pinnacle year reverberates with the frequency of the number nine – a year of summation, of closing chapters to allow new ones to be written. Conversely, the initiation of the three last pinnacles resounds with the frequency of the number one – a year brimming with fresh possibilities.

To discover these pinnacles, we look to numerology as a guide, a kind of divine arithmetic:

Example: August 5, 1967

- *First Pinnacle:* Month + Day of Birth (e.g., August 5: 8 + 5 = 13, Death)
- *Second Pinnacle:* Day + Reduced Year of Birth (e.g., 5 + 1967 (1+9+6+7) = 28, Two of Wands)
- *Third Pinnacle:* First Pinnacle + Second Pinnacle (e.g., 13 + 28 = 41, Ace of Cups)
- *Fourth Pinnacle:* Month + Reduced Year of Birth (e.g., 8 + (1+9+6+7) = 31, Five of Wands)

Calculating Pinnacle Durations

Note that the last year of the first three pinnacles ends in a nine frequency personal year, while the fourth and final pinnacle lasts for the rest of our lives. The first year of second, third, and fourth pinnacles all begin with a one personal year. The duration of your pinnacles is also the exact same for the duration of your challenges and the exact same duration of your positive and negative polarities. To calculate, reduce your spiritual path number to a single digit. For example, the birthdate of August 5, 1967 is 8 plus 5 plus (1+9+6+7) or 8 plus 5 plus 23 which totals 36 spiritual path number. Reduce this: 3 plus 6 is 9:

One: If your spiritual path number reduces to the single digit of 1: Then your first pinnacle starts at birth and lasts through to 35 years old, ending on midnight of your 36th birthday. Your second pinnacle starts on midnight of your 36th birthday, lasting up through and including age 44, ending on the midnight of your 45th birthday. Your third pinnacle starts at midnight of your 45th birthday and lasts up to and including age 53, ending on midnight of your 54th birthday. Your fourth and final pinnacle starts on midnight of your birthday at age 54 and lasts for the rest of your life.

Two: If your spiritual path number reduces to the single digit of 2, the duration of your pinnacles is as follows: First Pinnacle: From birth through and including all of your 34th year of life. Second Pinnacle: From midnight on your 35th birthday, through and including your 43rd year of life. Third Pinnacle: From midnight on your 44th birthday, through and including your 52nd year of life. Fourth Pinnacle: From midnight on your 53rd birthday until the rest of your life.

Three: If your spiritual path reduces to the single digit of 3, the duration of your pinnacles are as follows: First Pinnacle: From birth through and including all of your 33rd year of life. Second Pinnacle: From midnight on your 34th birthday, through and including your 42nd year of life. Third Pinnacle: From midnight on your 43rd birthday, through and including your 51st year of life. Fourth Pinnacle: From midnight on your 52nd birthday until the rest of your life.

Four: If your spiritual path reduces to the single digit of 4, the duration of your pinnacles are as follows: First Pinnacle: From birth through and including all of your 32nd year of life. Second Pinnacle: From midnight on your 33rd birthday, through and including your 41st year of life. Third Pinnacle: From midnight on your 42nd birthday, through and including your 50th year of life. Fourth Pinnacle: From midnight on your 51st birthday until the rest of your life.

Five: If your spiritual path reduces to the single digit of 5, the duration of your pinnacles are as follows: First Pinnacle: From birth through and including all of your 31st year of life. Second Pinnacle: From midnight on your 32nd birthday, through and including your 40th year of life. Third Pinnacle: From midnight on your 41st birthday, through and including your 49th year of life. Fourth Pinnacle: From midnight on your 50 birthday until the rest of your life.

Six: If your spiritual path reduces to the single digit of 6, the duration of your pinnacles are as follows: First Pinnacle: From birth through and including all of your 30th year of life. Second Pinnacle: From midnight on your 31st birthday, through and including your 39th year of life. Third Pinnacle: From midnight on your 40th birthday, through and including your 48th year of life. Fourth Pinnacle: From midnight on your 49th birthday until the rest of your life.

Seven: If your spiritual path reduces to the single digit of 7, the duration of your pinnacles are as follows: First Pinnacle: From birth through and including all of your 29th year of life. Second Pinnacle: From midnight on your 30th birthday, through and including your 38th year of life. Third Pinnacle: From midnight on your 39th birthday, through and including your 47th year of life. Fourth Pinnacle: From midnight on your 48th birthday until the rest of your life.

Eight: If your spiritual path reduces to the single digit of 8, the duration of your pinnacles are as follows: First Pinnacle: From birth through and including all of your 28th year of life. Second Pinnacle: From midnight on your 29th birthday, through and including your 37th year of life. Third Pinnacle: From midnight on your 38th birthday, through and including your 46th year of life. Fourth Pinnacle: From midnight on your 47th birthday until the rest of your life.

Nine: If your spiritual path reduces to the single digit of 9, the duration of your pinnacles are as follows: First Pinnacle: From birth through and including all of your 27th year of life. Second Pinnacle: From midnight on your 28th birthday, through and including your 36th year of life. Third Pinnacle: From midnight on your 37th birthday, through and including your 45th year of life. Fourth Pinnacle: From midnight on your 46th birthday until the rest of your life.

The Seasons of Life

These aren't just numbers; they are signposts along a life journey. For our August 5, 1967 example:

- **First Pinnacle:** *Death (13)* – Age 0 to 27
- **Second Pinnacle:** *Two of Wands (28)* – Age 28 to 36
- **Third Pinnacle:** *Ace of Cups (41)* – Age 37 to 45
- **Fourth Pinnacle:** *Five of Wands (31)* – Age 46 and beyond

The Transformative Force of Pinnacles

The pinnacles are not arbitrary but rich with symbolic meaning. The first pinnacle in our example from August 5, 1967, signified by the number 13, carries the weight of transformation. It's a period of turbulence, ripe with trials that promise growth if navigated well. It is the stage where a person realizes the weights they have to drop to keep moving, just as they might have felt burdened by familial expectations or flirted with self-destruction before finding their path.

The second pinnacle in our example, symbolized by the Two of Wands, is a time for taking a stand. Here, a person learns to walk on their own, embroiled, perhaps, in legal battles for child custody or caring for a deteriorating parent.

The third pinnacle, marked by the Ace of Cups, awakens a profound sense of love and emotional richness. It's the chapter where a person unearths soul connections, explores passions, and considers legacy projects like writing a transformative book.

The final pinnacle, the Five of Wands, illuminates the complexities of relationships and the need for a legal resolution. It invites a person to break free from codependency and to rebuild, whether that means a new business venture or an overdue divorce.

Through these pinnacles, we see how each year, each pinnacle comes not as an arbitrary point on a timeline, but as a crucial classroom – each with its own curriculum tailored for our soul's progress. The journey may not always be smooth, but it's during these pinnacles that we are most ripe for transformation. And that's what makes life both fascinating and subliminally beautiful.

Another Example and Elaboration

Let's unfold another layer of this cosmic narrative using the birthdate of September 9, 1999. What are the pinnacles that govern this individual's life journey?

Example: September 9, 1999

1. The Moon glimmers in the First Pinnacle: a sum of the birth month and day (9 + 9 = 18).
2. King of Cups holds the chalice in the Second Pinnacle: day and the sum of the reduced birth year unite (9 + 28 = 37).
3. Ace of Swords cuts through in the Third Pinnacle: a synthesis of the previous two pinnacles (18 + 37 = 55).
4. The King of Cups returns for an encore in the Fourth Pinnacle, hinting at recurrent themes throughout this individual's life (9 + 28 = 37).

The Pinnacles Unveiled

The following is a brief synopsis of the breakdown of the pinnacle meanings. Also read the non-reduced double-digit number of your pinnacle in the delineation section for the in-depth breakdown of each of your pinnacles.

Frequency 1 Pinnacle: It's time for new beginnings. Exercise leadership. Make things happen. Act now. This is your moment under the spotlight, carving out a solo performance on the stage of life. It whispers the urgent phrase: "Time to act, do it now." Lead with audacity, embrace independence, and initiate new beginnings like a sculptor molds raw clay into art.

Frequency 2 Pinnacle: Retreat, but not in defeat. Play a supporting role. This period is a sanctuary for your intuition and creativity. In contrast, the symphony of Frequency 2 demands you play the supportive violin, not the lead guitar. This is your cue to listen, observe, and serve as a linchpin for others. Don't misconstrue this as inferiority; it's merely different. Think of yourself as the stagehand who ensures the show must go on. A time of intuition and microcosmic beauty – like the intricacy of poetry or the cellular ballet in a petri dish.

Frequency 3 Pinnacle: The spotlight seeks you. You're the toastmaster, the influencer. Fertile ground for inspiration. Rise again to the limelight. You become the captivating storyteller, the social catalyst, fueling inspiration and proliferating causes worthy of attention. An aura of abundance envelops you – this is your season to blossom.

Frequency 4 Pinnacle: Discipline reigns. Systems fall apart only to be reconstructed stronger. Adhere to the rules. The canvas of life isn't always vibrant; Frequency 4 saturates it in a monotone of discipline and hard labor. It's the military drill sergeant, exacting, unyielding, teaching you to value the foundation over the frills. Respect authority, lay strong groundwork, and beware – the pitfalls are tests, not punishments.

Frequency 5 Pinnacle: Wander, wonder, expand. It's a carousel of learning, sensory experiences, and changes. The chameleon in you emerges; you morph with change and travel. The narrative veers into exploring realms physical and metaphysical, from the taste of exotic cuisines to the textures of new experiences. This period is a playground for the senses, so whether it's about reclaiming bodily joy or taming exuberant tendencies – balance is key.

Frequency 6 Pinnacle: It's a tale of love, of home, and long-term aspirations. If 5 is the adventurous bachelor, 6 is the committed spouse. From courtship to community, it's about forging enduring ties and long-term plans. You are a homemaker in the largest sense of the word – building relationships, not just dwellings.

Frequency 7 Pinnacle: Reconnect with your inner monk. The external dims so your spirit can luminate. Imagine a monastic retreat: your phone is off and the door is bolted. This is the sanctuary of the soul where you soak in metaphysical elixirs – meditation, prayer, ancient wisdom. You explore the invisible – sound waves, light waves, the echoes of the universe. Conventional healing yields to alternative approaches; it's the time to let your spirit roam freely.

Frequency 8 Pinnacle: You're the maestro of a material world orchestra. It's time to manifest your vision. The pendulum swings to worldly conquests. As if you're fueled by some cosmic espresso, you're acutely focused, executing plans with the precision of a master chess player. This is the energy field of CEOs and athletes – manifestation in its most palpable form.

Frequency 9 Pinnacle: Farewells fuel future beginnings. Endings aren't terminations but transitions. Finally, the circle closes. A farewell party for the life chapter you're leaving behind, but also an overture for what's coming next. This is your cosmic clean-up, a yard sale of emotional and material baggage. Your old world must disintegrate to fertilize the soil for new beginnings. You went from initiate to adept, to Teacher.

In the intricate dance of numbers and energies, every pinnacle and frequency informs a distinct chapter of our life story. How will you navigate yours?

Challenges

In our multifaceted world where light contends with darkness and good wrestles with evil, the notion of existence without challenges seems inconceivable. Why venture into life if not to test our mettle to the fullest? It's in this rigorous testing that our presence on this earth challenges itself – ideally, facing only what aligns with our spiritual readiness. Let's delve into the challenges you've unconsciously chosen, perfectly synchronizing with your pinnacles. Each pinnacle corresponds with one distinct challenge. As your life unfolds through four pinnacles, so too will you encounter four challenges. When deciphering pinnacles, we added numbers. Now, to unearth your challenges, we subtract.

To uncover your first challenge, subtract your birth month from your birth day, always deducting the lesser from the greater.

Take Roberta's birth date: August 5, 1967.

Here, the first challenge is 8 minus 5, yielding 3, symbolized by The Empress. It reflects the enduring challenge of self-worth, a battle with Roberta accepting that she deserves love and goodness. It is a formidable struggle that threaded through many years and numerous relationships.

The second challenge emerges from subtracting your birth day from your reduced birth year. With Roberta's birthdate, it's 5 minus (1+9+6+7), or 5 - 23. With 23 being the higher, we subtract 23 from 5, resulting in 18, The Moon. This challenge manifested as Roberta's mother's mental and physical health concerns. Her mother's well-being rested solely on Roberta's shoulders, a burden that tested her to the core.

Amidst full-time work and single parenthood, Roberta's resilience frayed. The nights were long, the days a haze. Each doctor's visit, each silent plea to the heavens, marked Roberta's descent. Yet, survival came – a testament to miracles – when a doctor's decision led her mother to a nursing home, inadvertently granting Roberta salvation.

Your third challenge is the difference between the first and the second challenges. Roberta's first being 3, and the second 18, we subtract the former from the latter: 18 - 3 equals 15, The Devil. Looking back with a touch of irony, this period coincided with a pinnacle that promised true love. The man Roberta met, who bore the birth date of the 15th, played the proverbial Devil to her unwitting enabler. Their paths have since diverged, leaving Roberta with invaluable lessons and gratitude in his wake.

For the fourth and final challenge, subtract the sum of your birth year digits from your birth month. (1+9+6+7) minus 8 gives us 15 again, The Devil, signifying another period of personal captivity, not by evil, but by the unexamined self. Roberta's concurrent pinnacle was the 31, the Five of Wands – symbolic of the need for patience, cessation of conflict, and the pursuit of harmony to realize tangible success. In this phase, two men, akin to 'devils', entered her life. She views them now as soul contracts – mirrors reflecting the parts of herself hidden in shadow, pushing her toward a deeper self-awareness.

I note it this way:

Pinnacle	Challenge	Duration
1. 13 death	3, Empress	Born - 27 years old
2. 28, 2 of Wands	18, The Moon	28 - 36 years old
3. 41, Ace of Cups	15, The Devil	37 - 45 years old
4. 31, 5 of Wands	15, The Devil	46 on

Reminder:

Pinnacle 1 is Month + Day you were born
Pinnacle 2 is Day+ Year you were born
Pinnacle 3 is Pinnacle 1 + Pinnacle 2
Pinnacle 4 is Reduced Year+ Month you were born

When you change the plus signs to minus signs, that is the Challenges calculation. Always subtract the smaller from the larger number:

Challenge 1 is Month - Day you were born
Challenge 2 is Day - Year you were born
Challenge 3 is Challenge 1 - Challenge 2
Challenge 4 is Reduced Year - month you were born

Polarity

The universal law of polarity is the epitome of the dual nature of all things. It asserts that every aspect of existence has its pair of opposites, identical in nature but differing in degree. These opposites are two inseparable aspects of the same continuum, such as hot and cold – one cannot exist without the potential for the other. Their unity creates a whole, striving for balance and harmony. This law manifests in our lives daily, influencing conditions, circumstances, and events, urging us to maintain equilibrium between the extremes.

> Power v. Force
> Acceptance v. Resistance
> Dark v. Light
> Good v. Evil
> Right v. Wrong
> Angel v. Devil

Key dualities like power versus force, acceptance versus resistance, and good versus evil illustrate this concept. Even personal events, as demonstrated by numerological assessments based on birthdates, reveal the play of polarities. For instance, the birthdate of August 5, 1967, yields specific numbers known as pinnacles and challenges, which, when combined according to certain rules, reveal one's positive and negative polarities. These polarities mirror the events and phases of life, from childhood homes to the birth of children and the intricacies of relationships.

Retrospectively, we can dissect how polarities have sculpted our existence. The positive and negative aspects, whether they relate to family dynamics, career paths, or personal growth, all stem from the law of polarity. It's through the lens of hindsight that the influence of these numerological milestones becomes evident – from the sudden loss of a loved one to the transformative experience of motherhood, and even the trials of enduring challenging relationships. From the Hua Hu Jing on polarity: "The Tao gives birth to One. One gives birth to yin and yang. Yin and yang give birth to all things. Now forget this. The complete whole is the complete whole. So also is any part the complete whole. Forget this, too. Pain and happiness are simply conditions of the ego. Forget the ego. Time and space are changing and dissolving, not fixed and real. They can be thought of as accessories, but don't think of them. Supernatural beings without form extend their life force throughout the universe to support beings both formed and unformed. But never mind this; the supernatural is just a part of nature, like the natural. The subtle truth emphasizes neither and includes both. All truth is in tai chi: to cultivate the mind, body, or spirit, simply balance the polarities. If people understood this, world peace and universal harmony would naturally arise. But forget about understanding and harmonizing and making all things one. The universe is already a harmonious oneness; just realize it. If you scramble about in search of inner peace, you will lose your inner peace."

To calculate your polarity, you need your pinnacles and Challenges. For the birthdate of August 5, 1967:

   Pinnacle 1=13   Challenge 1=3
   Pinnacle 2=28   Challenge 2=18
   Pinnacle 3=41   Challenge 3=15
   Pinnacle 4=31   Challenge 4=15

For the positive polarity, add Pinnacle 1 to Challenge 1: 13 + 3 which equals 16, The Tower. For the negative polarity, subtract Pinnacle 1 and Challenge 1, again always subtract the smaller number from the bigger number. In this case, 13 - 3 equals 10, The Wheel of Fortune. Both the positive and negative polarities have the same duration and timing as the pinnacles and challenges. So the timing of both Pinnacle 1 and Challenge 1 is the same timing as the Positive Polarity1 and Negative Polarity 1 and so on. I note them in this way so it's easy for me to see:

P1=13   C1=3   +P=16   -P=10   Birth - 27 years old
P2=28   C2=18   +P=46   -P=10   28 - 36 years old
P3=41   C3=15   +P=56   -P=26   37 - 45 years old
P4=31   C4=15   +P=46   -P=16   46 - rest of life

In Roberta's first pinnacle, the positive polarity is 16, The Tower. In retrospect, she can easily relate the 16 Tower to the death of her stepfather. It was sudden, very Tower-like. He literally went to the ER thinking he had gallstones and it was discovered he had pancreatic cancer. He was gone in six weeks. This completely directed the course of Roberta's life. He did not have a life insurance policy. Roberta's mom sold their house and had to go back to work. Roberta, determined to help out with the situation, started court reporting school a week or two before her 16th birthday and got her first job at 16 as a teacher's aide at a school.

The negative polarity is 10, the Wheel of Fortune. Roberta was heartbroken to no longer have the house she grew up in. She has since owned homes, lived in apartments, and even gone through a foreclosure but she still has a deep emotional attachment to her first home. The Wheel of Fortune is a change for the better. It is in her negative polarity. Roberta misses that home, still. But having to work from the age of 16 on and having a court reporting career literally saved Roberta from starvation.

In her second positive polarity, 46, the Six of Cups represents children, and the importance of the past. June 22, 1995, just two months before her 28th birthday, the start of her second pinnacle, her niece came to live with her. This became permanent. Roberta does not consider her a niece, but a daughter, her firstborn, in fact. The niece was just 13 months old when she came into Roberta's life. Roberta's first mother experience. She then met the father of her children and had a son in 1999 and a third and last child in 2004 – the positive polarity of the 46 bringing children into her life – three of them. Roberta had always wanted to be a mom.

In her second negative polarity, she has 10 again. The challenge of the 10 represents the fact that Roberta never married the father of her children. She was a single mom, raising her children while taking care of her sick mother and maintaining a full-time job. It was insane! The 10 likes to develop independence and become a leader. Roberta did not feel like a leader and she did have help, now and then, taking care of her mother. In hindsight, she mostly felt completely sleep deprived and on the edge of a nervous breakdown the whole time.

At 37 years old, her pinnacle was 41, the Ace of Cups. She fell in love, just as is represented by the Ace of Cups. Her challenge is 15 – the Devil. And that's who she fell in love with. He was also a homeopathic practitioner. Her Positive polarity is 56, the Two of Swords. This fit with Roberta's blindness to the narcissistic aspects of this man whom she would eventually marry and divorce. Roberta relays that she felt completely stuck in the last year that they were together.

The positive polarity is 26 which is responsibility, karma, and inheritance. In the end, Roberta did not inherit any money, but she did learn homeopathy! 26 requires great strength and courage which is exactly what helped Roberta to get away from him, eventually.

At 46 years old, Roberta started her last and final pinnacle of 31 which requires patience and learning how to get along with others – in her case, along with 15, the devil yet again. Here, there was a positive polarity of 46, the Six of Cups, and a negative polarity of 16. In this phase of her life, a second devil rescued her from the first devil. The father of her children literally came to save Roberta and her daughter from her ex-husband. The positive polarity of 46, the Six of Cups, brings the past back to us. The father of her children is now back in their lives. On November 12, 2021, Roberta fell off of a horse and broke her neck and back. She needed help and moved in with him, and he has very kindly and generously helped her a lot to this day. Roberta has felt both stuck and grateful to have a place to live away from her ex-husband. She never, ever would have believed that she would be living out on his property in the desert with him and their two children. The past and children are both aspects of the 46.

Through retrospect, it can be seen how the pinnacles, challenges, and polarities shaped Roberta's life. Each polarity presents a learning opportunity, a mirror reflecting our life's journey marked by distinct phases – such as stepping into independence, embracing the role of a parent, and confronting the complexities of love. Even through adversity, like health crises, the law of polarity teaches resilience and adaptation. It serves as a constant reminder that every moment of our life is a dance of duality, and our awareness of these forces shapes the narrative of our personal history.

Personal Year

Your personal year commences on your birthday and extends to the eve of your subsequent birthday. Annually, a fresh calculation is pivotal to ascertain the energy or frequency that will envelop you in the coming year. This cyclical change is of essence – it arms you with foresight about the duration of any given frequency's influence over your life. Each year unfurls differently – some years present relentless challenges, others you navigate with ease and triumph. I am particularly vigilant during years governed by a '1' energy, signifying beginnings, or a '9' energy, indicating conclusions. In a year resonant with the energy of '4', I counsel my clients to exercise self-compassion; this frequency often thrusts us into the realms of authority, legalities, meticulous detail, and laborious work.

The energy of '16' is another which I approach with caution, advising slow, deliberate steps. Every frequency we encounter serves as a gift, though its true purpose may elude us during its presence.

Retrospect and hindsight are great teachers. Any significant year that you can remember, whether for very joyful reasons and in particular for very challenging reasons should definitely be calculated so you can see exactly what personal year you were in. One's personal year should be viewed in tandem with their numerological chart. There will be years that mirror the frequencies of your core numbers – karma, heart, personality, destiny, or spiritual path. Such alignments are profound, with those reflecting your spiritual path heralding significant, lasting events that align with your divine blueprint. Doing such a comparison usually helps answer the question: "What the bleep is going on and how long will it last?"

Conversely, some years may present as oppositional to the numbers in your personal chart. For instance, a '3' heart energy yearning for joy and spontaneity might be at odds with a '4' personal year urging discipline and structure. For instance, your 3 heart wants to shop and spend money and have a party, but your 4 personal year is having you set up a budget, stick to a healthy diet and be organized and disciplined for the entire year. One of the most serious times in life, some have an 8 or 8 frequency pinnacle, and when they get to the 8 personal year of that 8 pinnacle, it's very intense. You will find yourself in a personal year that is also the same or same frequency of your pinnacle. As an example, you might be in a 28 pinnacle, a one frequency, and the very first year of that 28 pinnacle is also a one frequency personal year. This totally intensifies the new beginnings. You are required to be independent, start the project, or several projects. These periods can be arduous but are imperative for growth.

Each number carries its distinct connotations. Here is a brief synopsis breakdown, but, as always, look up the exact number in the delineation section for the most accurate information. And always, anything can happen at any time - God is in charge.

1 is for beginnings and assertive action. This is all about you and what you want to establish, create, produce, and begin.

2 beckons cooperation and intuition. You find yourself helping others, often under the radar. This is a highly, intuitive, sensitive, and receptive time. Trust your own intuition and your ability to hold or make use of secrets. This is a time to be a diplomat.

3 calls for social interaction and expression. This is a time to socialize, to be seen and heard, to advance a cause worthy and dear to your heart. The spotlight is on you, in front of the camera communicating, singing, speaking, fundraising, celebrating, and more.

4 demands hard work and order. Play time is over; this is a period marked by work, discipline, authority, military and law enforcement, government, focus, study, organization and repair, planning, budgeting, and responsibility. Keep your eye on your goals.

5 heralds change and exploration. This marks travel, escape, new groups of people, moving a home or job, technology and advancement.

6 represents commitment and community. This is a time marked often by marriage or commitment, children, family, and staying in one place; being and creating a center of community, taking on long-term goals, and building or purchasing a home.

7 is strength of the spirit. Invites introspection and spirituality. Seven is marked by quiet, peace, meditation and the spiritual plane. Shut your door, drink more water, and do not answer the phone. Take naps. Do not run a marathon. Travel, but to other planes of consciousness. Often, business and money slow down so the spirit can be your focus.

8 is strength of the physical realm which emphasizes power and material achievement. The eight offers intensity, focus, personal power, growth, business and financial success, the setting of personal and financial boundaries, sudden events and the building of strength.

9 marks completion and humanitarianism, saying goodbye, clearing out the old, letting go of relationships and other situations that have run their course.

Calculating your personal year involves a simple sum of your birth month and day with the year of your last birthday. This number holds the key to understanding the energies at play. With this calculation, you can quickly determine for any time period - past, present, or future - the personal year energy you are in.

For instance, someone born on August 5th would calculate their personal year by adding their birth month and day (8 + 5 = 13) to the sum of the digits of the year they last celebrated a birthday. If they are calculating for 1995, they would add 1 + 9 + 9 + 5 to get 24, and subsequently add these figures (13 + 24) to arrive at 37. This means the 37 personal year started as of midnight on August 5 of 1995 and ends on midnight of August 5 of 1996. This means in 1995 before August 5, the personal year calculation must use the year of 1994, or 8+5+(1+9+9+4) to determine the personal year influence during, say, February of 1995.

It is paramount to remember that this personal year stretches from one birthday to the next. Prior to your birthday, the calculation must reference the year of your last birthday.

As an illustration, for a Christmas-Day birth, to ascertain the personal year for 2022, you would add the month and day (12 + 25 = 37) to the year 2022 (2 + 0 + 2 + 2 = 6), resulting in a personal year of 43, which would start on your birthday, December 25 of 2022 and lasting until December 24 of 2023.

Remember, the only number that is broken down is the year. The month maintains its number whether it's a 3 for the month of March or an 11 for the month of November. The day of the month is also maintained, whether it be the 9th of the month, that remains a 9, or the 31st of a month, which remains 31.

This chapter elucidates the intricate dance between our birth numbers and the unfolding years, guiding us to harmonize with the energies at play. Understanding these patterns can provide clarity, helping us to navigate our journeys with greater awareness and intention.

For the World

A very simple, useful, and profound tool is to determine the year the world is in. As an example, if the current year is 2024, add 2+0+2+4 = 8 for the world, which is all about physical and financial strength, setting boundaries in all the most positive and the most destructive ways possible to the 8. You can do this calculation for any year, past, present, or future as well to understand world-wide issues.

Personal Month

To ascertain your personal month within any year, simply expand upon the calculation used for determining your personal year.

Add the month you were born to the day you were born to the personal year you were in during the month in question, then add the month in question.

Remember your personal year starts as of midnight on your birthday and ends on midnight of your next birthday, year to year. What if we want to know the personal month that also happens to be the same as the birth month?

For example, someone born in September curious as to their personal month in September. Let's use the example of September 10 as the birthday. First, determine the personal year. Let's say we are curious to know the about the month of September of the year 2017. So 2017, use the previous year of 2016 to determine the personal year for September 1 through September 9, as this person is still in their personal year from 2016.

So Month of birth (9), plus day of birth (10) and personal year we must use for September 1 through 9 was 2016, so add (2+0+1+6): 9+10+9 and we get 28, Two of Wands as the personal year this person was still in from September 1 through 9. Now add September, or 9 to determine the personal month calculation: day of birth, plus month of birth, plus personal year, plus month in question: 9+10+9+9=37, King of Cups personal month up until midnight of September 10.

As of midnight on the birthday of September 10, the personal year will then use 2017 for the calculation: Month of birth, plus day of birth, plus personal year, plus month in question: 9+10+10+9=38 personal month that started literally on midnight of September 10 and for the rest of September.

Begin with the month and day of your birth. Factor in the personal year relevant to the month you're examining – use the preceding year's personal year for months before your birthday, or the current year's for those on and after. Add the numerical value of the month in question.

Example 1: January 2026

Birth Month and Day: August 5 → 8 + 5 = 13.

Year of Last Birthday (2025): 2 + 0 + 2 + 5 = 9.

Month of January: 1.

Calculation: 13 (Birth Month and Day) + 9 (Year of Last Birthday) + 1 (January) = 23.

Personal month for January 2026: King of Wands (23).

Example 2: October 2014

Birth Month and Day: August 5 → 8 + 5 = 13.

Year of Last Birthday (2014): 2 + 0 + 1 + 4 = 7.

Month of October: 10.

Calculation: 13 (Birth Month and Day) + 7 (Year of Last Birthday) + 10 (October) = 30.

Personal month for October 2014: Four of Wands (30).

Example 3: August 2000 (Birth Month)

Birth date: August 5 → 8 + 5 = 13.

Personal year for (2000): 2 + 0 + 0 + 0 = 2.

Month of August: 8.

Calculation for post-birthday in August: 13 (birth date) + 2 (personal year) + 8 (August) = 23.

Personal month beginning August 5, 2000: King of Wands (23).

For the days preceding your birthday in August:

Personal year for 1999: 1 + 9 + 9 + 9 = 28.

Calculation for August 1-4: 13 (birth date) + 28 (personal year 1999) + 8 (August) = 49.

Personal month from August 1 to August 4, 1999: Nine of Cups (49).

On August 5, transition occurs from a personal month of Nine of Cups (49) to King of Wands (23).

For the World

Just as we did for the personal year of the world, you can easily determine the personal month for the world and then look up the number in the delineation section. If you are curious about the month of January in the year 2025, here is how you would explore it:

Add the year (2+0+2+5) to the month in question, January. 9+1=10. Therefore, The Wheel of Fortune is the month the world is in during January of 2025.

Personal Day

Personal day calculations are very helpful in retrospect. As an enlightening exercise, jot down dates you know by heart from your own past. Some of these dates likely will have significance for being incredibly life altering such as weddings, graduations, funerals, the birth date of any of your children. As children are master teachers for us, as well as we are for them, see what your own personal day calculation is of the day your child was born. This reveals the gift and lesson they bring to you. I also note the personal day of extremely emotionally upsetting days as well as uplifting and joyful days. See any pattern? Are any of your personal day numbers the exact same or a similar frequency as your heart number or your destiny, spiritual path or your karma numbers?

Use this personal day calculation to choose a wedding day, launch a business. Always remember, anything can happen at any time, God is in charge. This is a very helpful tool to identify you personal patterns.

To calculate your personal day:
1. Combine the month and day of your birth.
2. Add the personal year you were in for the day in question, noting the rule that if the day in question falls before your birthday in any calendar year, you must calculate using the previous year.
3. Include the numerical value of the month in question.
4. Add the specific day you're interested in.

Example: Birthday in 2023

Want to know your personal day for August 5, 2023?

Here's how:

1. Calculate your personal year:

Month + day you were born + year in question
August   5   (2+0+2+3)
   8   5   7   = 20

2. Calculate your personal month:
   Personal year from above (20) plus 8 for August = 28

3. Calculate your personal day:
   Personal month from above (28) plus 5 = 33

Personal year: 20 (Judgment).

Personal month: 28 (Two of Wands).

Personal day: 33 (Seven of Wands).

Example: December 31, 2029

What's special about December 31, 2029?

Personal year for 2029: August 5 → 8 + 5 + (2 ı 0 ı 2+9) = 26 (Page of Wands).

Add December: 26 + 12 = 38 (Queen of Cups).

Add the day: 38 + 31 = 69 (Ace of Pentacles).

Example: January 1, 2030

Looking into January 1, 2030:

Personal year from 2029: 8 + 5 + (2+0+2+9) = 26 (Page of Wands).

Add January: 26 + 1 = 27 (Ace of Wands).

Add the day: 27 + 1 = 28 (Two of Wands).

Putting It All Together

Now that you have calculated every aspect of your personal chart and you easily see all the subtotals, grand totals, pinnacles, years, months, and days, it is time to put it all together. In the pursuit of understanding oneself through the lens of numbers, one embarks on an introspective journey. It is through the comparison of various numerological aspects within one's own chart that the dance of alignment and opposition reveals itself. This exercise unfolds the intricacies of our personalities and destinies, the nuanced ebb and flow of our existence. I first take note of:

> **Identical Numbers:** When numbers repeat, they resonate with a heightened intensity, signifying areas of life where one's energy is markedly concentrated.
>
> **Same Frequency Numbers:** Numbers sharing the same vibration complement each other, fostering an environment of support and harmony. See Base Frequencies.
>
> **Opposing Numbers:** Diametrically opposed figures signal areas ripe for growth, demanding patience and focus.

Significantly, the alignment of your spiritual path number with other aspects of your chart heralds the presence of life's overarching themes. Embrace the full spectrum of experiences this offers, in particular, comparing your heart, destiny, personality and karma to your spiritual path, pinnacles and personal year. The most significant of all of these is your spiritual path. Any time your spiritual path number is an exact match to any other number, expect long-term life themes to show themselves. Embrace the challenges and the joys. As your spiritual path number, you get the full spectrum of the frequency.

For Roberta Joanne Schlender, the chart reads:

```
    6 5 1      6 1   5      5      5
    ROBERTA    JOANNE  SCHENDLER
    9 2 9 2    1   5 5    1 3 8  3 5 4 9
```

Heart Number: 12 + 12 + 10 = 34
Personality Number: 22+11+33=66
Destiny Number: 34+23+43=100

Karma Number: 7

Spiritual Path: Calculated from birth date, August 5, 1967, results in 36.

Pinnacles:

   First: 13 (Death)
   Second: 28 (Two of Wands)
   Third: 41 (Two of Cups)
   Fourth: 31 (Five of Wands)

Personal Year: The narrative is penned in a 19 personal year.

In this study, the heart reveals two passions of similar intensity – both rooted in service and healing. The heart's duet with the personality (66, resonating with the 3 frequency) echoes a nurturing presence, one attuned to familial healing.

The 34, surfacing in both the external facade of the first name and the grand total of the heart, underscores this personal narrative. Similarly, the 43 in Schlender's personality and the 7 of karma blend to unveil an enduring love for homeopathy, influenced by personal relationships.

The narrative diverges with the Wheel of Fortune, represented by 10 in the surname's subtotal, not matching directly but resonating with the destiny number of 100 – signifying a love for independence and the path of self-employment.

Master numbers – 11, 22, 33, and 66 – punctuate the chart with profound personal lessons learned through relational challenges, marking a soul's agreement to the rigors of self-mastery.

Notice the pattern of 4s: the disciplined 22 in the first name's personality and the pinnacles of 13 and 31 highlight the areas demanding diligence and laborious commitment, particularly in the realm of numerology.

Contrasting numbers pose a dichotomy: the 34 (7 frequency) of the heart craves solitude and contemplation, while the 66 (3 frequency) personality shoulders familial responsibilities and social engagement.

Moreover, observe how personal years interplay with the chart, revealing alignments, frequencies, and oppositions, providing insight into the evolving journey of the self.

In sum, one's numerological chart is a tapestry woven with numbers – each thread a reflection of potentials and challenges, a guide to the conscious shaping of one's life narrative.

Compatibility

Compatibility forms the crux of our interpersonal tapestry. It's not just a matter of choice, but a dance of numerical resonance. In the realm of digits, evens harmonize with evens, and odds with odds – a numerical ballet dictated by innate qualities.

Adjacent, diverse, or opposite numbers often strike a contrast, revealing complementary dynamics:

1 and 2: One is the pioneer, while two lends its supportive grace.

2 and 3: Two cherishes the hush of solitude; three thrives in the company of others.

3 and 4: The third is a patron of extravagance, while four is the custodian of prudence.

4 and 5: Four meticulously crafts the plan; five seeks the thrill of spontaneous adventures.

5 and 6: Five relishes in unbridled liberty; six anchors in the harbor of familial bonds.

6 and 7: Six weaves the fabric of home, whereas seven yearns for the quietude of solitude.

7 and 8: Seven finds solace in repose; eight conquers through strength and structure.

8 and 9: Eight is the architect of material realms; nine, the benevolent giver, reaches beyond self.

9 and 1: Nine is the harbinger of conclusions; one heralds the dawn of initiatives.

Within the 3-6-9 trinity, however, there's a seamless fusion of love's threefold path: Self-love and personal validation in three, the duty and care encompassing six, and nine's impartial, boundless affection for all.

Partners ideally resonate at similar frequencies in their spiritual path number, allowing for balance between sameness and contrast, ensuring both comfort and growth.

Professional pairs might share a destiny number, but not necessarily their workplace. An inventive one may thrive with a supportive two, or an executive eight may find kinship with an inventive one – each complementing the other's strengths.

Diverse number pairings invite growth. Enlightened souls embrace their partner's contrasts, expanding their energetic arsenal. Yet, ego may present obstacles – prompting us to seek relationships that challenge us to evolve.

Moreover, the purpose of many connections is transient, meant to serve a specific exchange. Once fulfilled, these relationships may dissolve without negative residue.

In assessing compatibility, analyze both individuals' charts, starting with the spiritual path number – the keystone of our numerical being. Identical or similar frequency spiritual path numbers in any relationship can signify a united journey toward a common goal, though the outcome – synergy or rivalry – hinges on the consciousness level of those involved.

Romantic bonds tend to endure not when they are oppositely matched in spiritual numbers, but when there's a shared frequency or number, fostering mutual support rather than discord.

About karma and compatibility: You might have a spiritual path number of 44 and your partner might have 4 or an 8 karma. This would mean the connection you have is one of helping to balance the the karma of your partner. We always find the absolute perfect master teacher to help us find again the wholeness of our own selves. There are also often instances when a female client marries and the married name she takes on has the number that was the woman's karma. For example, a woman who has no B, K, or T in her name marries and changes her last name to Smith and Smith has the letter "t" thereby balancing her karma. And, male or female, often we are guided to use or change our name later, or adopt a professional name as well. With numerology you can decide for yourself what new name resonates best for you whether you feel guided to change your given name or you want to know what business name works best for your particular profession.

Ultimately, for romance, seek similarity in the spiritual path number, occasionally finding the exact match, which ensures the strongest connection and understanding. An exact match of spiritual path numbers for romantic partners is very rare.

The Quickie

"The Quickie" is an exhilarating and enlightening experience, blending spontaneity with depth in an on-the-spot reading. It begins with an invitation:

Choose the first three numbers that spring to mind, from 0 to 78. This seemingly simple act taps into the subconscious, allowing it to communicate via numbers. Each selected number is a piece of a puzzle, revealing insights about the individual's current state and preoccupations.

In interpreting these numbers, one uncovers the silent narrative hidden within. The meanings of the individual numbers offer a mirror to the soul, reflecting the nuances of the individual's journey and challenges. This process isn't just for the curious querent; it's a tool I often turn to myself. Before I can glean the insights of my own numbers, I must step out of the intellectual noise, clear my mind, and let my subconscious speak.

The "climax" of this numerological adventure is the summation of the three numbers. Their combined total transcends their individual messages, synthesizing them into a broader revelation. This sum serves as a beacon, illuminating a path forward and often presenting a perspective that is both surprising and profoundly useful. "The Quickie" isn't just a party trick – it's a quick dive into the psyche, a flash of clarity in the chaos of everyday life.

The Quickie gives you direct and immediate access to your subconscious through the numbers you choose. You are literally asking your subconscious for guidance when doing this exercise.

There are two ways I use The Quickie - one way is just clearing my mind and allowing the first three numbers to come through. The other way I use The Quickie is to set an intention, such as holding the following thought before I ask myself for numbers: Dear inner wisdom of mine, or Higher Self, please show me numbers that align with my question, then insert question here.

Allow me to share personally the following inner dialogue I have used before choosing numbers: Dear Inner Wisdom of mine, please share with me three numbers that best represent the current stuck patterns I have directly relating to my personal relationship choices. This is setting your intention and accessing the Best source of all time - your higher self. When I ask myself this question, I intend for the first number I choose to represent the pattern; I then intend for the second card to show me how I try to mask my pattern; and I intend for the third number I choose to be what is most beneficial for the healing of said pattern. The total of the three numbers is the outcome of me listening to myself.

None of this is set in stone. This is what I do personally for myself and my clients. Anything you set up with the intention of healing and love will be right for you. Maybe you want to pick five numbers and label them as follows: the first could be the query; second could be your own hopes, dreams, and fears; the third could be what is beneficial in the healing; the fourth number you choose could be labeled as what keeps you stuck in the pattern; and fifth could be the positive outcome of following your own guidance.

The Ultimate Cure for Road Rage

While driving, when someone cuts you off, Don't get mad - Get the message!!! This is super simple: Merely make note of the last two numbers/letters of the license plate that cut you off. This is a message from your guides! I also take this further - on road trips, I take note of the number(s) and or letter(s) that seem to be directly in front of me, particularly if the same number(s) and/or letter(s) keep showing up. Then look up the numbers in the delineation section here. Not while driving, please. Translate the letters to their assigned number so everything gets broken down to the numbers. Enjoy and drive safely!

I take it really far - I enjoy noting the number on my receipt at In-N-Out, or the number I pull at the bakery counter. Nothing is random and it's really fun and enlightening to try this. My guides appreciate when I get the message they keep trying to share with me.

PART TWO:
The Delineations

Section One:
The Major Arcana

1: The Magician

Tarot Symbolism: A man is holding a wand. Much like an antenna, the wand serves to focus and channel energy. The wand is neither positive nor negative, much like our own subconscious, and does our bidding. He holds the wand up indicating inspiration and creative ideas. He wears a white robe representing purity, newness, beginnings. On his table is a symbol from each of the tarot archetypes indicating all the elements at his disposal. Above his head is the lemniscate, or figure eight symbol that represents making manifest his ideas. The snake around his waste is biting its own tail signifying the cycle of life, death and rebirth.

In *The Secret Teachings of All Ages*, Manly P. Hall presents the Magician, or Le Bateleur, as described by Court de Gebelin. The Magician represents the concept that the fabric of creation is but an illusion, a divine juggling act with existence and life as a continuous gamble. Nature's wonders are mere cosmic trickery. Humanity, in this analogy, is akin to a ball – seemingly disappearing at the command of the juggler, who retains it secretly in his hand. Omar Khayyam refers to this figure as 'the master of the show,' suggesting that the enlightened understand and control natural phenomena without being misled by appearances.

The Magician is depicted standing behind a table laden with symbolic items, including a cup suggestive of the Holy Grail and Joseph's gesture to Benjamin; a coin representing both tribute and the master craftsman's pay; and a sword reminiscent of Goliath's and the philosophical sword discerning truth from falsehood. His hat is shaped like the lemniscate, emblematic of creation's inaugural movement. The Magician points to the earth with his right hand and raises his wand with his left, asserting dominance over the world. This wand is Jacob's rod and the blossoming staff, representing the spine topped with the orb of creative thought. In a variant, the pseudo-Egyptian Tarot, he dons an uraeus on his brow, stands before a cubic table, and wears an ouroboros belt, symbolizing eternal cycles.

When the number 1 or a frequency of 1 surfaces in your heart, personality, destiny, or spiritual path, its significance is deeply personal. From the biblical notion of God creating light on the first day, the number one represents initiation, the emergence of the self from the source, embarking on the cycle of life, death, and rebirth. It's a call to the Magician within, urging the creation of something from seemingly nothing – a testament to the profound potential and dynamic energy that number one carries. This number embodies the essence of leadership, independence, and a forward-driven spirit, echoing the exploratory zeal of Captain Kirk on the USS Enterprise. You, aligned with one, are poised to command, to innovate without dwelling on the past or the minutiae but to set into motion ventures that shape the future.

For those experiencing one in a pinnacle, year, month, or day, the message is clear: focus narrowly on what kindles true desire, bypass distractions, and channel your boundless ideas into tangible creations. This period calls for entrepreneurship, for being the architect of your dreams, where persistence is key, and the universe aligns with your steadfast vision. Partnerships are less favored now, as your path demands individuality and personal direction. Beware, though, the nuances of a one personal year can lead to a rushed pace and an inclination toward the color red, signaling energy and urgency.

However, if one is absent in your name – without an A, J, or S – karmic challenges may arise, manifesting as hurdles to self-expression and autonomy. Your efforts may feel directed for others' benefit, overshadowing your desires. Bradley Nelson's *The Emotion Code* associates this with heart or small intestine issues and a spectrum of emotional states from abandonment to vulnerability.

In tarot symbolism, The Magician is depicted channeling universal energy through his wand, an emblem of boundless creativity and potential. The insights from "The Secret Teachings of All Ages" describe the magician as the master illusionist who understands and directs the flow of Nature's mysteries, with the earthly realm under his dominion – echoed by the wand he wields, symbolic of the spine crowned with the globe of creative consciousness. Thus, the Magician archetype, draped in the masculine, represents the seed of possibility – limited or unlimited – by the Magician's own making.

2: The High Priestess

Tarot Symbolism: A young woman, or virgin, is depicted sitting alone, signifying her preference for solitude with her thoughts, intuition, and creativity. She is the protector, sitting on a throne that serves as a gateway between this world and the next, guarding the unseen and sacred. She is the custodian of esoteric wisdom, traversing other dimensions to collect and safeguard healing knowledge. Access is not granted to all; she discloses only to those who are earnest and prepared, providing just enough to handle. Her moonlit feet signify mastery of divine femininity and intuition. Flanked by black and white pillars, she symbolizes the balance of dualities – yin and yang, light and dark, and the lessons derived from their harmony. Pomegranates around her embody potential awaiting fruition, safeguarding the divine feminine essence. Her crown suggests vision extending beyond the physical realm. Draped in white and blue, her attire reflects purity, serenity, and connection with the elements of air and water. The partially concealed Torah on her lap indicates that knowledge is imparted only to the truly dedicated at the proper time.

From *The Secret Teachings of All Ages* by Manly P. Hall, a mysterious story is told of the Female Pope, La Papesse, intertwined with the legend of Pope Joan, the woman who, disguised in male garb, is said to have ascended to the pontifical throne and met a brutal fate when her deception was unveiled. This tarot card encapsulates the image of a seated woman, adorned with a tiara crowned by the lunar crescent, a symbol of her clandestine wisdom. In her possession, she holds the Tora or the book of the Law, its contents partially obscured, while the keys to the secret doctrine, one gold and one silver, rest in her left hand. She is flanked by the pillars of Jachin and Boaz, with the varied hues of a veil stretched between, as she sits upon a throne grounded by a checkerboard floor. In certain renditions, Juno replaces La Papesse, embodying the female hierophant of Cybele's Mysteries, a representation of the Shekinah or Divine Wisdom. This priestess of the pseudo-Egyptian Tarot is veiled, symbolizing the partial revelation of truth to mankind, with her book equally shrouded, suggesting that only a fragment of life's enigma is within our grasp.

GotQuestions.org sheds light on the historical and symbolic significance of the pillars of Jachin and Boaz, which adorned the entrance to Solomon's Temple's vestibule. The construction of this majestic temple in Jerusalem, beginning in 966 BC and reaching completion seven years later, is chronicled in the biblical books of 1 Kings 7 and 2 Chronicles 3. Jachin, meaning "he will establish," coupled with Boaz, translating to "in him is strength," served as a powerful testament to the belief that God's presence would fortify the temple and worship within its hallowed walls.

If 2 or a 2 frequency is a number for your heart, personality, destiny, or spiritual path, then this applies to you: On day two, God created the atmosphere and the firmament. Pause, listen, help, assist, peace, intuition, duality, opposites. You are a highly sensitive individual and acutely aware of others and their energy, as the High Priestess can see and hear both sides of any situation, which is why you second-guess yourself. You are the diplomat, the peacemaker. Your sensitivity can be so highly attuned that you are frequently the medium due to your ability to listen and hear which often extends to the spiritual realm as well. Seeing and hearing spirits can be commonplace for you. You are the softer, quieter feminine energy. You have absolutely no desire for world domination. You are perfectly happy taking second chair, being the assistant. You are the adage "Being of service is the highest calling."

You love meditation, art, poetry, symmetry, and architecture. You do well in any customer service capacity, or as a mediator dealing with angry, upset, or hostile people because of your calming nature. Because of the duality, two sides, you are constantly weighing, deciding, judging. You are your own harshest judge. You can be painfully shy and quiet. Your nervous tension happens when you haven't had your meditation and quiet or when you have not heeded your inner guidance. It's about trusting yourself. You have learned that appearances can be deceiving and that you must listen to your intuition which has never been wrong. You are required in this lifetime to make many decisions as Two represents turning points. The High Priestess archetype is a virgin indicating the protection of ideas and concepts before they are made manifest which is why our High Priestess is so connected with the realm of spirit.

In some Tarot decks, the High Priestess has her back turned to us indicating She has no desire for the material side of life, she is turned toward the spiritual realm. Jimmy Carter helped Bill Clinton by getting Russia to sign a peace agreement just in time to stop our attack. A perfect example of diplomacy under pressure and bringing others around to a peaceful resolution. The gift/lesson of our High Priestess is, "I am here to help and assist wherever I am needed, I trust myself, things are not always as they appear, my intuition is right."

The word Shaman has a heart number of 2, the ability to quietly observe and travel to other realms of consciousness and bring back useful, healing energy. A negative High Priestess is always second-guessing and judging herself, holding onto and regretting the past and has lots of nervous energy. When she is positive, peace rules. You like to collect things as well. You have a love of words and small things, sometimes miniature. You know the details are important and that which is very small has a large profound effect on everything around it, such as molecular biology, the study of atoms. You are an excellent historian, museum curator because you feel the need to protect, honor and preserve beauty in all its forms. You are the protector of memories. You would be an excellent librarian, genealogist, poet, author, artist, painter, sculptor.

If 2 or a 2 frequency is a number of a pinnacle, year, month, or day of yours: Two is the chrysalis, the stage of quiet and stillness before the caterpillar becomes a butterfly. It's now your job to assist others. You are the strength and support, quiet and stabilizing. You find yourself taking second seat, the observer behind the scenes. You are the protector now, of people, of ideas. You are at a crossroad usually more than once during this time period where you are making major decisions about your life due to the restless energy you feel. It is time for a decision and you intuitively know you must wait out the nervous energy you are feeling and then take action based on what gives you peace. You are weighing, measuring, deciding, mediating. The right decisions bring long-lasting peace with this energy. This is not a time for assertiveness. Receptivity, gentleness, patience are called for now. Choose your words carefully as situations are resolved with the utmost tact and diplomacy from you. You may well find yourself in the middle of some chaos, disorganization, hostility and your role is diplomat. This is where you are now needed to restore order, balance, and peace. This is a time of charity and service for you. The challenge of this period is akin to navigating your way through landmines armed with only your intuition to guide you and you masterfully, peacefully, calmly make it through. The gift of this time period brings you much greater intuition and much needed and deserved peace.

If you do not have a **B, K,** or **T** in your name, then you have no 2 or 2 frequency and this will signify karmic lessons you have chosen to experience. There is an absence of peace and trust. This is a time of decision-making where you find yourself second-guessing every decision you make and frequently the decisions are based on an emotional reaction rather than intuition. The lesson here is you are to navigate through these emotions, this turbulence and come out with a clear understanding and tranquility. The Emotion Code, by Bradley Nelson, associated this with the spleen or stomach, anxiety, despair, disgust; nervousness, worry, failure, helplessness; hopelessness, a lack of control, and low self-esteem.

3: The Empress

Tarot Symbolism: Our Empress wears a crown of twelve stars indicating the realm of the mystical guiding her. She is not skinny. She is full figured, curvy and pregnant. The flowers are in full bloom around her. She represents fertility and mother earth. She is the mother energy. She is very well dressed as she loves luxury, and because she has taken care of and tended to mother earth, the Empress is bountiful. Her white robe of purity is adorned with pomegranates representing sacred divine feminine and fertility.

In *The Secret Teachings of All Ages*, by Manly P. Hall, the card known as L'Imperatrice, or the Empress, is presented as an embodiment of the divine feminine, bearing resemblance to the 'woman clothed with the sun' from the Apocalypse. This tarot card showcases a winged woman of authority, her presence commanding yet serene as she sits upon her throne. In her right hand, she holds a shield adorned with the image of a phoenix, symbolic of rebirth and continuity, and in her left, a scepter topped with either an orb or a floral motif, signifying her reign over creation. Sometimes, a crescent moon is depicted beneath her left foot, adding to her mystique. The Empress wears a crown, or her brow is encircled by a diadem of stars. Occasionally both adorn her, radiating her sovereignty. Known as Generation, she is the essence of the spiritual realm, giving rise to the physical world. To those initiated into the higher mysteries, she is the Alma Mater, the nurturing figure from whom initiates are symbolically reborn. In the variation found in the pseudo-Egyptian Tarot, the Empress sits upon a cube embellished with eyes, a bird poised upon her left forefinger, while a golden nimbus envelops her torso, illustrating her as the progenitor of the visible cosmos, often depicted in the fullness of pregnancy to signify her creative potency.

If the number three or its frequency is significant in your life – be it through your heart, personality, destiny, or spiritual path – the following insights are tailored for you: The number three has been emblematic of completeness and harmony throughout history and spirituality. It's the day God fashioned dry land and flora, and the day Christ triumphed over death with his resurrection. It's the number of the Three Wise Men, the triad of the third eye, and the Christian Holy Trinity – Father, Son, and Holy Ghost – as well as the linear flow of time: past, present, and future. If this is your number, it signifies you are an embodiment of unity, balance, and communication. Your spirit is one of joy, beauty, and artistic expression. Like The Empress in tarot, who is depicted as expectant amid flourishing flowers, you exude an energetic, outgoing nature, reveling in social interaction, creativity, and the art of manifestation. Your essence is steeped in expression – be it through art, conversation, or the simple joys of life such as fashion, gastronomy, and the pursuit of romance. You are openness personified; a spender, a socialite, and an artist with a compulsion to communicate in every form. Your charm and vivacity naturally draw others to you, making you the soul of any gathering, with humor as your companion. You might find your calling in the arts or any field that allows you to stand in the spotlight and uplift others.

However, if the number three is pronounced during a significant time like a pinnacle, year, month, or day, it signals a period of action, visibility, and fertility. It's a time to embrace social activities and express yourself, a stark contrast to the quietude of solitude. Symbolically, you've transformed from the stillness of a chrysalis to the vibrancy of a butterfly. It's a phase of being noticed, not only for your words but also for your aesthetic. Attention to personal grooming and style becomes paramount, as the world becomes your stage. Nonetheless, this cycle may bring waves of challenges, from emotional to financial, often all at once, prompting personal growth.

If your name lacks the letters C, L, or U, the number three might represent a karmic lesson, signifying a past struggle with self-expression and validation in your creative endeavors. As you mature, the lesson turns towards self-affirmation and expressing your truth, which is integral to your sense of self-worth and love. David Icke's philosophy resonates here, reminding us that seeking approval can lead to our entrapment, while "The Emotion Code" associates the number three with the lung or colon, highlighting emotions such as grief, defensiveness, discouragement, rejection; sadness, sorrow, self-abuse, and confusion – all of which can be overcome through self-empowerment and the articulate expression of one's truth.

4: The Emperor

Tarot Symbolism: The Emperor is married to the Empress, representing a union of opposites. He sits on a stone throne, symbolizing his connection to the earth element. His throne is adorned with four rams, emblematic of determination and a strong will. In his right hand, he holds an ankh, the symbol of life that amplifies energy and strength. The other hand grips an orb, signifying his dominion over the Earth. Cloaked in red robes that express passion, his white beard betrays his age and wisdom. His attire includes a suit of armor for protection, underscoring his direct, authoritative, and unemotional nature. Behind him rise mountains of achievement, testaments to the accomplishments borne of his strength, discipline, determination, and knowledge.

In *The Secret Teachings of All Ages*, by Manly P. Hall, the fourth major trump is called L'Empereur, the Emperor. Numerologically connected to the deity worshipped by the Pythagoreans as the tetrad, the Emperor's regalia and throne signify his role as the Demiurgus – the sovereign of the material realm. His armor-clad figure sits on a cubic stone throne, accented by a phoenix, further asserting his authority. The crossed legs of the Emperor are not without meaning, bearing either a scepter topped with an orb or carrying symbols of power in both hands. This orb is a testament to his role as the world's supreme ruler. Sun and moon symbols adorn his chest, representing the 'eyes' of the monarch in esoteric symbolism. His bodily posture and the arrangement of his legs evoke the symbol of sulphur, a nod to the revered alchemical king of yore. In the pseudo-Egyptian Tarot, this powerful figure is shown in profile, donning a masonic apron with a skirt that shapes into a right-angled triangle. His head is crowned with the Crown of the North, and his brow is marked by the spiraled uraeus, an ancient emblem of sovereignty and divine authority.

If the number 4 or the frequency of 4 resonates with your heart, personality, destiny, or spiritual path, then the following applies to you: On the fourth day, God created the sun, the moon, and the stars. You are the Magician all grown up. You have achieved much through reason, logic, study, and discipline – your essential tools. Your work ethic is strong, you plan carefully, and you adhere to a budget. With self-discipline at your core, you understand that daily effort is necessary to achieve your objectives, such as buying a home and securing financial stability. You consciously avoid debt, in contrast to our Empress who indulges in spending.

You embody the athlete, the dancer; your energy is physically robust. The nature of the number four is strong, solid, disciplined – salt of the earth. You stand as Mother Earth's guardian, overseeing agriculture, geology, and farming. You are the strong foundation, backed by education, knowledge, and skill, all of which you put to practical use. You recognize that a foundation's strength is contingent on its details, hence your meticulous nature. The concept of four relates to three-dimensional reality; with four points, we have our first three-dimensional figure, the tetractys. This is why the Emperor demands study, perfection, and a meticulous eye – so that the foundation laid can endure for generations. "Slow and steady" is your motto.

In proving a theorem in geometry, each statement builds upon the previous to arrive at a conclusion. This precision mirrors computer programming, where each entry must be exact. When achieved, the outcome is enduring and resilient. The Emperor's lesson, in stark contrast to the Empress, is to approach life with seriousness, to curb excesses, to formulate a plan and a budget, and to adhere to them. Our brave Emperors are found in law enforcement, the military, and the law – any sphere of life that lays a foundation. The Emperor's gift and lesson are to get serious, budget, exercise, become debt-free, plan meticulously, overcome addiction, and lay the groundwork for the future. A negative four can be bossy, dominant, or controlling.

If 4 or the frequency of 4 marks a pinnacle, year, month, or day for you, then you are in a phase of planning. Patience is crucial during this period as it seems everything that can break, will. This applies to your possessions and even your physical body, like your back, knee, or hip. Financially, it appears as though your resources are depleting quickly with repair bills surging beyond expectations. Authority issues may also arise. Avoid shortcuts; the trials you face now are setting a stronger foundation for the future. Perseverance is key. Plan for retirement and all financial matters. After this phase's intensity, you will find that everything is now stronger, setting an energized stage for future endeavors. Major purchases and retirement planning are favorable during this demanding time. Success will come from your efforts.

Consider the four elements — earth, wind, fire, air. Mastery over these is not about domination but discipline, study, and the judicious use of each, emphasizing recycling and eco-friendly practices. With four sides, we have a structure — opportunity to achieve much within the focus and boundary it provides. Yet, be mindful, as a negative four can also mean being bossy, dominant, controlling.

If your name lacks a D, M, or V, then 4 is your karmic number. This could manifest in various ways: perhaps you were raised by overly strict disciplinarians or bore the weight of life's realities early on, including financial or health issues. You might find yourself contending with a bully or control freak. Such a karmic number suggests a life of all work and no play, lacking a carefree childhood. Your purpose may be to challenge and change outdated laws, much like Susan B. Anthony, whose efforts enabled women's suffrage. *The Emotion Code* associates this with the liver and gallbladder, emphasizing emotions such as anger, bitterness, guilt, hatred, resentment; depression, frustration, indecisive, panic, and being taken for granted.

5: The Hierophant

Tarot Symbolism: Clothed in the regalia of spiritual authority, the Hierophant bears a triadic crown, each tier symbolic of mastery over the conscious, subconscious, and superconscious realms. He is the custodian of sacred knowledge, perched between the polar pillars of a temple, imparting esoteric wisdom to the acolytes before him. In his grasp, the papal cross, another trinity, symbolizes the Father, Son, and Holy Spirit – fundamental principles of creation, redemption, and sanctification. The Hierophant's attire, drenched in blue, white, and red, is not merely a sartorial choice but a visual testament to his attributes: blue for serenity, white for purity, and red for vitality and devotion. Beneath his venerable feet, keys lie in wait – the proverbial pass to the next echelon of spiritual evolution for the earnest seeker.

Drawing from *The Secret Teachings of All Ages* by Manly P. Hall, the fifth major trump card is the Hierophant, often equated with the Pope, the sage of the esoteric or exoteric enclave. This card is steeped in iconography: the tiara, the triple cross – a ruler's scepter over the worldly domain. With his stigmatized hand, he gestures an arcane benediction, a silent communion with the mystics who kneel in his presence. The throne itself is flanked by celestial and terrestrial insignia, denoting a command over the dualistic nature of existence. This tarot figure embodies the adept, one who has transcended to a plane of spiritual enlightenment, deciphering the enigma of life. In Hall's interpretation, the Hierophant is the 'spiritual physician' – the Pythagorean sage – armed with profound understanding to heal the ills birthed from illusion.

In a version that nods to ancient Egypt, the Master dons the ureaus, signaling supreme wisdom. A duality is presented in the supplicants – one white, one black – representing life and death, light and shadow, virtue and vice. Yet, above this dualism sits the Hierophant, an initiate who has achieved dominion over the ephemeral through the emblems of his sacred office – the tiara and the triple cross, the symbols of his sovereignty over the triune manifestation of the cosmos, birthed from the inscrutable Source.

If the number five is your heart, personality, destiny, or spiritual path – then consider the fifth day of creation: God crafted the birds and sea creatures, symbols of travel, transformation, and liberty. This biblical act echoes the essence of the number five, championing the break from the old and embracing the allure of distant shores and diverse cultures.

The quintet – senses, workdays ending in the liberation of Friday, even the evocative notion of five o'clock – exemplifies the concept of freedom, a core value to those who identify with this number. Take the Hierophant, an archetype of experience and the antithesis of stagnation. Freedom is not just a preference but a necessity for those who carry the energy of the five: a necessity for touch, for mental stimulation, and for incessant change to fend off the mundane.

This number is associated with versatility and wit, qualities that underpin the essence of technology's ever-evolving landscape. In numerology, where the number two signifies the High Priestess' feminine energy, five represents the High Priest, its masculine counterbalance. It's the number that fuels large organizations, ensuring they pulsate with life and never grow obsolete.

Consider the role of a family law judge, often tasked with the dissolution of unions that no longer serve those involved. It's in these circumstances that the influence of the number five is most needed – to dismantle what's broken and foster progression. Yet, there is a cautionary note: an excess of sensual indulgence can lead one astray, tipping the balance towards addiction and away from the wholesome enjoyment of life's physical delights.

If the number five marks a significant time for you – a pinnacle, a year, or even a day – it heralds a period ripe for transformation. It could mean the spark of new romances, the thrill of travel, or the bold step of altering life's direction. This phase encourages movement, bidding farewell to the stagnant and embarking on adventures that had once been mere entries on a bucket list.

Finally, if letters E, N, and W are absent in your name, five comes forth as a karmic challenge. This could manifest in an ascetic denial of pleasure or, conversely, an overindulgence in sensuality. It represents the struggle with addictions or a past filled with upheaval, challenging one to find stability and balance in the turbulence that the number five can bring. *The Emotion Code* associates this with the kidneys or bladder, and includes emotions such as blaming, dread, fear, horror; peeved, conflict, creative insecurity; terror, feeling unsupported, and wishy washy.

6: The Lovers

Tarot Symbolism: A naked man and woman stand in the Garden of Eden under Archangel Raphael, the angel of healing, representing the physical and emotional healing they achieve together. The apple tree with the serpent signifies mastery over the lower realms. The twelve flames on the tree behind the man symbolize time – 12 months in a year, 12 hours on a clock – representing the cycles of incarnation and reincarnation needed to overcome the lower self. The volcano behind them symbolizes passions igniting between two people. The man, representing consciousness, looks to the woman, the subconscious, who in turn looks up to the superconscious. As they each independently balance their energies, they can then come together in balance.

From *The Secret Teachings of All Ages* by Manly P. Hall: "The sixth numbered major trump is called L'Amoureux, the

Lovers. There are two forms of this Tarot. One shows a priest uniting a youth and a maiden in matrimony. Sometimes a winged figure above pierces the lovers with an arrow. The second form shows a youth with a female figure on each side. One figure is crowned and winged, the other wears vine leaves. They represent the dual nature of man – spiritual and animal – the angel and the demon. The youth faces 'the Parting of the Ways,' where he must choose between virtue and vice, eternal and temporal. Above is the genius of Fate, often mistaken for Cupid. If the youth chooses poorly, Fate's arrow will strike him. In the pseudo-Egyptian Tarot, the arrow points directly at the figure of vice, indicating that her path leads to destruction. This card reminds us that free will carries the burden of responsibility."

If the number 6 or the frequency of 6 is significant to your heart, personality, destiny, or spiritual path, this message is for you: On the sixth day, God created land animals and humans. Notably, the word "God" includes the vowel "O," which numerologically represents the number 6, and God epitomizes love. The Lovers card in Tarot, embodying the energy of 6, symbolizes unconditional love. Following the Hierophant's experiences, representing a wild, free-spirited phase with travel and exploration, one is often ready to settle down and nurture a family. The number 6 represents family, home, commitment, and children, emphasizing stability. It sees you as a community pillar, skilled in homemaking, real estate, and parenting – embracing long-term commitments, creativity, artistry, honesty, dependability, and loyalty. Your pursuits are enduring, such as raising a family, caring for an aging parent, or pursuing education. You value depth over fleeting connections, offering your whole self to your commitments and seeing them through to completion. You embody Mother Earth's nurturing essence. Children and stray pets are drawn to your protective aura. You prioritize family, placing their needs well above all else. Unconditional love is at the heart of your existence, while the negative aspects of a 6 can be domineering and controlling. When positively expressed, the energy of 6 is the muse for heartfelt love songs, offering a deep understanding of universal interconnectedness through love. Your charitable spirit fights for the voiceless – children, the elderly, animals – echoed in the Merkaba symbol's six-pointed star, representing the unity of the divine and earthly realms and the activation of the heart chakra.

If the number 6 appears in important dates or cycles of your life – such as pinnacles, years, months, or days – it signifies a period of familial support, assuming the role of caregiver for both younger and older relatives. You embody the maternal archetype, loaded with responsibility. The domain of the 6 encompasses all things home-related, from real estate and interior decorating to property management and community engagement. This phase calls for commitment and seeing things through, an ideal time for familial expansion or deepened commitments. However, be cautious of overextending yourself. It's crucial to set boundaries and prioritize self-care, ensuring you are equipped to fulfill the responsibilities of this period. A negative expression can lead to overbearing or dependent behavior. By meeting these responsibilities, you channel and manifest the unconditional love associated with the number 6.

If your name lacks the letters F, O, or X, the number 6 represents a karmic challenge. This may be reflected in early maternal responsibilities, complex parental relationships, or a lack of nurturing in your upbringing – challenges that echo the love and dedication represented by the number 6. Commitment may have historically placed you in the role of the responsible one, possibly leading to a sense of servitude or oppression within the home. Recognizing and addressing these karmic issues allows for the growth and expression of the nurturing, loving qualities of the number 6. *The Emotion Code* connects this with your glands and sexual organs, and associates this with emotions like humiliation, jealousy, longing, lust; overwhelm, pride, shame, shock; feeling unworthy and worthlessness.

7: The Chariot

Tarot Symbolism: The Chariot card signifies an openness to the Divine Source. The charioteer, depicted without reins in his hands, symbolizes control over the chariot through mental power. This image embodies mastery over one's lower emotional self, achievable through consistent meditation and prayer. Rather than being at the whim of his thoughts, the charioteer is his own sovereign, having seized the mental reins. He directs the two sphinxes, one white and one black, which embody the duality of life – positive and negative forces that are harmonized by our higher self's guidance. The stars adorning his crown symbolize the celestial guidance that is ours when we quiet the mind to listen. The moon phases on his shoulders reflect the emotional progression of humanity. Standing tall, not seated on a throne, the charioteer is poised for action. The river in the background represents a state of flow, while the square on his chest denotes fortitude. He exhibits control over the physical realm, with the constant support of the celestial, a testament to how he maintains equilibrium at all times, even without physical reins, steering dualities in the direction of his will.

Drawing from *The Secret Teachings of All Ages* by Manly P. Hall, the seventh major arcana card, named Le Chariot, presents a triumphant warrior wearing a crown and riding in a chariot drawn by black and white sphinxes or horses. The celestial dome of the chariot is sustained by four pillars. The card represents the Exalted One journeying in the chariot of creation, indicating that the seven planets serve as vehicles for the solar force, which prevails in their sphere. The four pillars symbolize the four great forces upholding the cosmos, illustrated by the starry drapery above. The figure wields the scepter of solar energy, and the moon crescents on its shoulders – known as the Urim and Thummim – denote divine guidance. The sphinxes embody the esoteric and unseen energies propelling the ruler across his domain. In some Tarot decks, this victorious figure embodies the enlightened individual, with the chariot's body as a cubic stone. The armored figure is not merely standing within the chariot but is ascending from the cube, signifying the elevation from the material to the spiritual – the '3' rising from the '4', much like the lifting of the flap on a Master Mason's apron. In the pseudo-Egyptian Tarot, the warrior brandishes Luna's crescent sword, sports a beard to show wisdom, and dons the collar symbolizing the planetary orbits. His scepter, representative of the tripartite universe, is topped with a square enclosing a circle framed by a triangle.

If the number seven or its frequency resonates with your heart, personality, destiny, or spiritual path, the following attributes apply to you: the Holy Spirit, spiritual awakening, the essence of water, depth of emotions, and a penchant for tranquility, healing, and reflective sojourns. God's rest on the seventh day, the presence of seven principal chakras, and the imagery of the charioteer in the Tarot Chariot card – all point to the significance of seven in controlling one's life through mental prowess rather than physical means.

This number denotes a methodical approach, compassion, unselfishness, eloquence, and a dignified reserve. Your attention to detail is meticulous, influencing even the subtleties of your attire, yet never to excess. The mind serves as your greatest ally and challenge, being the vessel for your innate mysticism. Historically, those whose spiritual paths totaled to seven were considered destined for temple life, owing to their deep spiritual understanding.

The 'seven' vibration compels you to explore beyond the five senses, towards that which is aged, hallowed, and enigmatic. You thrive in the pursuit of knowledge, especially in areas considered occult or atypical. Mental stimulation is crucial to your being, driving a continuous quest for understanding. Your nature is akin to that of a Gnostic, relentlessly seeking answers. Your engineering prowess stems from a curiosity to dissect and comprehend how things operate, contributing to your role as a free thinker and problem solver. Despite an aversion to crowds, your innovations significantly benefit humanity. A natural empath, you are sensitive to the energies of those around you, often at the expense of your own health.

The energy of seven fosters your mental faculties, allowing your body to seek repose. Physical exertion should be minimized under this influence, inviting you to delve into your spiritual talents. This energy shapes you into a healer, perhaps through sound therapy, with intuitive gifts awaiting your exploration. Financial gain may be sluggish, as your focus is drawn inward to the splendors of your inner landscape.

Interest in fields not mainstream – shamanism, numerology, astrology, and various forms of energy healing – aligns with your essence. Your daily rituals must include water and silence to maintain equilibrium; otherwise, you risk becoming irritable and unwell. Assertiveness in a seven vibration often leads to resistance, something you intuitively understand. In stillness and quiet, you attract remarkable experiences. You embody the philosopher, the thinker, the visionary. Traditional religious constructs may clash with your free-thinking spirit.

If you find yourself in a seven pinnacle, year, month, or day, it is imperative to rest and refrain from assertiveness. This is a time for spiritual retreat, not for bustling amusement parks but rather for tranquil sanctuaries. Physical activity should be gentle; allow your mind to wander through other realms. On the negative side, you might exhibit moodiness and withdrawal, engulfed in your emotional states. Financial dealings and legal matters require careful scrutiny during this period.

If your name lacks a G, P, or Y, then seven reflects your karmic challenges. These may manifest as a constant intrusion upon your solitude or an overwhelming isolation. Being unheard or restricted in expressing your thoughts can be part of this karmic lesson, urging you to utilize and hone the power of your mind. Samuel Hahnemann, the founder of homeopathy, is an example of seven karma in action. Isolated to ponder, he harnessed his solitude to develop groundbreaking medical philosophies. Your seven karma is a catalyst for mental development, a journey that may lead you through vision and insight far beyond the average scope. Take care of your eyes and ears as vision and hearing are key issues of the 7 frequency.

8: Strength

Tarot Symbolism: The woman is depicted alongside a lion. The lion symbolizes pride, courage, regality, self-assurance, leadership, and protection, as well as raw passion. She has subdued the beast with her dauntless spirit and benevolence. The infinity symbol above her head signifies her astuteness and sovereignty over terrestrial concerns.

In *The Secret Teachings of All Ages* by Manly P. Hall, it is described: The eleventh card of the major arcana, named Strength or La Force, shows a young woman donning a hat resembling an infinity symbol, with her hands on the muzzle of a seemingly fierce lion. There is some debate over whether she is closing or opening the lion's jaws. Most scholars agree that she is closing the mouth of the lion; however, upon closer examination, the impression may be that she is doing the opposite. The maiden embodies spiritual fortitude, and the lion may represent the animal nature she subdues or the esoteric knowledge she commands. The lion also represents the summer solstice, and the girl corresponds to Virgo, as the lion's strength wanes when the sun enters this sign. King Solomon's throne was adorned with lions, and he was compared to the king of the beasts, which held the key to wisdom in its jaws. Thus, the girl might be prying open the lion's mouth to retrieve the key, symbolizing that bravery is essential for acquiring knowledge. In the pseudo-Egyptian Tarot, the motif remains, except the maiden is portrayed as a priestess crowned with an elaborate headdress featuring birds and serpents, and an ibis. It is worth noting that the eighth card was once Justice and the eleventh Strength. The reason for this change is unclear. Having learned to recognize the eighth card as Strength and the eleventh as Justice, I continue to adhere to this arrangement.

If the number 8 or its frequency resonates with your heart, personality, destiny, or spiritual path, this message is for you: The essence of 8 is resurrection – embodied by the brave, bold, and fearless leader. Consider the spider and its eight legs: It represents the conquest of fears, and you embody this triumph. No obstacle is too daunting for you. Reflect on toll-free 800 numbers: symbols of corporate might, organization, and resilience. A standard workday begins at 8:00 AM, following a period of solitude and quiet – a time for recharging. As we transition to the energy of the 8, we find ourselves physically prepared and mentally sharp.

Your determination distinguishes you. In the financial realm, you thrive. Vigorous exercise, particularly outdoors, suits you best – be it horseback riding, marathons, gymnastics, or dance. Your innate talent to channel energy through your physique explains your affinity for sports, more so than any other number. Eights are renowned as stellar athletes, courageous and adept at taking calculated risks. You lead projects, organize effectively, and execute with precision. As an authority in your domain, your influence is undeniable.

The scale of the budget or challenge invigorates you, aligning with your focus on wealth, fiscal matters, and physical prowess. If this path is spiritual for you, it's about reclaiming your power and asserting yourself with love, defining your space assertively yet gently. Eights have masculine energy; thus, be wary of domineering or intimidating tendencies.

As an authority in your chosen field, you eclipse your competitors with unrivaled skill and focus. Efficiency is your hallmark – there's no room for downtime. The lemniscate, an infinity symbol and a figure eight on its side, represents karmic cycles: the eternal balance of giving and receiving, as exemplified in the Tarot with the woman and the lion – a narrative of leadership coupled with kindness.

Precision, be it in German or Swiss engineering, or an athlete's regimen, is your playground. Remember, routine and discipline are vital, but self-criticism must be tempered. Allow yourself moments of respite. Your executive prowess and ability to manage vast projects stem from this precision.

The Eight draws adversity, often prompting you to defend yourself or others. In harmony, you are the strong leader with a tender core, passionate about law and order on a global scale.

If the number 8 is a current pinnacle, year, month, or day – you may find that your youth was overshadowed by the gravity of an Eight's responsibilities. It's a time of work and defining your boundaries. Organizational needs may arise in all areas, from finances to physical fitness. This period may bring financial extremes, shaped by the Eight's karmic nature. It's a time to harness your focus, to make the most of the resources at your disposal.

Without an H, Q, or Z in your name, Eight's karma may manifest as past physical or financial trials. It is your task to navigate between submissiveness and aggression, channeling your anger through a potent yet healing expression. Remember, assertiveness over aggression, strength without domination. Your experiences might include encounters with bullies, often male, reflecting the Eight's masculine energy. Yet, wealth's burdens can be as challenging as poverty. Balance is the lesson: stand your ground.

With the number 8, you are called to be assertive, not aggressive – robust, not overbearing. Your task is to use your formidable energy in a manner that resolves your karmic debts instead of compounding them. As the 8 individual demands much from their own bodies, physical breakdowns are possible.

9: The Hermit

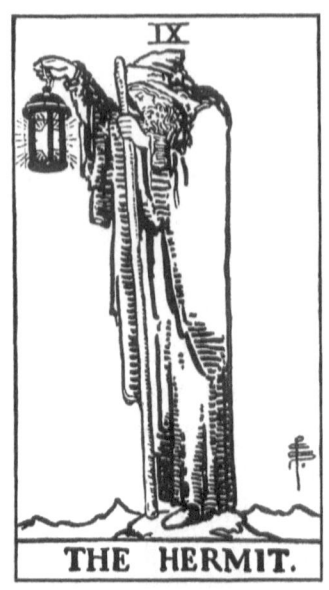

Tarot Symbolism: The elderly man leans on his staff, casting light to guide others. He stands atop a snow-covered mountain, symbolizing the isolation that comes with wisdom. His simple attire signifies the shedding of the superfluous on his spiritual journey. His white beard and venerable age speak of lifetimes of accrued wisdom. The staff, akin to the Magician's wand, signifies power and the awakened kundalini energy, denoting self-mastery. The light he shares, a symbol of generosity, reveals his role as a mentor, imparting wisdom to enlighten others on their path.

From Manly P. Hall's *The Secret Teachings of All Ages*, we understand the ninth tarot card, L'Hermit, or the Hermit, to depict an elderly man in monastic robes, leaning on a staff. This figure is often thought to embody Diogenes in his search for an honest man. Concealed within his cloak, he holds a lamp, symbolizing the secretive societies that have long guarded esoteric knowledge from those not initiated. His staff, occasionally marked into seven segments, subtly alludes to the mystical energy centers aligned with the human spine. In certain Tarot representations, the Hermit's careful shielding of his lamp behind his cloak underscores the philosophical notion that wisdom, if revealed to the uninitiated, might be extinguished just as a storm can snuff out a lantern's flame. The human form acts as a veil, only faintly revealing the divine essence within, like the obscured light of the lantern. It is through the Hermetic lifestyle of renunciation that one achieves depth of character and inner peace.

This passage reflects the intended sophistication and depth, eliminating redundancies and enhancing clarity, while maintaining the text's informative and descriptive nature.

If the number 9 or its frequency resonates with your heart, personality, destiny, or spiritual journey, then this message is for you: You possess profound wisdom, as symbolized by the Hermit's grey hair in tarot lore. Your essence is philanthropic and humanitarian, embracing responsibilities and seeing them through to their conclusion. You look past divisions of borders, race, ethnicity, gender, and sexual orientation; such distinctions hold no meaning for you. Your life's purpose is service to humanity and to our planet, Earth. You take charge where others may falter, concerned not with the origins of issues but with the solutions necessary to reestablish harmony.

You feel a strong calling to share your knowledge, born from countless lifetimes and experiences. The number 9 represents an impersonal life, urging you to let go of the personal and embrace completion, addressing unfinished business. Your intuition is keen, often accompanied by marked psychic abilities, and your inner voice is a clear guide. Generosity is your hallmark, with a belief that true value arises from sharing. As a teacher, you integrate your extensive knowledge into wisdom, forming the foundation of your compassion.

The Tarot archetype of the Hermit, which you embody, is a figure of simplicity, unconcerned with material trappings, and focused on illuminating the path for others. His wisdom sets him apart, and he leads without control. Your divine connection will bring tests in this lifetime, as you are meant to experience life impersonally, letting go of transient relationships and situations.

The number 9 signifies the completion of a cycle, much like the nine months of gestation before birth. Creativity and a penchant for the dramatic arts are intrinsic to this number, necessitating an environment filled with music, art, and teaching. The term "light," with "i" as its sole vowel, further emphasizes the heart-centered nature of the number 9. Your humanitarian spirit is indispensable in maintaining the world's equilibrium.

There are potential pitfalls, however, such as emotional turbulence and an overly generous spirit that can lead to self-neglect. The phrase "on cloud nine" captures the euphoric highs that can be reached by this energy. Your gentle, non-controlling approach to sharing knowledge raises collective awareness. The path of the 9 involves embracing acceptance, teaching, giving, and sharing. The personality number of Mohandas Karamchand Gandhi, which totals 81, resonates with the 9 vibration. Gandhi exemplifies both the highest and the lowest traits of a Nine. Similarly, the word "Soul," with the vowels adding up to 9, centers on a love for wisdom and humanity, underscoring the value you place on these virtues. As a wise old soul, you likely felt out of place in childhood, distinct from your peers.

Should the number 9 appear as a pinnacle, year, month, or day for you, prepare for additional responsibility, tests, farewells, and the act of letting go. This Nine vibration marks a period of completion for long-term goals, encompassing the experiences of numbers one through eight. It's a time for you to be the observer, recognizing and accepting endings and preparing for new beginnings.

If your name lacks the letters I or R, the number 9 represents a karmic lesson. It may manifest in an aversion to completing tasks, a lack of follow-through, or experiencing significant loss. Embracing completion, follow-through, and focus can be challenging but is necessary for growth. Spine and shoulder issues come up frequently for the 9 individual as the Hermit carries much responsibility.

Remember, the nature of the Nine is to conclude, not to begin. Embrace this time of giving and receiving, and allow yourself the space to receive as well.

10: The Wheel of Fortune

Tarot Symbolism: The card depicted does not feature a human figure, instead, it symbolizes help, assistance, and knowledge from celestial entities far beyond our earthly realm. At the heart of this message are the Torah's sacred texts, from which we glean knowledge. Yet, true wisdom is only birthed through living – engaging in the cycle of life, death, and rebirth. It's within this wheel, or circle, of existence that book knowledge transforms into the profound understanding that only real-life experiences can bestow.

The wheel's circularity is not mere happenstance; it's a divine blessing. It offers us the chance, time and again, to take human form and navigate through life's lessons until we grasp the wisdom the Divine wishes to impart. The snake on the card illustrates our spiritual descent to Earth, marking the start of our quest for enlightenment. Clouds shroud the future, veiling the lessons yet to be learned. Life's inherent cycles awaken us to our true nature, setting us on the homeward journey to the source of all. Immutable laws govern our time on Earth, symbolized by the books. Representing various facets of existence are the winged figures – a bull, lion, eagle, and an angel – while the sphinx atop the wheel wields the sword of justice.

Manly P. Hall, in *The Secret Teachings of All Ages*, describes the Wheel of Fortune as a wheel with eight spokes, echoing the Buddhist wheel of life. Clinging to its rim are Anubis and Typhon, representing good and evil. The sphinx above, signifying divine wisdom, holds the balance of justice amid these forces. As Typhon falls, evil rises; as Anubis ascends, goodness fades – depicting the perpetual flux between virtue and vice. The wheel signifies the material universe, with divine wisdom as its impartial judge.

In Indian tradition, the 'chakra' or wheel is tied to the vital centers of either a cosmos or an individual. The Tarot often portrays the sphinx with a spear and Typhon being cast down from the wheel. The solitary column seen beside the wheel, an allegory for the world's axis, supports the inscrutable sphinx – its sentinel. Occasionally, this cosmic wheel is depicted within a boat on the ocean, a metaphor for the bewildering sea of illusion that underpins the ceaseless wheel of life.

If the number 10 resonates with your heart, personality, destiny, or spiritual path, then this message is for you. For further insights, refer to the section titled "The History of Zero." Number ten embodies novelty, progress, innovation, strength, leadership, and transcendence. You are a natural leader, with a preference for self-employment due to your broad, visionary thinking. You easily grasp unconventional concepts and exhibit great creativity and inventiveness. The word 'impossible' captivates you, as you recognize that all is possible and relish a challenge. Your achievements stem from your leadership capabilities and innate intuition – you simply 'know.' You are destined to introduce something new to the world, with ambitions that are both noble and expansive. Like the turning wheel, progress and the realization of your dreams are inevitable.

However, if the negative aspects of this energy manifest, there's a risk of becoming self-centered or egotistical. The dichotomy of ten is common in its expressions: it signifies 'a perfect ten' for exceptional success or a measure on a pain scale, implying that you have access to the wisdom of all your past lives. With this knowledge comes the choice of direction – towards the positive or negative. Ventures in land and property can be highly profitable for you, and success and influence seem to come effortlessly. This is not due to chance but because you understand that reaching any goal is a matter of taking sequential steps. You are audacious and resolute in your pursuits.

As a spiritual entity, you've already honed your powers of manifestation over numerous lifetimes. Your bold ideas push humanity's progress forward. On this spiritual journey, you learn to assert yourself, to fulfill your needs, and to voice your desires. Starting projects and delegating tasks is your strength, and you're known within your family for challenging conventional beliefs and exploring unconventional knowledge, which can make you feel like an outsider. Introducing new concepts can be a struggle, as many prefer the comfort of the familiar, but you thrive in pushing these boundaries.

If the number 10 represents a significant pinnacle, year, month, or day for you, understand that you are on a specific mission. Your current role is to advance people, ideas, and concepts toward what is urgently needed, which entails leaving behind outdated methods. Your presence may not always be welcomed by those resistant to change. You are called to substitute the old and stagnant with the fresh, practical, and humanitarian. Now is your time to stand alone, to initiate action, and not to remain passive. With a strategic approach, focusing on one small step at a time, you channel your creativity into multiple projects.

This period is marked by intense activity and concentration, as you draw in the necessary people and resources. You're in a position of authority – leading, not following. Although both roles are equally important, this is your moment to lead. Your clear and straightforward communication garners support from those around you. Assistance and opportunities arise as you set your plans into motion. With a bustling agenda and a path of great significance before you, your success is virtually ensured. This marks a positive turning point.

11: Justice

Tarot Symbolism: Behind the throne is a purple veil, symbolizing the crown chakra, connection to the spiritual realm, and embodying compassion and wisdom. Lady Justice is seated between two pillars, suggesting another trial or initiation into mastery. In her hands, she holds the sword of discrimination, double-edged to slice through deception and achieve clarity of vision. The sword, held in her right hand and pointing upwards, signifies divine guidance. In her left hand, the balanced scales of justice are firmly grasped, reflecting her intuitive, logical, and compassionate nature. The square on her crown alludes to a logical mind, while her exposed white shoe signifies being grounded in purity. Her red robe represents dominance and the mastery over the lower self.

According to *The Secret Teachings of All Ages* by Manly P. Hall, the eighth numbered major trump is called "La Justice," or

Justice, and depicts a figure seated upon a throne, backed by two rising columns. Crowned, Justice wields a sword in her right hand and scales in her left. This card serves as a reminder of the soul's judgment in the hall of Osiris, teaching that only balanced forces endure and that eternal Justice eliminates the unbalanced with its sword. Justice is sometimes shown with a braid of her hair fashioned into a noose, subtly suggesting that humanity may engineer its own downfall – our actions, symbolized by our hair, becoming our undoing. In the pseudo-Egyptian Tarot, Justice sits elevated on a dais of three steps, indicating that true justice can only be administered by those who have ascended to the third degree. Justice is blindfolded to ensure that sight does not influence judgment. (For reasons he deemed beyond his readers' understanding, Mr. Waite swapped the positions of the eighth and eleventh major trumps.)

If the number 11 resonates with your heart, personality, destiny, or spiritual path, then this message is for you: Your journey is inherently spiritual. You possess acute observational skills and favor tranquility, silence, and a position away from the spotlight. As a diplomat, you play the crucial role of peacemaker, whether within your family or on the global stage, fostering peace where war might otherwise erupt. Your presence is essential, often in profound darkness, yet it's best you remain unaware of the energy of these places, for your work is vital there. You heed an internal command, one not issued by others, but from within. Your mission is clear, and you accept it without question. When you trust this inner guidance, all aligns; when you ignore it, disarray ensues. This master number is potent. You've sought to be tested, as if opting to be blindfolded in life to enhance your profound inner dialogue and vision. Your psychic and intuitive abilities are significantly heightened, and it's likely you possess advanced psychic skills.

The challenge lies in trusting not others, but yourself. You must delve beyond appearances, heeding your inner voice's counsel. With the power of the dual ones, your leadership manifests through peace, tact, and diplomacy. Words are your tools; with them, you craft change and influence for the better. Courageous, you confront injustice, often advocating for others over yourself. As a protector of ideas and ideals, you face numerous trials, navigating them with finesse, precision, clarity, and factual acumen.

Legal matters gravitate toward you, necessitating changes for the collective benefit – a challenge you do not shy away from. Notably, the word "Healer" resonates with the number 11 in the heart and 20, or Judgment in personality numerology, both sharing the 2 frequency that restores balance, emotionally and spiritually. William Griffith Wilson, co-founder of Alcoholics Anonymous, walked a destiny path of 11, bringing light and healing through his struggles. You, too, serve as a beacon for many, unwavering. Service is your ultimate vocation.

With an abundance of 11s in your chart, sleep may elude you, as you stand like twin pillars rooted in the earth yet open to the heavens, akin to lightning rods awaiting inspiration's strike. Grounding and rest are crucial.

If 11 marks a pinnacle, year, month, or day for you, it heralds a time for legalities, justice, and resolution. In the face of conflict and injustice, you're compelled to pursue the moral high ground, ensuring improvement through legal channels. Your intuition peaks, guiding you unquestionably toward the right path, one that illuminates the way for all. You lead with your carefully-chosen words, providing the peace so desperately needed by others. You face upheaval and injustice with your innate sense of justice, and through this, balance will be reinstated. This is your test.

As a visionary, your unwavering adherence to your ideals sways others to your perspective, requiring patience, firmness, strength, and tact – qualities you possess in abundance. This period is marked by psychic awareness, meditation, creativity, and artistic expression. You may find yourself awakened with urgent words that demand to be penned down. Like Mozart, who professed to simply transcribe the music dictated to him, you have access to various realms of consciousness and must express these experiences so that others may be inspired by your insights.

12: The Hanged Man

Tarot Symbolism: The Hanged Man is literally upside down, gazing at his reflection in the water below. This signifies a mirror image or reversal, suggesting that things are not as they seem. A deeper search for truth is imperative. The Hanged Man is ideally poised for this introspection; he is detached, not engaging with his surroundings. Despite his inverted state, he achieves clarity. His crossed leg forms the number 4, echoing the Emperor, which signifies the need for logic, reason, and order. His composure remains intact; calm and serene. His hands, folded behind him, create a triangle, and a halo around his head signifies enlightenment.

From *The Secret Teachings of All Ages* by Manly P. Hall, "The twelfth numbered major trump is called Le Pendu, the Hanged Man, and portrays a young man hanging by his left leg from a horizontal beam, the latter supported by two tree trunks from each of which six branches have been removed. The right leg of the youth is crossed in back of the left and his arms are folded behind his back in such a manner as to form a cross surmounting a downward-pointing triangle. The figure thus forms an inverted symbol of sulphur and, according to Lévi, signifies the accomplishment of the magnum opus. In some decks, the figure carries under each arm a money bag from which coins are escaping. Popular tradition associates this card with Judas Iscariot, who is said to have gone forth and hanged himself, the money bags representing the payment he received for his betrayal. Lévi likens the hanged man to Prometheus, the Eternal Sufferer, and declares that the upturned feet signify the spiritualization of the lower nature. It is also proposed that the inverted figure denotes the loss of spiritual faculties, as the head is positioned below the level of the body. The stumps of the twelve branches represent the signs of the zodiac, divided into two groups – positive and negative. The imagery thus conveys polarity temporarily prevailing over the spiritual principle of equilibrium. To ascend to the heights of philosophy, one must reverse (or invert) the order of his life, leading to the loss of personal possession as he renounces the rule of gold in favor of the golden rule. In the pseudo-Egyptian Tarot, the hanged man is suspended between two palm trees, symbolizing the Sun God who dies perennially for his world.

If the number 12 resonates with your heart, personality, destiny, or spiritual path, the following insights are for you: Surrender, reversal, sacrifice, submission, observation, awareness, and clarity. Your life's mission is to serve others. The number 12 is woven into our lives with twelve months in a year, twelve jurors in a panel, twelve disciples of Jesus. Following Jesus' ascension, his disciples endured numerous trials before earning the right to teach. The number 12 signifies a person adept at a particular skill. It carries an energy that is soft, quiet, loving, and knowing.

You may have embraced a challenge, be it an illness, a relationship, or a circumstance that appears limiting and restrictive. Yet, you are undaunted by commitments or the pursuit of education, investing time and effort to master your field, be it through obtaining a degree or attending classes. Your passion might lie in the healing arts; whether you are a surgeon, nurse, spiritual healer, or massage therapist, you possess an intimate understanding of your craft. Precision is not just a requirement but a standard you set for yourself. Your best work emerges under pressure, maintaining calm amid chaos.

The inclination towards the healing arts comes from a desire to alleviate suffering, a calling you hold dear. Your heart is expansive; your observational skills are sharp. Representing this is the Hanged Man tarot card, which symbolizes seeing the world from an unconventional, 'upside down' perspective. Your views may not always align with the mainstream, but they often offer a more accurate and profound understanding. Drama, unrest, and illness may find their way to you, but your task is to observe rather than engage. In silence, you align with the universe's perfection.

Nonconformity is your norm; the unconventional and alternative spark your interest over the traditional, which you find limiting. Innovation and patience are among your virtues. Embracing acceptance liberates your mind, allowing knowledge, skill, awareness, and peace to flow through you and onto others. Volunteering your expertise is second nature.

Water plays a critical role in the imagery of the Hanged Man, reflecting back at him his own image. In your submission and acceptance lies the serene strength of this figure. Your mental fortitude and precision enable you to excel in meticulous and demanding tasks. You carry your burdens with remarkable love and compassion, showing tolerance for all beliefs without judgment. Others seek your wisdom, comfort, and guidance. As a gnostic, you quest for answers without casting judgment, finding the most joy in serving others. Interestingly, the heart number of the word 'doctor' is 12, which may explain your affinity for the healing sciences. The simple act of being is the gift you offer the world.

If 12 appears as a significant pinnacle, year, month, or day for you, embrace the principles of sacrifice, reversal, and submission. Now is not the time for active change; rather, it's a time for stillness and observation. Any feelings of being stuck, whether due to illness or a challenging assignment in a remote location, are part of your current journey. Unusual and demanding situations may arise, offering little control. Utilize meditation and observation as tools to return to inner harmony and peace amidst apparent turmoil. You might find yourself responding to a call to volunteer your services. Remember, engaging in surrounding dramas is not your role. Inactivity paradoxically serves better than action. Your mere presence is healing, provided you remain detached from the drama. In this period of 'just being,' you find your gift and lesson, both for yourself and for others. Success comes through letting go, which, counterintuitively, ensures victory and opens doors to gifts greater than those present at the outset of this journey.

13: Death

Tarot Symbolism: The skeleton represents the embodiment of death, which is indiscriminate, visiting all beings without exception. His armor bestows upon him invincibility. Mounted on a white horse, the skeleton symbolizes the purification process through death, transformation, and rebirth. A fallen royal on the ground, alongside other figures pleading for mercy, underscores the inevitability of change. The five-pointed flower on the skeleton's banner represents humanity and the beautiful cycle of change driven by our spiritual evolution, drawing us ever closer to Christ consciousness with each cycle of life, death, and rebirth.

The square banner alludes to the number four, The Emperor, and the earthly realm, suggesting that our earthly existence is akin to a classroom of our own creation, where we learn lessons chosen by our higher selves to master our being. The waters in the background are symbolic escorts of souls to the afterlife, while the sun represents the hope that each life offers, an opportunity to progress and awaken the Christ within us.

According to *The Secret Teachings of All Ages* by Manly P. Hall, the thirteenth trump card in the Tarot, known as "La Mort" or Death, depicts a reaping skeleton with a scythe severing the emerging heads, hands, and feet. Interestingly, the skeleton appears to have accidentally cut off one of its own feet in some decks, a detail underscoring the notion that imbalance and destructiveness go hand in hand. Symbolically, the skeleton represents the primary and supreme Deity, mirroring the body's foundation as the Absolute underpins creation. While death physically signifies an end, it philosophically embodies the natural impulse for all beings to merge back into the divine state pre-existing the illusory universe. The scythe's blade represents the moon and its crystallizing power, and the field of the universe wherein everything that rises from the earth will be returned to it. Death, the ruler of all visible and tangible parts of creatures, regards kings, queens, courtesans, and commoners equally. Some Tarot decks show Death armored atop a white horse, trampling both old and young, illustrating death's impartial nature. The pseudo-Egyptian Tarot adds a rainbow behind Death, symbolizing the transcendence of the body's mortality into the spirit's immortality. Death, though a destroyer of form, cannot annihilate life, which is ever-renewing. This card stands as an emblem of the universe's ceaseless renewal - a cycle of disintegration and reintegration at higher levels of existence.

If the number 13 is significant for your heart, personality, destiny, or spiritual path, the following is pertinent: It heralds a sequence of death, destruction, and, ultimately, liberation, leading to rebirth and renewal. This numeral rarely signifies an actual demise but rather a transformative process that is much needed. You embody strength, methodical precision, and an unwavering commitment to study and understand your subjects thoroughly. Your life decisions are grounded in your knowledge, education, and experience, with discipline being a cornerstone of your existence. You are conscientious of the far-reaching impacts of your choices, both on yourself and on others.

Duty and honor are not mere concepts to you but guiding principles. The presence of 13 in your numerological chart signals the areas of life where your serious nature comes to the forefront, where your choices are shaped by the wellbeing of all and driven by the noblest of causes. Death and transformation weave through your existence; you manage significant shifts that shape the fabric of life. In the realm of numerology, the 13 decomposes to a 4 (1+3=4), symbolizing the discipline of the mind and body, while 13 itself speaks to the evolution of the spirit. You are laying down a powerful, necessary foundation – solid, healthful, enlightened, and spiritually aligned. Change and transformation are your hallmarks.

Your experience is akin to that of Anne Sullivan, Helen Keller's teacher, whose destiny number of 94 (9+4) reduced to 13, a number encapsulating her role in guiding Helen through transformative darkness. When 13 influences your life decisions, you often find yourself in environments that deal with stark realities, such as the military, law enforcement, hospitals, or social work. Your innate gifts of discipline, focus, and transformation are called upon in these roles.

When the number 13 marks a pinnacle period, year, month, or day, you encounter an expansion of consciousness. 13 is the Christ, or the Christ-consciousness, and whenever the 13 experience is in charge, your consciousness is opening, expanding. Under its influence, your awareness broadens, and change is constant. There could be upheavals like relocating or tackling long-term projects. This period can be demanding but is necessary and ultimately rewarding. Conditions that have grown stagnant are revitalized; anything negative is swept away to allow for the infusion of new, positive energy. This is a time of complete commitment – there's no halfway.

Preparation for this phase involves a thorough examination of your life's constituents, as most will undergo positive change. Any signs of breakdown, whether in material possessions or personal health, indicate a need for repair or transformation. This is a call to discipline, organization, education, and personal growth. You are answering a higher call to align with a Christ-like consciousness. Every creative, intuitive, and focused effort you make now is fine-tuned, propelling you to excel in your field, whether it be as a musician, social worker, or any other vocation.

Anything that undergoes the purifying process of 'death' is sanctified, echoing the touch of the divine. The white horse symbolizes purity and every transition through death and rebirth is an ascension, an alignment with higher consciousness. Release self-judgment and embrace the transformative journey.

14: Temperance

Tarot Symbolism: The androgynous angel, depicted with dual cups, meticulously transfers water between them – symbolizing the blending of emotions. This act represents a profound opportunity to combine feelings such as anger with forgiveness, fostering deep compassion and wisdom. Emblazoned upon the angel's attire is a square containing a triangle, illustrating the synthesis of the number four, The Emperor (indicative of tangible manifestation), and the number three, The Empress (representative of harmony).

The angelic figure stands poised with one foot immersed in water and the other grounded on land, embodying the pursuit of equilibrium – the imperative to ground emotional experiences in reality to find a balanced, middle path. The vibrant red wings echo the transformation from intense emotions like anger and wrath to states of compassion, forgiveness, and profound understanding. In the tableau's background, a path denotes life's myriad experiences, akin to the vital kundalini energy one is destined to master. This trail meanders towards the sun, emblematic of the gifts garnered through life's journey – balance, moderation, strength, compassion, and wisdom. Foregrounded white lilies symbolize the purification that comes from the tempering of the self.

In *The Secret Teachings of All Ages*, Manly P. Hall elucidates the fourteenth tarot card, La Temperance. It depicts an angel with a solar emblem upon her brow, endlessly pouring from one urn to another, a cycle that mimics the celestial rhythm of life – flowing from the unseen to the seen and back again, a cycle uninterrupted and eternally sustained. Whether in Tarot decks where the liquid assumes the Aquarius sign or the pseudo-Egyptian Tarot's male counterpart, the essence remains – the descent of divine forces into earthly realms, illustrated by the golden and silver urns. This potent imagery captures the interchange of life energies within the cosmic framework, directed by a solar force that lifts water to the heavens, only for it to descend as rain in a perpetual loop, representing the flow of human vitality between the poles of existence.

If the number 14 is with your heart, personality, destiny, or spiritual path, the following traits are likely to be characteristic of you: You possess a charming, witty, and dynamic personality with a clever and versatile mind. You are drawn to intellectual challenges and have an innate magnetism. Historically, the number 14 has been associated with the scribe, a figure with access to extensive knowledge across various subjects and adept in handcrafting manuscripts. You learn optimally through direct, hands-on experiences, always seeking to delve beyond appearances to test and verify truths for yourself.

The essence of the number five, derived from adding the digits in 14 (1+4), signifies a drive for freedom or a significant shift – be it a major life transition, overcoming an addiction, or a release from anger. Your approach to sexuality and sensuality is one of enjoyment and embrace. This notion is symbolically paralleled in the Temperance card by the angel's balanced stance, one foot in water and the other on land, symbolizing the deliberate testing of emotional waters. Patience and adaptability are your tools for navigating new circumstances, which lead to peace and balance.

When out of balance, a propensity for excess – such as in indulgence in sex, alcohol, or gambling – may surface. However, as a moderator, your balance brings temperance to the fore. Your emotional life experiences, particularly those that involve water (a representation of emotion), are opportunities for transformation, where anger can be alchemized into compassion – a lesson learned through lived experience.

In your natural state of compassionate temperance, life seems to align in your favor. Your mind is quick, and your dexterity serves you in both physical and intellectual pursuits. You thrive on knowledge and are not one to blindly follow rules – freedom and first-hand experience are vital to you. As such, boundaries and limitations often feel restrictive and foreign. Boredom is anathema to your vibrant nature, and others are invariably drawn to your compelling presence.

Elvis Presley's name, containing the number 14, exemplified this charm and magnetism, alongside the risk of excess. The life path under this vibration starts with testing the waters and progresses through chakra alignment, blending experiences with compassion to awaken the kundalini life force, culminating in wisdom – symbolized by the mountains behind the angel in the Temperance card.

In business and speculation, your quickness and accuracy, provided you have thoroughly vetted your facts, make you formidable. Slowness can prove challenging, so it's essential to intersperse periods of calm to maintain your health. Avoid hasty speculation without the necessary groundwork to prevent potential losses. Your preference may lean towards day trading rather than long-term investments, as you handle rapid change better than most. Careers in mediation, family law, research, entertainment, photojournalism, storytelling, racing, or judging could align well with your attributes.

If 14 is prominent in a significant pinnacle, year, month, or day, you may find yourself confronting emotional challenges. These periods are destined to temper and balance you, offering gifts of wisdom, compassion, and the freedom to move beyond past patterns and emotional constraints. You may encounter pivotal life events, but the ultimate aim is to achieve emotional liberation, forgiveness, and the release of judgment through diverse experiences. During this time, your persuasive power, intuition, and influence peak, guiding you towards internal harmony and the assertion of your boundaries when necessary. This is a highly fertile time, so keep this in mind for family planning.

15: The Devil

Tarot Symbolism: Baphomet is depicted as a hybrid creature, part human and part goat, symbolizing the juxtaposition of opposites like good and evil. The dark backdrop signifies the absence of enlightenment, representing ignorance. The inverted pentagram in this context is a symbol of power corrupted. The torch held in Baphomet's left hand, paradoxically, emits no heat or comfort.

The figures of a man and woman, representing duality, appear shackled to the devilish figure. Yet, their chains are not tight; they could liberate themselves if they chose to. The grapes and flames at their tails, along with the tails themselves, suggest that their bondage intensifies as they fail to strive for freedom. It is through the act of breaking free from their self-imposed chains, looking beyond superficialities to seek deeper truths, and learning to find humor in self-reflection that they transcend. This liberation transforms them into teachers and exemplars for others.

Manly P. Hall, in *The Secret Teachings of All Ages*, describes the fifteenth tarot card, Le Diable, as a figure resembling Pan with ram or deer horns, human arms and body, and the legs and feet of a goat or dragon. This creature stands on a cube, to which two satyrs are chained. Baphomet wields a torch, an emblem of the astral light's magical powers reflected in a distorted, infernal manner. The figure's bat-like wings associate it with the night and lower, obscured realms. The chained male and female elementals represent humanity's baser instincts, bound to the base of the figure. The torch symbolizes the misleading illumination that leads the unenlightened to ruin.

The alternative depiction in the pseudo-Egyptian Tarot is of Typhon, an amalgam of various animals symbolizing destruction, brandishing the torch of chaos. This figure is portrayed standing amidst the havoc it has wrought, a metaphor for the consequences of mankind's vices which, when turned against their creator, lead to his downfall.

If the number 15 shows up in your heart, personality, destiny, or spiritual path, this message is for you: It embodies the roles of captor and captive, slave and master, highlighting the contrasts of freedom and bondage, reality and illusion, desire and restraint. Themes of addiction, instant gratification, sin, sex, lust, and temptation tie into the number's significance, leading one into the deepest, darkest places filled with secrets, shame, and guilt. It represents a dire need for the next "fix."

Both Capricorn and Baphomet – pagan icons often associated with the devil – symbolize the amalgamation of our animalistic and human sides, the elegant equilibrium of dominating our base instincts. Absent this equilibrium, enslavement is imminent. We, as humans, often find the anguish of perpetual torment more bearable than the rigors of change. With the devil as your emblematic number, comfort and complacency are luxuries you can't afford. In Christian doctrine, Lucifer, once the Angel of Light and God's highest angel, fell from grace, leading a rebellion and drawing others with him. It's a battle to reclaim balance.

The term "hell," a word synonymous with all forms of damnation, doesn't appear in the original texts of the Bible. Instead, translators employed it to encapsulate the myriad torments. When harnessed for good, the attributes associated with the number 15 – power, energy, charm, and manipulation – can make positive, indelible marks on your community and the wider world. Conversely, the same attributes can manifest as cruelty, control, dominance, and intimidation.

In tarot, the Devil card in the heart position suggests a love that should be unconditional, from a parent, spouse, or similar figure, is instead withheld, leaving one feeling entrapped in the relationship. This imagery of slavery, of feeling utterly stuck, is depicted by the devil standing over a manacled couple, a representation of varying degrees of entrapment. For instance, one client found herself prematurely assuming maternal duties due to her mother's illness, embodying a kind of indentured servitude.

The devil also personifies our addictions, the personal devils to which we feel enslaved. Yet, the chains that bind the couple to the devil in tarot are loose – they can achieve freedom at any time. The devil's power is derived from our own free will, and understanding this is the first step in reclaiming our autonomy, initiating a liberating shift in consciousness. Facing this test, as Jesus did in the desert, is about reclaiming your humanity through intense, powerful energy. Your task is not to succumb to life's gravity but to find humor in your situation and liberate yourself from bondage.

James Buchanan, the 15th President of the United States, controversially believed in the constitutional right to own slaves, and his inaction contributed to the Civil War. Avoiding confrontation can lead to greater conflict. Taking a stand is critical for liberation.

If the number 15 marks a significant time for you, such as a pinnacle, year, month, or day, expect a liberation from addiction, depression, and bondage. This is not a time for complacency. Significant changes are on the horizon. Exercise charm and influence with caution. Embrace laughter and freedom but act with discernment to avoid jumping from one problematic situation to another. This period is an opportunity to break free from whatever personal devils bind you – addictions, toxic relationships, or harmful habits. Choosing growth leads to exhilarating freedom; choosing inaction could intensify your struggles. This is an all-or-nothing crossroads. Be prepared for a profound personal transformation from bondage to liberation, embracing human frailties, releasing judgment, and discovering the joy of unburdening yourself. This is the dark side demanding your attention.

16: The Tower

Tarot Symbolism: Lightning strikes the Tower, igniting a blaze. A man and a woman are seen plummeting headfirst from the burning structure. This image symbolizes not only chaos and destruction but also sudden enlightenment – an abrupt revelation of what was once hidden in shadows. The obliteration signifies an irreversible departure from bygone secrets and destructive patterns, now shattered or consumed by the inferno sparked by lightning. The Tower also echoes the Tower of Babel narrative, where language barriers led to incomprehension, highlighting a newfound necessity for alternative communication methods.

The lightning, striking at the Tower's summit, represents an awakening in the crown chakra, the seat of knowledge. The twenty-two flames, reminiscent of the Fool card numbered 22, signal reconstruction. Now, with a focus on spiritual integrity, a durable new foundation can be established. This is the inception of a radical shift in mindset, the release from spiritual captivity.

Manly P. Hall's *The Secret Teachings of All Ages* describes the sixteenth trump card, Le Feu du Ciel or the Fire of Heaven, as a crowned tower fractured by a divine bolt, the crown's diminutive size possibly hinting at its inadequacy, leading to its downfall. The bolt, occasionally resembling Scorpio's zodiac sign, hints at phallic symbolism, with the tumbling figures representing humanity's fall from grace. This card is a metaphor for humanity's spiritual descent, taking on the illusions of material existence. Here lies an allegory of sexual mystery, with the tower's "gold coins," suggestive of latent potential, spilling out due to the lightning's impact.

In certain decks, this tower is depicted as a pyramid with its apex cloven by lightning, alluding to the missing capstone of the Universal House. Corroborating Eliphas Levi's view that this card is linked to the Hebrew letter Ayin, the foreground's descending figure bears resemblance to this sixteenth character in the Hebrew alphabet.

If the number 16 resonates with your heart, personality, destiny, or spiritual path, then the following is pertinent to you: Sudden destruction, like a lightning strike, reveals truths previously obscured. The force of lightning is anything but gentle, and when it strikes, it brings about instant illumination. In the metaphorical darkness before the strike, the tower is hit, and someone falls – it's both inevitable and necessary. This is the intensity of the experience.

The cover of night or darkness symbolizes the unknown – secrets, complex matters, or elusive aspects of life such as hidden infrastructures or intricate relationships. If you embody the qualities of quietude, intensity, and magnetism, it's a time to avoid risks and speculation. Your adeptness with words suggests you could excel as a writer, detective, or undercover operative. Your energy aligns with the emergency room's demands, addressing sudden or critical situations, akin to a bomb squad technician. There's a thrill in maintaining composure amid turmoil – you're the poised first responder, managing crises with ease and grace. You step in when storms are unavoidable, showcasing remarkable skill and focus under pressure. Such aptitudes could also serve well in hostage negotiation, with a flair for handling hidden, secretive, or undercover situations.

Your experiences with the Tower imply resilience, akin to the Rock of Gibraltar, vital in recovering from destruction. Abraham Lincoln, the 16th President, embodied this energy by denouncing slavery – sometimes, it takes a lightning bolt to shatter our bonds. This intense process encourages disentanglement from all destructive relationships and habits, representing the Tower's redemptive aspect as you atone for past misjudgments.

The calamity you face is directly proportional to internal strife; they compete to overshadow all else. Yet, in this chaos, you rediscover the serene guidance within. When external validation loses its grip, an inward journey begins, unveiling the Tower's true gift. It's as though just as you gain stability, the rug is pulled from beneath you, but this cycle is necessary to clear the way for new growth, demanding a fresh mindset.

The Tower's purpose is to expose and dismantle anything selfish, manipulative, or harmful. In this role, you're akin to a shaman or demonologist, confronting the darkest creations and transforming misused energy by bringing darkness to light. Ceremonial practices, sounds, and truths become tools for healing and reclaiming what was lost. For some, shamanic ceremonies are crucial acts of liberation and healing for places once overshadowed by darkness. The number 16 is emblematic of such intense transformation, sometimes resulting in psychic awakenings.

The Tower experience often strips away material comforts, leaving us with only our words and true selves. Detachment from material desires and external validation paves the way for introspection – this is the Tower's powerful, isolating gift.

If 16 marks a significant pinnacle for you, a year, month, or day, exercise caution, avoid risks, and slow down. Your foundation is about to undergo seismic shifts, revealing what may have been inherently flawed. Everything that's corrupt or harmful is set to collapse, whether it be in relationships, health, or structural integrity. Such change is abrupt and appears destructive, but it is essential for growth. Meditation can help connect with new, peaceful philosophies.

Losses may occur, but they precipitate the fall of oppressive powers and the old, harmful order. You're tasked with rebuilding from scratch, establishing new principles that will foster your gifts of communication, possibly leading to wealth or recognition. Your role as a first responder, spiritual guide, or leader is to forge this new foundation. Once the upheaval settles, there's no reverting to old ways – the transformation is profound and positive. The Tower signifies awakenings, drawing out your best, dormant qualities.

Take Abraham Lincoln as an example; he guided America through its direst trials, preserving the nation and abolishing slavery, epitomizing the Tower's spirit. Your part in this could vary – from a liberator like Lincoln to someone releasing or being released from bondage. The Tower shines a light on all such roles, and the ensuing destruction balances karmically. Negotiation is redundant; it's a time for complete renewal.

17: The Star

Tarot Symbolism: A naked woman kneels with her left leg bent on land, representing reason, logic, and intellect – symbolized by the number four. Her right foot stands in water, embodying the subconscious, emotional, and intuitive. Her exposed form conveys innocence, vulnerability, purity, faith, and hope. With two urns, she pours water from her right hand, or conscious mind, into the pool at her feet, ensuring life's continual cycle and nurturing Mother Earth. From her left hand, aligned with the subconscious, she directs water onto the land, dividing into five streams symbolizing the senses that guide humanity's quest for knowledge.

Surrounding her are seven lesser stars, denoting the energy points or chakras, and a prominent eight-pointed star of revelation and rotation.

Manly P. Hall, in "The Secret Teachings of All Ages," describes the seventeenth tarot card, Les Étoiles (the Stars). It shows a young girl balancing between water and land, pouring from two urns into both. Above her, eight stars shine, the largest of which may represent Sothis or Sirius, accompanied by seven sacred ancient planets. The figure is thought to be Isis, initiating the Nile's flood with the Dog Star's ascent. Isis's nudity suggests that Nature is bereft of verdure until the inundating waters unlock the vegetative life. Symbols of growth and resurrection – a bush and a bird, or perhaps a butterfly – accompany the water's rise. In some interpretations, the star contains a juxtaposed black and white triangle, and the bush becomes a tall plant with a threefold crown upon which a butterfly rests. Here, Isis takes a triangular form, and the urns transform into shallow cups. The water and earth beneath her feet represent the balance of opposites in Nature, both equally blessed with divine abundance.

If the number 17 resonates with your heart, personality, destiny, or spiritual path, the following traits are likely yours: You approach problems distinctively, breaking free from restrictive belief systems and terrestrial confines. For you, "impossible" is a non-entity. Your insights reach beyond the earthly, drawing on celestial or even extraterrestrial wisdom. Interstellar communication, a quest for knowledge across planets, galaxies, and solar systems, aligns with your spirit, encompassing healing, peace, the occult, and the vastness of space.

However, when the shadow side prevails, it manifests as a deficit in faith, giving way to despair and depression. The unordinary captivates you, fueling your aspiration to realize space and time travel, to pierce through dimensions. Your reverence for Earth is profound, yet it's the expanse beyond the horizon that truly captivates you. In the arcane, you search for keys to unlock portals to other realms.

Your intuition is pronounced. To you, a single star illuminates the night for many. Numerologically, the one stands alone; seven spans the cosmos; together, they sum to eight. It's in solitude and brilliance that your strength shines. With singularity of purpose and intuitive clarity, your gaze is fixed on the otherworldly.

Silent yet formidable, your movements are stealth, focused, and precise – a strategist by nature. Your intellectual acuity is matched only by the keenness of your observation, and your actions are executed with meticulous accuracy. Words are chosen with equal care.

Drawn to the mysterious, you could excel as a ghost hunter, chemist, curator of the curious, guide, astronomer, healer, or voyager of the cosmos. The enigma of the unknown beckons, and you cannot resist its allure. The quest for discovery, the beckoning of celestial bodies – these are points of light that affirm the transformative power of the universe.

A star signifies more than a distant light; it's proof of other realms, a testament to the multidimensional nature of reality. You thrive amidst collectives, potentially excelling as an executive or project manager.

"The heavens declare the glory of God; the skies proclaim the work of his hands. Day after day they pour forth speech; night after night they reveal knowledge." - Psalm 19:1-2. This scripture mirrors the mystical wellspring of your knowledge.

Darkness, dreams, night – they do not intimidate you; you are the bearer of light. You comprehend life's cycles – life and death, day and night. In the void, ideas germinate, thoughts take root, and from the void's point of light, knowledge unfurls, guiding journeys of healing and inspiration.

Every night ushers in the stars, every dawn the sun's ascent, affirming the steadfast, loving guidance and restoration of this force. Your thought processes are radical, unconfined. Solitude is necessary for your contemplation and meditation, opening channels to entities from other dimensions – an experience you frequently embrace.

```
   6           = 6
  GOD             6 + 11 = 17
  7 4         = 11
```

The concept of God aligns with the numerology of 17, a number denoting destiny. Your inherent kindness and compassion not only attract the support you require but also empower your ventures into the depths of quantum physics and extraterrestrial realms. Your passion lies in the exploration of worlds and dimensions beyond our immediate perception, finding splendor in the black canvas of the night sky, where the distant stars emit their faint glow. Such boundless curiosity and groundbreaking discoveries often lead to a legacy that outlives its originator, cementing fame that endures through time.

If 17 marks a significant pinnacle for you, a year, month, or day, you are aligned with meditation, healing, focus, clarity, support, and journeying. You possess a self-awareness of your value, and as if by design, the right people and opportunities align with you within this harmonious frequency. Your physical strength, emotional equilibrium, and the financial means for substantial and meaningful projects come together seamlessly. Should you have faced imbalance or health concerns previously, 17 heralds a time of recuperation and renewal. You become the focal point, unrestricted in thought, scaling mountains previously unseen, propelled by this newfound vitality. Remember, inheritances, too, may find their way to you under the auspice of 'The Star.'

Your healing journey not only illuminates your path but also serves as an inspiration to those around you. Your guidance is drawn from the unseen realms and the infinite expanses of space. Amidst these explorations, personal revelations and scientific breakthroughs are yours for the taking. Doubt has no place here – trust in your capacities.

18: The Moon

Tarot Symbolism: Welcome to the enigmatic realm of the subconscious, a place where appearances often deceive. Under the muted glow of the full moon, its 32 rays symbolize the Kabbalistic Tree of Life, while the 15 yods cascading downwards invoke the imagery of the Devil card, emblematic of the internal shackles we strive to liberate ourselves from.

Dominating the landscape, two lofty towers stand, edifices of the ego's making, symbols of perceived confinement. The surrounding waters serve as a mirror to our subconscious depths. Emerging from these depths, the crayfish embodies our primal nature, embarking on the serpentine path towards the pinnacle of self-realization. The path, ever-narrowing as it ascends, signifies the increasing demands placed upon us as we venture further on our spiritual quest – a journey demanding patience, as true progress defies haste.

Flanking this path, the contrasting presences of the wolf and the dog reflect our personal trials in cultivating self-mastery. The untamed wildness of the wolf and the domesticated obedience of the dog mirror the inner battle between our untamed instincts and the virtues of compassion, love, and kindness that we aspire to embody.

If the number 18 resonates with you – whether in matters of the heart, personality, destiny, or spiritual journey – then the following insights apply:

The Moon governs healing, dreaming, and the elusive dream state – realms unseen by most. If 18 is your number, you likely have an acute awareness of these domains, experiencing levels of perception that remain inaccessible to the majority. Your dreams, potentially distressing since childhood, are vivid; your emotions, profoundly deep. The Moon's influence drives a quest to understand the mind, particularly the elusive subconscious. It's a realm beyond our direct control, yet it fascinates you, especially in relation to emotions, psychology, and psychiatry.

The mind is a domain where you feel most at home, though at times it resembles a rollercoaster that necessitates occasional retreats from the world. You possess a profound understanding of mental health, keen to explore conditions such as bipolar disorder and PTSD. The Moon's guidance has illuminated the profound connection between mind and body, showcasing how unseen forces can profoundly affect us.

Intuitive and possibly possessing psychic abilities, you are a healer. Your visual acuity suggests you'd excel in photography, capturing the interplay of light and shadow. You recognize that true healing requires sleep – that darkness is not malevolent but a time for regeneration.

Braving the depths of our own subconscious is not for the faint of heart. For those under the number 18, there might be a struggle with mental health or merely a need for more rest. It's a restlessness familiar to all human experience. We may crave change, yet find ourselves delving deeper into our own psyche. In this space, we shine our light of awareness, mending the disconnections that have severed us from our most authentic selves. Some may feel trapped by their emotional state, glimpsing little hope. But here lies the opportunity for self-reclamation.

The Moon, once named Sin – reflecting the ancient moon deity – suggests that the so-called 'sinners' were simply under its sway. Yet, the Moon also rules over inspiration and spiritual revelation, governing the night – a time for visions, dreams, and the unconscious. It reminds us that darkness is merely a reflection of our own fears, while daylight symbolizes control. This natural-supernatural cycle serves to balance us.

Referencing historical and spiritual texts like the Aquarian Gospel, we see night as a time for otherworldly encounters, a tradition spanning back to the revelations received by Moses on Mount Sinai – 'the mountain of the moon.'

If 18 is a number of a pinnacle, year, month or day of yours: There can be a debilitating illness. Things are not what they seem. Take care to get enough rest. The mind is the journey now. You know you want a change, but wait until your signs are clear for this change. Perhaps a new job, new location are in the works. Change may beckon, but wait for clarity. This number suggests a time for reconnecting with past endeavors and harnessing your intuitive strength. In this phase, myriad voices may seek to influence you, but it is the voice of your Spirit that should guide you. This is a time of profound, intuitive healing. As you venture into the depths, you're not succumbing to darkness; rather, you're bringing light to your darkest places, embarking on a journey of renewal, realignment, and empowerment. It is a cleansing process, turning down the volume on the inauthentic and tuning into your deepest wisdom.

19: The Sun

Tarot Symbolism: The nineteenth card of the Tarot, Le Soleil, or The Sun, signifies the culmination of the 9's journey in the number 19 – there's no returning to what once was. The brick wall symbolizes this final farewell. Yet, within its confines bloom four sunflowers, embodying hope and peace – the sunflower's most vital symbolic messages – and signaling love and friendship. These sunflowers, integrated into the wall, are testaments to the beauty forged from the act of letting go. Their vibrant presence offers a beacon of your influence and the expansive reach of your message to all passersby.

A naked child rides unbridled upon a white horse, embodying the unspoiled purity, innocence, and delight of our inner child; the horse, too, signifies purity. Above, the sun beams down, a harbinger of new beginnings, divine support, and personal resolve. It shines as a guide, a symbol of fruitfulness, joy, and abundant prosperity.

Manly P. Hall's *The Secret Teachings of All Ages* describes the Tarot's nineteenth card. It depicts two children, perhaps the Gemini twins, in a floral-ringed garden with a brick barrier at its edge. The sun ascends beyond the wall, its alternating straight and wavy rays casting thirteen droplets. Lévi, interpreting the dual imagery as Faith and Reason, parallels it with bipedal balance, binary cosmic forces, and the duality of sexes. These twin pillars, Jakin and Bohas, uphold Solomon's temple. As the solar truth illuminates the world's garden, these children, embodiments of perpetual forces, stand sentinel. Worldly harmony is sustained by the interplay of mind and heart, perennially represented by these dualities.

In an alternate depiction – the pseudo-Egyptian Tarot – the children are replaced by a youth and maiden, crowned with a solar halo featuring the phallic symbol of generation, underscoring the sign Gemini's governance by Mercury. These figures echo the entwined serpents of the caduceus, a symbol of commerce and negotiation, harmonizing dualities within the emblematic staff.

If 19 resonates with your heart, personality, destiny, or spiritual path, consider its significance: You are a figure of intensity and focus, self-forged through the fires of early adversity. The hurdles you've surmounted attest to a familiarity with loss and an early fostering of independence. In this lies the necessity of farewells, often prematurely, paving the way for superior opportunities. Such experiences may include an early departure to boarding school, either through necessity or choice, which sharpens your acquaintance with loss, emotion, and self-reliance. The 19 persona is particularly suited to therapy, channeling insights into the hopeful renewal that follows every ending.

Your profound empathy and intuitive connection to others enhance your therapeutic potential. Clarity and determination define your path to leadership, making you a nexus of influence. In equilibrium, your presence is luminous, offering illumination to those around you. If 19 is your personality number, you likely attract those in emotional turmoil, reflecting the sun's nature to draw both light and shadow.

The strength of the 19 lies in leading and innovating, using one's experiences and knowledge to foster healing, especially emotional. The necessity for challenges is like the contrast between the sun's brilliance against the void of space; it is within the darkness that your light is most needed. You weave the narrative of release from the nine with the creative spark of the one, birthing beauty from inspiration and invention. As an autonomous spirit, your path might wind through the realms of the arts or philanthropy, guided by the 9's generous spirit and the auspicious favor that luck bestows.

If 19 marks a significant time for you – a pinnacle, year, month, or day – the prospect may include a fortuitous union or the dawn of prosperity. Such a period demands self-reliance; heed your intuition over the counsel of others as you chart a novel course. Amidst the flurry of activity, maintaining equilibrium is key; too much ambition, like Icarus, can lead to downfall. The dynamism of the one seeks progress, while the discernment of the nine prunes away the superfluous, fostering continuous rebirth. Embrace the cycle of constant beginnings and culminations; the changes you encounter are monumental but ultimately for the best, as essential as the sun's energy to our world. Now is your season to radiate invention and action.

```
    3              = 3
    SUN               3 + 6 = 9
    1   5          = 6
```

The word "Sun" embodies a numerological triad of 3 for heart, 6 for personality, and 9 for destiny – a symphony of self-awareness, community bonds, and the courage to embrace solitude with wisdom as one's compass. Here, your capacity for manifestation is amplified. What wonders might you craft – a towering empire, a new world, or an unforeseen life? Indeed, the potential is boundless.

20: Judgment

Tarot Symbolism: Archangel Gabriel, named for "God is my strength," graces the sky in depictions, horn in hand, summoning people to their higher selves – beckoning them to embrace the celestial love and guidance. Below him, a trio – a man, woman, and child symbolizing the conscious, subconscious, and superconscious – rouse to a fresh existence presented to them. This scene signifies a departure from old consciousness, a transition from shadow to light, our inherent state. The mountains in the distance symbolize the trials that, without divine turn, would seem insurmountable.

Referencing *The Secret Teachings of All Ages* by Manly P. Hall, the twentieth major trump card, Le Jugement or the Judgment, depicts a scene of awakening. Three figures appear to ascend from their tombs, with only one casket in view. A glorious winged entity, likely Angel Gabriel, heralds their awakening with a trumpet blast. This imagery is a metaphor for the release of the human spirit's tripartite nature from the confines of the material world. Since only a fraction of the spirit inhabits the physical vessel, the card suggests a partial, rather than complete, resurrection. Court de Gebelin contends that the coffin might be a later addition by card designers, suggesting the scene symbolizes creation rather than resurrection – concepts that are near interchangeable in philosophical discourse. The trumpet's sound epitomizes the Creative Word, the utterance of which frees man from earthly chains. In the pseudo-Egyptian Tarot, the notion that the figures are aspects of a single entity is reinforced by the portrayal of three mummies rising from a single sarcophagus.

If 20 resonates with you – whether it's a number connected to your heart, personality, destiny, or spiritual path – the following insights are for you. See "The History of Zero" for foundational knowledge. Think of 2020: a year marked by social distancing, revelations, and androgyny. It was a tumultuous period where polar opposites endeavored to find equilibrium. This is the influence of the number two, magnified.

The Judgment tarot card signifies an epiphany, an awakening, and thus a period ripe for decision-making. This represents rejuvenation. All that has lain dormant or obscured now emerges, aimed at healing and achieving tranquility. The choices have been made: what to keep and what to relinquish. Whatever fosters harmony and balance will stay. Imagine tending to a garden where the soil is fertile, primed to nurture life, prosperity, and momentous transformation. In this culled garden, all that is beautiful and true shines under the dawn's light.

The number two in 20 symbolizes the minute, the microscopic – viruses, subtle energies, unseen frequencies, the essence of poetry and art. Your inner work paves the way for the celebration and manifestation of new realities. Now, the minutiae command attention, and what was once concealed is now apparent. The ostensibly insignificant becomes vital – acts of kindness, pets, seeds, even particles like germs and atoms, and energies such as zero point or nuclear. It's a time when love and relationships are appreciated in their fullness.

If 20 is a number of a pinnacle, year, month, or day, you're now fully alert to the fine details of your existence and ready to discern what stays and what goes. Judgment rejoices for it bestows the clarity to connect deeply with what genuinely brings joy. This period heralds transition. It prompts you to assess your relationships, your career, your home – and welcomes the inevitable transformations that come from such introspection.

An individual influenced by the number 20 radiates an angelic and mystical allure. Healing has transpired, paths have been cleared, and decisions made. It's a celebratory era where peace and compassion carve new roads and mend past rifts. This renaissance honors balance, beauty, and the essence of Earth and self-worth. The old has paved the way for the new. With fresh understanding, the tranquil path invites you to proceed with clarity and courage.

This time symbolizes rebirth and enlightenment – the breaking of dawn, the remaking of your life, embracing new job prospects, relationship dynamics, and living situations. Your life, along with your emotions, is transformed, rising from the remnants of the past – valued, yet ready to be surpassed.

21: The World

Tarot Symbolism: The divine cosmic consciousness serves as the guiding force in this context. Education now complete, the dissemination of knowledge commences. You find your consciousness reaching beyond the quotidian, embracing the extraordinary. This is the essence of the number 21, the final emblem in the Major Arcana, symbolizing both the culmination of a journey and the fulfillment it brings. The heightened awareness acts as a source of healing and inspiration, encouraging you to impart your wisdom. Represented by the element earth, a naked woman stands as a symbol of total confidence and the completion of a cycle, with a celebratory wreath encircling her. She stands surrounded, indicating that she has become a central figure, generously sharing her abundance with those around her.

Drawing from *The Secret Teachings of All Ages* by Manly P. Hall, "The twenty-first major trump is named 'Le Monde,' or the World, depicting a feminine figure. A wind-blown scarf adorns her, shaping into the Hebrew letter Kaph. Her outstretched hands, each grasping a wand, and her crossed legs take the shape of the alchemical symbol for sulphur. The figure is encased in a wreath resembling the vesica piscis (as in a Vinn Diagram), which Levi equates to the Qabbalistic crown, Kether. Occupying the corners of the card are the Cherubim from the vision of Ezekiel. This Tarot embodies both the Microcosm and the Macrocosm, encapsulating the multitude of forces that construct creation. The sulphuric emblem represents the divine fire at the heart of the Great Mystery, with the encircling Nature symbolizing the life-embracing fiery core. The Cherubim stand for the elements, worlds, forces, and planes emanating from this divine epicenter of life. The wreath also denotes the initiate's crown, bestowed upon those who transcend the four guardians and come into the unveiled presence of Truth. In the pseudo-Egyptian Tarot, the Cherubim encircle a wreath of twelve trifoliate flowers – symbols of the zodiac's decans. Beneath this wreath, a human figure kneels, playing a harp with three strings, signifying that the spirit must first orchestrate harmony within its own tripartite nature to earn the solar crown of immortality."

If 21 resonates with you – whether it relates to your heart, personality, destiny, or spiritual path – this message is meant for you: It's centered on expression and being vocal. It speaks to liberation, freedom, and the allure of travel. Your potential shines in numerous realms – you could be a remarkable scientist, a creative artist, or a captivating singer. Fortune smiles upon you, acknowledging your stewardship of Mother

Earth, rewarding your respect for her natural laws with abundant grace. Your attunement to the Earth's energies fosters a brilliant scientific mind, particularly in earth sciences. The balance inherent in the number 21, with its combination of two's harmony and one's initiative, ensures a yin and yang that you naturally honor, steering clear of unnecessary drama. Distant destinations beckon, promising serenity upon arrival.

The equilibrium of yin and yang, enhanced by the progressive force of the one in 21, heralds new beginnings rich with potential, brought forth by tranquility and equilibrium. Conflict is a relic of your past; now, peace is sovereign. Charged with this serene energy, you're destined to pioneer new discoveries and share enlightening insights, focusing particularly on scientific and artistic advancements. The essence of your work radiates joy, renewal, and love, drawing from the abundant harvest of your diligent past efforts. Now opportunities for travel and financial reward present themselves, and you must heed their call. Aligned with the cosmic flow, you possess the intuition to know when it's time to embark on new quests.

Your calling may place you at the forefront – whether through public speaking, teaching, or performing – sharing your artistic and scientific gifts to elevate others. By imparting wisdom through harmonizing with nature's laws, you help alleviate burdens, teaching others to move with the natural world rather than against it. It's your mission to restore the natural balance, intertwining the well-being of humanity and the Earth. Your influence endures, rooted in the sacred knowledge of words and intention, wielding language as a tool for healing. Like honeybees, whose intricate dances lead their kin to nectar, your life's work restores equilibrium and sweetness to the Earth each time you share your gifts with fearless candor.

On the flip side, embracing the negative aspects of this energy can lead to hypercritical attitudes, stifled intuition, and a stubborn resistance to the transformative calls of travel and exploration, compelling a need to be incessantly correct.

If the number 21 marks a significant pinnacle, year, month, or day in your life, it signals a time ripe with liberation, celebration, and the crossing of new frontiers. Now is the time to amplify Mother Earth's voice and the wisdom you've gleaned. The stage is set for public engagement, vocal performances, scientific ventures, and possibly cosmic exploration. Projects culminate with success, and travel opportunities are abundant – keep your luggage and passport within reach. Your efforts are weaving a global tapestry of unity, and the world is your platform to share your convictions, creativity, and healing. This is the fruition of your labor; embrace it. If you succumb to the negative, opportunities may go unnoticed, familial bonds could feel like chains, and emotions may fray. But returning to positivity, this energy bolsters marriage, infusing it with security and fruitfulness.

22: The Fool

Tarot Symbolism: The Fool, historically the court's entertainer, exhibited a carefree demeanor. However, this persona concealed his extensive real estate portfolio and a tendency to eschew conventional norms in law and healthcare, suggesting a deeper wisdom. Governed by the element of air, the Fool embodies logical thought and innovative problem-solving. His depiction as a wanderer, ready to embark on an odyssey, signifies fresh starts and the unblemished anticipation of a significant new voyage. In tarot, the Fool is aligned with the numeral zero, symbolizing not emptiness, but rather the potential for divine intervention. It is a leap of faith, unburdened by human expectations, that propels the Fool, while divine providence steers his path, enabling his unorthodox accomplishments.

Manly P. Hall elucidates in *The Secret Teachings of All Ages* that positioning Le Mat at the beginning of the Tarot sequence hints at an imminent journey through life's spiritual lessons. The Fool is poised to traverse the cards, much like a neophyte blindfolded before initiation, standing on the precipice of an extraordinary quest – a passage through the sacred gates of enlightenment.

If the number 22 resonates with your heart, personality, destiny, or spiritual path, this message is for you: You are here to disrupt the established order. Your journey on Earth is marked by a mission to challenge and revolutionize systems synonymous with law, justice, and governance. Your approach to conformity is atypical; you possess a robust moral compass, yet it veers away from traditional systems and structures. This master number demands more from you, setting you on a path to reflect society's imperfections and outdated norms back to itself – including those within your own family. Your role is not to demolish what exists but to ready the world for a more enlightened existence by highlighting areas where change is imperative.

Your presence inherently reveals flaws, yet this is not a detriment but a part of your unique path. Bearing the number 22 is a formidable undertaking; it seeks to uncover weaknesses to lay a more resilient foundation. This number embodies duality: emotional depth coupled with a propensity for secret knowledge, shaping your childhood as an acute observer of the imperfections in your immediate environment. Rather than a curse, consider yourself humanity's reflective surface, where even minor fissures can herald significant transformation.

Your existence is pivotal in the construction and reformation of relationships, structures, and institutions. You are the groundwork upon which future worlds are based, tasked with cultivating the soil of our collective psyche and legislative landscape to foster what is essential for humanity's advancement. Health and alternative healing are at the forefront of your interests, leading you to seek wisdom beyond conventional education and practitioners. Your mentors are often those deemed unorthodox, echoing your innate sense that progress requires a departure from the established order.

Your skepticism of entrenched systems – be they bureaucratic, legal, or medical – is justified by your observations of correlation between progressiveness and societal ill health. Your moral compass is steadfast, guiding you to explore and adopt practices that may be deemed controversial, thereby illuminating new paths for others. In this quest, your courage does not falter before offense or opposition. The challenge for you is to balance your pioneering spirit with self-care and understanding for those not aligned with your fervor.

The 22's capability to forge new enterprises and communities is immense, motivated not by ego but by a vision of a more efficient, healthier way of life. With high intuition and emotional strength, your true sensitivity remains shielded behind a facade of resilience. Loyalty and protectionism define your stance towards family, while your life's work is to expose and mend the flawed and dysfunctional in all spheres.

In your pursuit of the ideal, vigilance against burnout is essential; your dedication can sometimes border on the tyrannical if left unchecked. Remember, your legacy is not just the strong foundations you build but also the humane approach you embody. While 22 holds the potential of the Tarot's zero – a conduit for transformation – balance and pacing are vital.

When 22 features prominently as a pinnacle, year, month, or day, anticipate direct confrontations with authority and the status quo. Your life's work oscillates between the masterful 22 and its foundational 4, drawing you into crucial, world-altering projects. The crumbling of old systems provides fertile ground for your efforts, though the magnitude of these tasks can be daunting. Challenges with authority are inevitable, yet they are a testament to the necessity of your endeavors. Stand resolute, even against the Goliaths of our time, and pace your progress; the world awaits the changes only you can implement.

Section Two:
The Wands

23: King of Wands

Tarot Symbolism: The King sits upon his throne, his gaze cast outward, cognizant that adventure and transformation are on the horizon. Embodied within him is the essence of pure, fiery masculine energy. In his grasp, his wand flourishes, a testament to the fruitful changes and positive perspectives that lie ahead. Adorning his cape are emblems of lions and salamanders, symbols of his driving passion. Protected and sagacious, he heeds counsel before embarking on decisive action.

If 23 resonates with your heart, personality, destiny, or spiritual path, then the following is pertinent to you: a tapestry of safety, security, and the richness of a multi-cultural, multi-lingual world interweaving with the tenets of fair trade and business – all underscored by the motif of water. As the central axis where diverse cultures converge for commerce and exchange, you often find yourself at the water's edge, the bustling ports. Your charm is magnetic, and your intelligence, wit, and cleverness are as striking as they are influential. Vigilant care for your physical well-being underpins your values; marriage and progeny stand paramount in your life's landscape. You are ensconced in guidance and protection, with a charm and sincerity that summon the support necessary to bring your ideas to their prosperous completion. Those in positions of authority lend their aid effortlessly.

You are never bereft of ideas, finding delight in the challenge of transforming them into financial gain. Your soul hungers for adventure, for the tapestry of different cultures. Given that 23 vibrates with the energy of a 5, you seek out the excitement of travel and the stimulation of intellectual challenges. Delving into a single book is an inadequate pace for your voracious mind; you are typically engrossed in multiple narratives simultaneously. Education, particularly in foreign languages and cultures, is not just appreciated but sought after fervently. You could stand as a sterling ambassador. Yet, whatever your endeavor, it is transient, giving way to the allure of your next vibrant idea, and so a new journey begins. Your reputation for fairness fosters trust, cementing the foundation of your triumphs. A penchant for intrigue could steer you towards investigative work, with unsolved mysteries of the paranormal drawing your keen interest. No single endeavor can captivate you for long; your mind craves puzzles and challenges. Distant places call to you, perhaps even to undertake clandestine missions aiding refugees or hosting exchange students. You find your life immensely enriched by the broadened horizons that come with embracing other cultures, ensuring you love, protection, and respect. Your insight could make you an exceptional reporter of global affairs or a visionary in international business. It's the amalgamation of your maturity and zeal that promises success. Your aptitude could shine in the realms of science and mechanics. There are also negative aspects, such as ruthlessness, impulsivity, rudeness, boorishness, acting like a tyrant, being unreliable, being a bully or giving away your power.

If 23 marks a pinnacle, or a year, month, or day in your life: Protective forces are especially potent around you now. An imperative for travel and change is upon you – stagnation is antithetical to this period. Heed the guidance of those who lead, and move forward with the confidence of assured success in your next venture. Money, adventure, and cultural diversity are all woven into this time's fabric. Opportunity is beckoning. Whether you're the student studying abroad or the missionary untethered to any religious institution, you're poised for the enrichment that comes with immersion in novel environments and new tongues. Now is a moment for binding agreements, promising journeys, and affluence. The commitments you form now are set to be lucrative and equitable. A social whirlwind accompanies this time of excitement – new acquaintances, knowledge, wealth, lands, and treaties await. It is time to commit with your whole heart and leap forward boldly.

24: Queen of Wands

Tarot Symbolism: The Queen of Wands reigns from her throne, flanked by lions that symbolize the fire element within her. In her right hand, she firmly grips the wand of power, an emblem of her authority. Her left hand clasps a sunflower, reflecting the Leo element's vibrant energy and her connection to its radiance. A black cat at her feet signifies her renowned telepathic and intuitive prowess, an advisor in the shadows. The two stately lions that stand sentinel behind her embody strength and the establishment of safety and boundaries. Rising beyond her, the trio of mountains signifies her mastery over self and her acute awareness of the three planes of consciousness – a testament to her profound dominion.

If 24 is a significant number in your heart, personality, destiny, or spiritual path, then the following insights resonate with you: The Queen of Wands governs from her heart, and in turn, the world responds with tenderness, ensuring a loving home, fulfilling relationships, and happy children. Your intuition is sharp; you defend your realm with valor and heart. With an unyielding spirit, you broadcast your message to the world, unafraid of the consequences, driven by the belief that truth liberates. You're drawn to service, feeling the pull of a higher calling, perhaps leading a congregation or spiritual community. The role of a parent is sacred to you, irrespective of gender, and you cherish the maternal bond. Your home is an oasis of calm, diligently nurturing the minds, bodies, and spirits of those in your care. Qualities like steadfastness, loyalty, and love define you. You rule with logic and love with all your heart, ensuring the stability of Mother Earth's foundation. Your care extends to the environment, feeling the imperative to nurture the planet with the same fervor. Relationships flourish under your care, with motherhood being a cherished responsibility. Your household reverberates with laughter and love, and you wield your authority and resources for the family's betterment.

Teaching your children the revered ways of Mother Earth is essential to you. You excel in professions that fortify homes and lands, instilling in your children the importance of living in harmony with nature. Your well of creativity nourishes your health. Travel holds little allure for you; your home is your sanctuary, attracting others with its restorative aura. You might find great success in feng shui, given your affinity for harmonious spaces. Fertility is your gift; you value early education, understanding that peace is the origin of all things. Your home and family are testaments to this tranquility. Your drive, organization, and ability to affect your surroundings inform your mood and creativity. Commitment comes naturally to you, understanding the profound impact of nurturing over time. This is the secret to your enduring relationships and the high regard in which you're held by your community. Your home is a magnet for joy and care, even stray animals sense a haven at your doorstep. You embody the Divine Feminine on Earth – spirited, valiant, and steadfast.

If 24 marks a pinnacle, year, month, or day, you're entering a period of growth and deep-rooted connections. Family expands, and the Sacred Feminine takes center stage. Your protective instincts peak, inspiring leadership, especially in spiritual realms. Home becomes a creative sanctuary, reflecting love and care. Marriage flourishes, and teaching or community leadership may call to you. Real estate and sustainability may become priorities, reinforcing self-sufficiency. Creativity thrives, but focus on what's realistically nurtured. Your role as the emotional cornerstone strengthens—invest wisely now for lasting generational impact.

You may find peculiar circumstances surrounding your family. You may connect with your biological parents; you may adopt children. You may learn you have siblings you never knew about. You are very protective of your family and will defend them from adversity.

25: Knight of Wands

Tarot Symbolism: The Knight of Wands, an embodiment of the fire element, is astride his steed, poised for swift action. His journey is extensive, laden with tasks to accomplish. Clad in a suit of armor for defense, he wears a yellow robe adorned with salamanders – a symbol of fire. In his right hand, he holds a sprouting wand, signifying the success awaiting him after his arduous endeavors. The barren landscape behind him suggests a vast field of work yet to be undertaken.

If 25 is a number close to your heart, personality, destiny, or spiritual path, then this applies to you: You're in for the long haul, unfazed by obstacles that may arise. Your intuition is blooming amidst the turmoil in your life. You follow a unique rhythm, tasked with significant achievements. Expect to travel; your intuition will guide your way. Attend to your health for unusual conditions. Keep sage at hand to dispel negative energies. With the influence of 25, you journey both physically and astrally, dedicated to restoring peace and harmony. No challenge is too daunting for your perceptive and tenacious spirit.

You possess a unique knowing beyond logic. Emotional intensity is your norm, and you find calm within the storm to establish equilibrium. While your physical presence may be transient, your spiritual vision is acute. The number 2 within 25 heightens your emotional and spiritual guidance, while 5 propels you on necessary journeys. Your healing abilities, coupled with deep wisdom, are now in active service. Your psychic talents are evident; you are clairvoyant, and your dreams are prophetic. Water is essential for you – in consumption and as a place to dwell. You've invited chaos to refine your spiritual and psychic skills, to test and trust your discernment. This path is tumultuous, but your intuition leads you to intense experiences where your skills are vital.

Respect for ancient traditions guides your path. Your role may be akin to a shaman, energy healer, or exorcist, where you don't resent but understand the need for your unique abilities. Your philosophy is one of peace, your bags always packed for the unexpected. Intuitively, you know your purpose. Your sensitivity to disruptive energies demands that you engage in realignment and purification wherever you are. Material concerns are secondary to you; however, you find the means for your spiritual quests. You delve into ancient texts on healing and the metaphysical with zeal, welcoming challenges that further open your psychic senses. Your mission transcends the ordinary – you are a savior of souls, mastering spiritual elements in your journey toward success and fulfillment.

If 25 is a pinnacle, year, month, or day for you: Gear up for relocation; swift, unforeseen events may compel you to move. You'll surmount several hurdles in this transitory phase, emerging triumphant through arduous efforts. You will adeptly manage emotionally charged situations. This period is tempestuous; action is necessary, rest is scarce. Unpredictable circumstances will call you to rescue, enlighten, and save. Health issues may be elusive but can be resolved within this period of deep insight. Scrutinize documents thoroughly before committing. Maintain focus on your vision as you confront and conquer myriad challenges. You've never felt more vital, more necessary. This era is a turning point toward a profound, divine trajectory, bringing light to darkness, paving the way for healing and a newfound direction with clear, strong, divine guidance.

26: Page of Wands

Tarot Symbolism: Element: Fire. A young man examines his wand intently, observing the burgeoning sprout at its tip – a symbol of potential, growth, and fertility. He is at a stage of testing his confidence, capabilities, and power. Draped in a robe adorned with salamanders, he is shielded by the garment which symbolizes fire, passion, transformation, and healing – a nod to the soul's odyssey through life. The desolate landscape around him suggests a canvas of opportunities, and he is charged with determination to revitalize the barren land.

If 26 is a number for your heart, personality, destiny, or spiritual path, then this applies to you: Strong, disciplined, focused, unexpected, marriage, children, inheritance, responsibility, karma. Be prepared for life's surprises. Inheritance may feature significantly in your journey, so maintain a keen interest in your familial bonds. Outdoor activities will be vital for your well-being – your focused and determined nature thrives in such environments. Leadership comes naturally to you, and your capabilities position you for roles that demand resilience, such as a broker, banker, athlete, or politician. Stress and tension do not deter but rather fuel you, pushing you towards success.

You exude poise under pressure, and your inexhaustible energy seeks out substantial projects – or perhaps they find you. Your integrity and reliability are key to your prosperity and influence. Thriving in stress, you often seek it, understanding that it shapes and hones your confidence. Fairness is your guiding principle, knowing that karmic balance is real and significant. However, temper your drive with caution, as not everyone can match your pace, and even you need respite from your own critical standards. Balance your intense focus with outdoor pursuits to maintain mental clarity and avoid undue stress on yourself and others.

If 26 is a number of a pinnacle, year, month, or day of yours: Inheritance, recognition, karma, fertility, marriage – all are within your realm of experience during this period. Responsibilities will mount, stemming from an inheritance or sheer diligence. Embrace these new challenges; they will bring growth and fulfillment. Steer these responsibilities wisely, making informed decisions that will beautifully shape your future. Ground yourself with expert advice, then proceed with conviction.

Parental and spousal roles may emerge or strengthen during this time, so prioritize outdoor activities that engage your mind entirely – this is your form of meditation. Financially, it is a prosperous phase, urging you to reassess and fortify your fiscal strategies, including your will. Relationships founded now will have enduring positivity. Embrace the good news and foster partnerships, especially those with familial ties, for they promise great rewards. Guard against impulsive actions that could undermine the positives. If you remain mindful and measured, anticipate the very best outcomes.

27: Ace of Wands

Tarot Symbolism: The Ace of Wands embodies the tree of life, symbolizing a profound connection to the earth and an openness to divine inspiration from above. As the tree sheds its leaves, each leaf transforms into a spark of divinity, carrying a creative seed that finds its home in fertile ground. In various tarot interpretations, the Ace of Wands is depicted not as a tree but as the hand of the divine, presenting a living wand that burgeons with life and bloom. This card conveys the essence of pure spiritual power, consciousness, and creativity. It is held by one who seeks neither possession nor dominion but instead serves as a conduit for the extraordinary creative force symbolized by either the flourishing wand or the life-sustaining tree.

If 27 is a number for your heart, personality, destiny, or spiritual path, then this applies to you: Intensity, beauty, artistry, inspiration, depth, soul-focused, divine guidance, expression. You are innately driven by divine inspiration, a true artist at heart. Your profound artistry evokes deeply moving sentiments, with dreams serving as a boundless well of inspiration. A multitude of projects beckons, and you shall fulfill them. Your creative force is not fueled by the desire for recognition or wealth, though they may find you without effort. Instead, you choose to convey, through your chosen artistic avenue, the poignant mix of beauty and melancholy that stirs your soul. Your work becomes a vessel, translating ineffable emotions into a form that captivates and transports your audience to the source of your muse. This is your unique contribution: to inspire and be inspired from a place of deep emotional, spiritual, and healing insight. Inspiration surrounds you, and though you may view the world through a lens tinted with optimism, you do not shy away from its darker emotions but rather embrace and transform them into art. You resonate with roles such as an art teacher, healer, or musician – any profession that channels our deepest sentiments into creative expression.

The quietude of the numbers two and seven combined attunes you to the subtleties of the unseen, heightening your sensitivity. There's a fragility in this blend – the two's association with duality and the seven's quest for tranquility. Meditation and the presence of water are essential for your equilibrium. Engaging with the material world may seem burdensome; however, your true joy lies in the act of creating – be it through painting, drawing, teaching, healing, or gardening. Your artistry carries a humanitarian spirit, fearlessly highlighting social injustices and stirring the status quo, much to your satisfaction. Confident in the messages you craft, you embrace social change through creativity, embodying the essence of a humanitarian. Family is significant to you, and though many connections may be fleeting, there is potential for a lasting love, ideally with someone who complements your stability and shares your secure grounding. You are here to shift global consciousness with your extraordinary creative talent, merging practicality with social reform and artistry. Should the negative aspects take hold, a lack of action on your creative impulses may lead to indecision, judgment, and confusion. Your creations stand as a clarion call to return to justice, harmony, and beauty.

If 27 is a number of a pinnacle, year, month, or day of yours: Birth, marriage, creativity, fertility, change, joy, expression. You're in a phase of inspiration and creation, with life's fertile grounds ripe for new endeavors. Now is the time to plant the seeds – literally or metaphorically – for a garden or a new business venture, and to engage in humanitarian efforts that promise to benefit the world. Divine inspiration flows freely to you, inundating you with innovative ideas. Your connection to Mother Earth is stronger than ever. If employed by others, a promotion looms on the horizon. Conditions are ripe for your ideas to take form, gain support, and flourish. The period ahead might well lay the foundations of your fortune, especially as what you undertake now springs from humanitarian values. Your sincerity, zest, and purity of intention compel the universe to pave the way for your inspired concepts. You become a beacon of inspiration, rallying the support you require.

28: Two of Wands

Tarot Symbolism: The man is holding the world in his hands, symbolizing boundless potential in any direction he chooses. Two wands, firmly rooted in the earth, signify the solid strength of his conviction. He has yet to depart from his castle, a testament to the significant achievements that await him. Ahead lies a landscape both fertile and rugged, heralding the challenges he is poised to surmount and the abundance that awaits him.

If 28 is a number for your heart, personality, destiny, or spiritual path, then this applies to you: New, beginning, surprise, unusual events. At the heart of your experience lies a competitive relationship. It may not embody the ideal of support and trust, but its presence spurs you to advance with vigor and self-assurance. This connection, potentially enduring a lifetime due to its 'one' energy, pushes you to evolve, to set limits, command your space, articulate your truth, and maintain your stance. With 28, expect a spectrum of extremes – tranquil productivity one moment, assertive boundary-setting the next – as you pave the way for a dynamic inception. A visionary with the zeal to achieve monumental and noble objectives, you find meditation in physical exertion and grow restless without productivity.

Leadership comes naturally to you; no task is too daunting with your unwavering focus on the end goal. Your creations are intended to assist others, powered by a lucid, focused mind attuned to the equilibrium necessary in all pursuits. Your realm includes self-defense, empowerment, balance, science, space, and discovery. If negativity takes hold, it manifests in dominance, coercion, and misjudgment. Yet, your purpose is to trust your intuition and discernment, knowing your potential to contribute significantly to humanity. Your insatiable curiosity, alongside your intuition, propels you toward discoveries that revolutionize the world with your inventions or creations.

Balancing the intuitive '2' and the assertive '8' is a dance of opposites for you, merging ideas into tangible reality. At your prime, you harmonize the tender with the robust, the masculine with the feminine, the yin with the yang – gentleness with firmness, kindness with confidence. Your influence reshapes the world. Your incessant activity leaves scant time for rest, driven by a quest to make life more efficient. Your practical innovations stem from a personal quest for speed, health, efficiency. Direct and optimistic, wealth and prosperity find you, for your pioneering spirit benefits others and, in return, your endeavors, fostering positive karma. Your passion and vitality draw others into your vision, eager for the new and better that you constantly seek.

If 28 is a number of a pinnacle, year, month, or day of yours, the '2' suggests decisions rooted in intuition, while the '8' denotes matters of significant ventures, finances, and organization. You're at a crossroads, contemplating long-term alterations. Brace yourself – life's pace is accelerating with much to achieve and unearth. Relationships present themselves, possibly enduring yet not necessarily affectionate, driving you toward more logical, practical discoveries. Competition looms, with outcomes in land, property, relationships veering towards profit and inspiration or total loss – your intent is pivotal. If positivity guides you, expect favorable results. There's no middle ground, only heightened results, good or bad. Embrace courage, integrity, confidence. Out with the antiquated, in with the novel. Define your boundaries, assert yourself. This period is not for idleness; it's an era of remarkable finds and origins. Tread carefully, and your finances will flourish. Unforeseen situations will challenge your judgment – stay alert and discerning, compile facts, then decide.

29: Three of Wands

Tarot Symbolism: A man stands with his back to us, a gesture of spiritual confidence; he trusts in his own resolve, needing not the confirmation of sight. He faces the work ahead, aware of the tasks at hand. The trio of wands symbolizes his spiritual strength. The unyielding land before him represents the cultivation he is poised to begin. Meanwhile, the water embodies emotion, the subconscious, and intuitive forces. He has departed from the familiarity of home, gazing into the journey that lies before him. By embracing his spiritual prowess, he walks with certainty and assurance.

If 29 is a number for your heart, personality, destiny, or spiritual path, then this applies to you: You are regal and joyous. Your infectious enthusiasm and keen eye for beauty elevate our spirits. You possess the wisdom of an old soul, which has led you to embrace life's trials. Smooth sailing does not appeal to you; it lacks the fire to forge your spirit. Yet, when calmness graces your life, it's a pause, not the play. Your soul vibrates with excitement for the courageous paths you've selected — those demanding valor, focus, truth, clarity, and merit. You are the venerable soul on a quest for self-worth. Trust becomes an odyssey until you realize your inner quietude had charted the course rightly from the start. The '2' in your 29 endows you with a profound artistic intuition and a penchant for the creative current. This is the tranquil aspect that revels in creative flow, be it through words, paint, or craftsmanship. You comprehend the universe's microcosm within you.

Conversely, the '9' in your 29 grants you an understanding of humanity's vast tapestry and the interconnectivity of all. Through your grasp and valorization of beauty, expression, and the arts, you teach us. For you, finesse and tact are imperative. When the negative surfaces, explosive anger can sever trust, disrupting your belief in the safety of intimate, transparent, and loving relationships. Positively, your peaceful influence is profound, steering us toward seeing the divine in all beings and things. You act as a unifier, coaxing forth the best of humanity. In a singular, poignant moment of recognition, you remind us that even the minute deserves our protection and appreciation. Your affinity lies with the undersized, the endangered, and the elemental — from atoms to ecosystems, suggesting you might well work with a microscope.

Words are your chosen instrument, wielded with the sanctity they command. Your vocation is to nurture peace and preserve light, perhaps through poetry. Self-trust is your crowning virtue, guided by the hushed voice within, rather than the cacophony of confusion. 'Know thyself' — your mantra and power. Your mediumship allows you to perceive what eludes others, making you a beacon for those seeking counsel.

Your acumen turns profitable, visioning the unseen. You're meant for wealth and accomplishment, often in partnership. A heightened sensitivity to the energies around can manifest as nervous conditions or anxiety attacks – a byproduct of your profound empathy. Thus, moments of solitude are not just a respite but a necessity, allowing you to sift through the torrent of emotions and discern their origins. Your energy is receptive, contemplative, not assertive. Peace is your precondition for decisions, guiding you to move with assurance, without the shadows of doubt. When serene certainty is your compass, trust that your chosen direction is true.

If 29 is a number of a pinnacle, year, month, or day of yours: This period signifies a crucible of learning and discernment. A decision looms, presenting a crossroads with little external aid; the guidance must come from within. The energy surges, carrying a weight of expectation, potentially stirring personal turmoil or unrest. Yet, your carefully chosen words can shepherd others. The current tension, possibly poised on a knife's edge, demands your tranquility and vision. When you trust yourself, you transcend disappointment. Anxious energies transmute into a poised and confident drive toward your new trajectory as you radiate assurance. Your authenticity is now our beacon. Remain vigilant, receptive to the aid and insight that comes your way. The partnerships you encounter now may be instrumental. Exercise discernment and welcome the support that presents itself. Your words carry weight; wield them wisely, for they have the power to either uplift or cause misunderstanding. Steadfastness in your authentic self steers you – and by extension, others – toward a profound mutual enlightenment.

30: Four of Wands

Tarot Symbolism: This fire element symbolizes a jubilant couple dancing before a majestic castle. Four wands, firmly planted in the soil and adorned with garlands of flowers and fruit, represent the fruits of past labors now ripe for celebration. This scene is an emblem of safety, comfort, fertility, prosperity, and the heart of home.

If 30 is a number for your heart, personality, destiny, or spiritual path, then this applies to you: Refer to the section "The History of Zero" for foundational understanding. The essence of 30 embodies beauty, grace, and elegance on a scale of extravagance. It's a number that resonates with worthiness and the flourishing of art – through words, song, speech, acting, and writing. You are endowed with creativity, which brings joy, happiness, and prosperity, marking times of fertility, engagements, celebrations, weddings, and even auspicious shopping excursions. Your unique talents lie in communication; like the Empress amplified by ten, you use words to inspire and elevate the causes dear to your heart, commanding attention.

Each encounter with the zero signifies divine protection and destiny, an assertion that socializing, singing, and self-expression are paramount. With the Four of Wands as a backdrop, your voice acts as an advocate for the voiceless, positioning you as a prime candidate for roles such as a lawyer, judge, artist, actor, orator, or singer. Your presence attracts both children and animals, indicative of your nurturing spirit and creative eye for beauty, art, science, and fashion. Your presence injects hope into our lives, elevating us through your advocacy and articulate nature.

This number's fertility brings love and offspring into your sphere with ease, alongside a magnetic attraction to both people and financial prosperity. Your sexual magnetism, cleverness, and wit are unmatched. Tarot iconography suggests the completion of work and the joy of a couple basking in their hard-earned success. You are the epitome of self-worth and joyous self-expression, with a heart generous enough to champion the welfare of animals and children. In excess, this energy may lead to gossip, overindulgence, or extravagance in vices. You are, at your core, a connoisseur with likely collections of wine, art, and poetry. Your love for opulent fabrics and vibrant colors reminds us to celebrate love and life in all its forms.

As a creator, you must channel your talents, whether in law, advocating for children, or pioneering fertility treatments.

The divine protection of zero may find you in extraordinary situations, championing the vulnerable, be it children or animals. You embody joy, and in moments of need, no challenge is too great for you to overcome in bringing others back to safety and love. Your works in systems, law, and science are acknowledged and celebrated.

If 30 is significant in terms of a pinnacle, year, month, or day for you: Now is the moment for jubilation – love, romance, and the realization of dreams take center stage. It's a time when fertility flourishes, leading to pregnancy and the joy of children. Love and marriage prevail during this prosperous period. Expect accolades, attention, and recognition, as well as the impetus to create and innovate. Indulge in music, jewelry, and fashion, but enjoy these blessings with moderation to prevent excess. This is your time to relish in the fruits of your efforts – a period of contentment at home and perhaps the chance for a significant acquisition. Your creativity is not only flowing but also garnering appreciation. Celebrate your achievements; moderation is key to ensuring the enjoyment of your successes.

31: Five of Wands

Tarot Symbolism: Five young men, each brandishing a wand, appear locked in battle. This card symbolizes intense and undirected youthful energy. The underlying lesson is one of diversity and potential: despite their varied backgrounds, religious affiliations, and political ideologies, collaboration among these individuals could yield astonishing results. They stand atop a hill, signifying that considerable effort is required to achieve great feats. The call to action here is for cooperation, respect, and patience.

If 31 resonates with you – be it related to your heart, personality, destiny, or spiritual path – the following traits are significant for you: patience, order, structure, determination, loyalty, a flair for the dramatic, leading by example, addressing special needs, working with the youth, engaging with government, and publishing. You are summoned to exercise extreme patience. At this time, your energy surges, and if not channeled correctly, it can lead to strife. Such vigor calls for a methodical lifestyle with an emphasis on unity, empathy, and collective action. An obstinate streak may present itself, but remember, it is through the repetitive exercise of patience, community-building, guidance, and understanding that a unique force for benevolence emerges, leading to transformative shifts in attitudes and actions.

There is a birth cycle inherent in the Five of Wands – a labor of love that births outcomes which, while seemingly miraculous, are the product of concerted effort, influencing generations. This is akin to averting wars or crises through peace treaties – a union of differing minds. Where turmoil exists, so too does the potential for diplomacy, tact, and a new order. Your role is to unify, particularly those with little common ground, by finding and reinforcing our shared humanity, keeping peace and advancement at the forefront. Your energy forms the backbone of communities, peace marches, and global movements. The Five of Wands' ultimate aim is peace, not conflict; it is about recognizing our shared human essence and celebrating diversity, rather than imposing singular perspectives.

Your wisdom, lived experiences, patience, and capacity to inspire others define you. Without the composed, authoritative presence of the Five of Wands, disputes would spiral unchecked, instead of being channeled towards agreements and unity. You comprehend the need for respect across differing belief systems, religions, and political affiliations, teaching us to value our diversity. You take up causes close to your heart and advocate alongside others, irrespective of gender or sexual orientation, illuminating prejudices and guiding us towards a common ground that endures.

You are often the first to challenge tyranny, inspiring others by your stance. Your journey is marred by personal struggles, and you possess a tendency towards impulsive confrontations. As a beacon of love and light, you aim for a harmonious blend of opposites to foster global change. However, beware of becoming too rigid, cynical, or dogmatic. Your role is to balance intense energies towards a collective goal. Peace and significant progress hinge on your leadership. Concerns like ADHD, anxiety, stress, and autism resonate deeply with you, underscoring the importance of developing coping strategies for well-being. Your experiences make you an exceptional therapist, and your curiosity may lead you to explore the realms of emotions, balance, and the psychology of criminal behavior.

If 31 is a number of a pinnacle, year, month, or day of yours, organization is key. Legal matters are likely to conclude favorably, provided your integrity has been steadfast. Collaborative efforts will move mountains at this time. You'll find yourself in the company of those you assumed you lacked patience for, yet you consistently evoke their best with your composure. This is a time of serious endeavor and remarkable productivity, where cooperation is instrumental. In this dynamic, your success is guaranteed as you elevate not only yourself but those around you.

You're not a solitary worker; you're collaborating with individuals from whom you are learning tolerance, including self-tolerance. Heed expert advice and welcome support from others. You're laying the groundwork for a significant initiative centered on peace and tolerance. The energy is raw, often laced with prejudice and intolerance, and you are tasked with leadership to nurture the best outcomes. Your influence in reshaping a chaotic environment, whether it's societal, professional, or mental − be it yours or others' − is profound. Through your efforts on important social issues, you channel intense energies into unity. Your effectiveness benefits the community immensely, ensuring both your professional success and the success of your business, bolstered by your commitment to inclusivity and your rejection of bigotry and bias.

32: Six of Wands

Tarot Symbolism: A horseman sits proudly atop his steed, wielding a wand crowned with a wreath. He finds himself at the heart of a celebrating throng, embodying victory. Acknowledged by his community, the horseman understands that their combined efforts culminated in success, though he rightfully basks in the praise for his courageous and principled leadership. With a creed of leaving no one behind, the ensemble faced peril with honor and unity, striving for the utmost good of all — an ambition gloriously realized. The path chosen was not of ease but of righteousness.

If 32 is a number for your heart, personality, destiny, or spiritual path, then this applies to you: Dynamic, beautiful. The unique aspect of this lovely number vibration is the 3, which represents prosperity, beauty, and recognition or fame, merged with the 2 – embodying balance, kindness, and the grace of manners. This synergy spurs action, travel, adventure, and notable success. Unlike some vibrations, 32 is distinguished for its visible fruits of labor, which are both acknowledged and rewarded. You teach us that beauty transcends the superficial; it shapes our emotions, removes stigma from glamour, and refocuses it on empowerment.

You cannot be subdued, and you extend the same respect for others' ideas and concepts. You possess the talent to transform what's deemed trivial into a healing balm, silencing critics. In industries where beauty, cosmetics, or fashion reign, which directly affect our self-perception, you spotlight joy and happiness as deserved indulgences. Your innovative spirit thrives in the duality of 32 – balancing multiple projects with an infectious magnetism. We're drawn to your storytelling; you're an artist with the human body as your canvas. Perhaps you're a tattoo artist or a skilled plastic surgeon, especially drawn to healing scars and birth defects, enhancing beauty in unexpected places. You resonate with endeavors and charities which align with your spirit of expansive aid.

The wealth that flows to you is a boon, fueling further humanitarian projects. Your dexterity and eagerness to learn shield you from boredom, pushing you to multitask. Your aptitude shines in scientific research, emanating confidence. You've scaled peaks, earned degrees, and garnered awards, all signifiers of a journey well-traveled and deserving of accolade. If 32 marks your spiritual path, embrace recognition and the limelight; hiding or diminishing your achievements is not your calling.

If 32 coincides with a pinnacle, year, month, or day: anticipate love, success, and acknowledgment. In relationships, it brings strength; in solitude, it promises supportive companionship. You are now celebrated for your endeavors, drawing admiration and taking center stage. Your radiant confidence is both potent and inspiring, especially for the naturally reserved. Embrace the spotlight, relish the applause, and let your efforts be furthered by this affirmation. Your current project culminates in triumph, with serendipity bringing the right collaborators to your path. Shine boldly; your earned recognition sustains and amplifies the impact of your work.

33: Seven of Wands

Tarot Symbolism: A young man stands alone atop a hill, his courage distinguishing him from others. Vital and youthful, he is well-equipped to face the battle he's already engaged in. With a wand in hand, he doesn't seek violence but defense of what is just. His elevated position offers not only a strategic advantage but mental clarity as well, allowing him to perceive the truth of matters. And it is with this wand of truth that he asserts his protection.

If 33 is a number for your heart, personality, destiny, or spiritual path, then this applies to you: Courage, sacrifice, vision, service, bravery, commitment, charity, sacred heart. This master number demands more from you. You are innately responsible, wise, and dependable. Confronted by injustice, you're compelled to act – it's your calling. Your home becomes a sanctuary for stray animals and lost souls, reflecting your inability to ignore suffering and your dedication to those in need. While you might be seen as bossy or controlling, it's your approach to advocating for those without a voice.

Material possessions hold little allure for you; their worth lies only in how they can alleviate the hardships of others. You face controversy with indifference, propelled by important causes and pure motives. Your connection to higher powers often brings about timely and mysterious aid. A robust spiritual practice is crucial for you, offering solace amid chaos. You plunge into situations of tragedy, war, unrest, and oppression, driven by a desire to support the disenfranchised.

Your grace under pressure is evident, even as you encounter adversaries – not through intent but because your stance on benevolence and universal rights invites challenge. Life presents constant uphill battles, not as punishment but as opportunities to challenge the status quo. The divine connection you possess is not only your lifeline but also a beacon for humanity.

The challenge you face is your relentless drive, often spreading yourself too thin. You must learn to say no, allowing yourself respite from your world-saving endeavors. Personal relationships might be difficult, but not unattainable. In your business ventures, you thrive not because of financial ambition but due to your dedication to service. Your success is a testament to your commitment to love and dedication, guarding it against opposition. Your causes garner attention, awakening society to pressing issues, akin to a protective mother bear ensuring her cubs' safety. Your presence is vital; only unconditional love will suffice.

If 33 is a number of a pinnacle, year, month, or day of yours: Arm yourself for defense and protection of your core values. Guard against burnout from the strenuous journey ahead. Your task is to highlight and challenge significant flaws and deceptions. Reward comes not in monetary form but from the fulfillment found in selfless giving. Be prepared for a path devoid of ease, requiring unwavering determination and focus.

You undertake a sacred duty, providing essential services to humanity at this critical juncture. The recognition you receive is not fiscal but a profound sense of self in doing what is morally right. You may find yourself shouldering heavy responsibilities, such as caring for an ailing relative or managing an important charity. Remember, while immersed in the welfare of others, your own needs are just as important. Take time to tend to yourself amidst your benevolent endeavors.

34: Eight of Wands

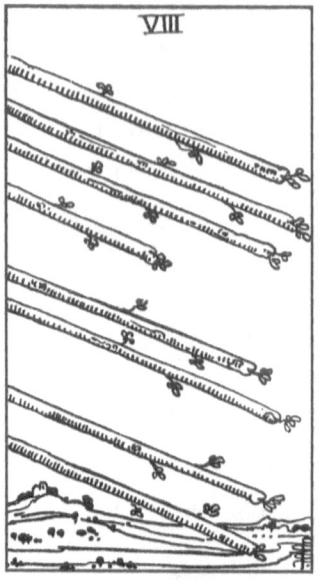

Tarot Symbolism: Eight wands soar swiftly over water, all pointing east. The foremost wand grazes the water's surface, symbolizing the harmonious fusion of water and sky – mirroring the axiom "as above, so below." This imagery heralds a tide of positive transformation, a movement towards light. It signifies the boon of divine aid and the establishment of celestial order.

If 34 is a number that resonates with your heart, personality, destiny, or spiritual path, then this is for you: Imagine travel, success, healing, movement, resolution, and completion suffusing your life with joy. You are the embodiment of beauty, charm, and wit, and your ability to concentrate is unrivaled. The ascent is complete, the peak surmounted, and from this vantage point, the world unfolds in splendor. Your journey is celestial, buoyed by angelic forces. You're cut out to be a healer, with a knack that spans various practices – be it through psychic insights, acupuncture, herbal remedies, or intuitive healing. It's probable that you've faced personal health challenges, which have steered you towards the paths of healing you now extend to others. Staying hydrated and being amidst nature are not just preferences; they are your sustenance, counteracting the draining buzz of urban landscapes. The burdens you've borne have been transformed into a profound capacity to heal, and your experiences may well demand that you author a book, sharing your journey and insights.

You possess a rare synergy, merging the nurturing abundance of The Empress (3) with the sturdy foundation of The Emperor (4). This blend begets a life rich in joy and prosperity, yet anchored by structure, strategy, and discipline. Beware the pitfalls: an imbalance can lead to inertia or financial imprudence, trapping you in the mire of the mundane. Yet, that isn't your truth. Your passion lies in unraveling mysteries, devouring literature on the paranormal, and pioneering uncharted territories, especially within the healing arts. Your quest for knowledge is relentless and rewarding. The wisdom you impart, the discoveries that have benefitted you, become communal beacons of health and beauty. Your work distinguishes the genuine from the spurious, always cognizant of the energetic interconnections that bind us. As a psychic, empathic, and intuitive soul, you absorb the emotional frequencies around you. It's essential, then, to guard your space; let in only those who resonate with your healing ethos. Your life's message is a testament to hope.

If 34 marks a pinnacle, year, month, or day, it heralds a period of swift, exhilarating transitions. Expect the unexpected; fortuitous occurrences bloom as your past efforts bear fruit. The blooms symbolize a healing that weaves itself seamlessly into the fabric of your life, completing the picture without demanding your toil. The onus lies on you to seize these serendipitous offerings that may arise abruptly in this dynamic phase. This chapter of your life is marked by rapid movement and sacred discovery, an invitation to the wonders that await. Heed nature's call; embrace travel, healing, success, and the kinship of spirits aligned with your path. Stay vigilant and ready to act when intuition signals – these chances won't wait. Conversely, passivity could see them slip away. Meditation clarifies your trajectory, safeguarding against false trails. Embrace the potential that unfolds before you, for it exceeds even your grandest imaginings. Take a breath of courage, and leap into the new.

35: Nine of Wands

Tarot Symbolism: A man is depicted kneeling in prayer, clutching a wand – a plea for strength in his present struggles. The eight wands standing behind him symbolize the support he garners from allies as he perseveres in his quest. The leaves on the wands show the promise of life.

If 35 is a number for your heart, personality, destiny, or spiritual path, then this applies to you: Strength, duty, task, responsibility, endurance, focus, stamina, inspiration. You are the backbone of tangible achievements, drawing upon untapped wells of strength. The physical world demands your all – energy, depth, and soul – to meet the immediate challenges. Amidst the chaos, you stand firm, an anchor in the eye of the storm, pivotal to the healing and safety of others.

Victory is within your grasp. Cling to your faith, for you are destined to triumph. You are a natural leader, exuding self-respect and demanding the same from others. Your role often requires ejecting disruptive forces from your environment. You are the bulwark against bullies, embodying strength and conviction without falter. The fine line between assertiveness and aggression is your tightrope – walk it with care.

You are, by nature, a fighter for justice – whether as a debater, lawmaker, or athlete – unyielding to injustice. Yet, beware the seductive path of becoming the aggressor you seek to overcome. With exceptional focus and discernment, you dissect fact from fiction, ensuring your actions are measured and controlled. Embrace the wisdom of David R. Hawkins, who teaches that true power requires no force. You are protective and direct, with the courage to confront rather than conceal. Strong boundaries fortify your role as protector. Your sanctuary is the outdoors; it is here that your critical mind finds peace in activities like horseback riding or archery, silencing the inner critic. Stand firm against overwhelming odds, and embrace the tests of courage and faith that define your spiritual journey. The challenges are merely stepping stones to your ultimate success – a testament to your enduring spirit.

If 35 is a number of a pinnacle, year, month, or day of yours: Now is not the time for surrender. Embrace the tempest of emotional upheaval and hidden family truths. It's in these darkest revelations that your true strength is called upon for healing. Stand resolute against tyranny in any guise; this moment demands your unwavering courage. Maintain composure, for you are in the crucible of character. Face the oppressor – narcissist, bully, or tyrant – with the fortitude of the Nine of Wands. Your persistence ensures victory. Although unasked for, this challenge becomes your proving ground, and with the support of others, your path leads to success. Stand firm; this trial by fire will yield hard-earned peace and restore balance through your indomitable will.

36: Ten of Wands

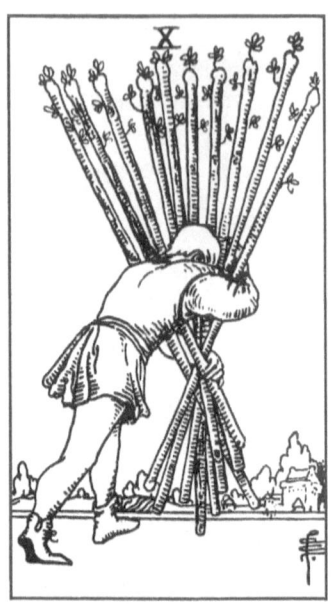

Tarot Symbolism: A man hunches, burdened by a heavy load upon his back. His journey is long, his load substantial, yet his resolve is unwavering. Through his perseverance, he becomes a beacon, inspiring others with his tenacity.

If 36 resonates with your heart, personality, destiny, or spiritual path, it signifies completion, endings, humanity, and responsibility. Your aspirations in this lifetime are expansive, particularly concerning personal relationships, forgiveness, and gratitude. There is a connection you share with the legal system, perhaps through the courts. With the number 36 as a nine energy, you are subject to extreme experiences – the peaks and valleys that compel you toward a delicate equilibrium, mastering yourself while learning to let go.

You rise to meet each challenge with grace, allowing your inner light to shine ever brighter. Invariably, you find yourself entrusted with responsibility at every turn. Your innate inclination to give and care for others is commendable. However, it's crucial to establish strong boundaries; balancing your generous spirit with attention to your own needs is essential. Confronted by continual tests of your service and selflessness, it's vital to ensure these attributes do not lead to being taken advantage of.

Your compassionate nature leads you to believe in your earthly purpose of caretaking for our planet and its denizens. Your soul's history is rich, embracing the journey of spiritual growth. People seek your support; you resonate with esoteric, ancient wisdom. As a teacher among teachers, you impart knowledge with empathy, advocating for second chances. Your creativity must be channeled, for your imagination is vast and fertile.

Financially, you regard money as a necessary instrument, not an end in itself. Your worldviews are altruistic; you engage with charitable endeavors and lead a life of simplicity. You have seen the folly in those who deify external forces. Your teachings are rooted in example, espousing nonviolence and peace, in stark contrast to seeking fame or wealth. Your wisdom draws others to you.

You are concluding a significant cycle of existence, seeking balance in all things. Legal resolutions, contracts, and family matters will find closure. Embrace your responsibilities with love, yet be wary of exploitation. See your tasks through with commitment. Your approach is methodical, valuing scientific and esoteric knowledge alike.

Your patience is legendary, and your humanitarian efforts connect you with diverse individuals. Romantic entanglements may be fleeting, typical of a nine energy settling past accounts. You carry your burdens willingly, paving the way for those who follow. Solitude and contemplation nourish you, and no endeavor is too burdensome if it serves the greater good.

Beware of narrow-mindedness and discrimination. Take care to avoid exhaustion; your physical health is as important as your spiritual well-being. Remember, it's okay to ask for help, to delegate, to rest. Establishing boundaries is critical for your personal well-being, avoiding codependency and pleasing others at the expense of yourself.

The 36 teaches the importance of saying "no" to undue servitude and maintaining personal ambitions. In service, you find fulfillment; in servitude, a diminishing of joy. You are deserving of a life filled with your own dreams and aspirations.

If 36 marks a pinnacle, year, month, or day, you will face a formidable challenge. The situation may seem daunting, but you embody the hope and light required for progress. You must lead by example, holding yourself accountable. Legal settlements and agreements will be part of your journey of surrender and release. Shouldering the care for an elderly parent or a significant cause may fall to you. Amidst these responsibilities, never neglect self-care, for it is the foundation upon which you can care for others.

Section Three:
The Cups

37: King of Cups

Tarot Symbolism: This king resides on his stone throne, cup of emotions firmly in hand, gazing toward the future. Positioned above the restless sea, his composure is unshaken – a testament to his dominion over his feelings. Adorned with a fish amulet, he signifies wisdom.

If 37 is a significant number for your heart, personality, destiny, or spiritual path, then the following insights resonate with you: Gentle, kind, and with a zest for life, you embody the nurturing spirit of the King of Cups. After the tumultuous journey of self-discovery, you've arrived at a place of emotional equilibrium. It's time to savor the rewards of your hard work; tranquility is now your companion. Your personality, a blend of the extroverted '3' and the introspective '7,' creates a harmonious duality, positioning you as both a raconteur and a sage. This unique combination, found in the persona of the King of Wands, paves the way for novel beginnings. Your fertility transcends mere progeny, enriching the earth and your endeavors. As a steward of the land, your approach to life is through care and nurture, eliciting a reciprocal bounty from the universe. Prioritizing people over profit, you steer clear of the rat race, instead finding your wealth in human connections, environmental stewardship, and the simple joys of life. Your lucky streak is not happenstance; it's the product of your innate equilibrium, as you deftly navigate life's dualities, seldom unsettled, ever appreciative of life's fleeting beauties. This appreciation is your strength, spurring creativity and tranquility in love and art. Your diplomatic flair and your profound understanding of balance make you an advocate for healing and environmental conservation.

If 37 marks a pinnacle, year, month, or day in your life, expect a harmonious fusion of intellect and emotion. This period heralds a union of passion and practicality, a time ripe with romance and fertility. Leadership comes naturally to you now, fostering unity and highlighting the best in diverse elements. Disputes are resolved, lands are cultivated, and under your influence, creativity and serenity reign. Embark on ambitious endeavors, such as purifying water sources or campaigning for ecological preservation. Your initiatives are likely to prosper, bearing lasting benefits for many. This phase is a symphony of aesthetics and reason, a testament to your ability to balance heartfelt emotion with thoughtful control.

38: Queen of Cups

Tarot Symbolism: The Queen sits upon her throne, her feet resting at water's edge, a testament to her deep connection with emotion. Her chalice is sealed, symbolizing the profound intuition and psychic abilities that originate from within. The handles of her cup are adorned with the figures of celestial messengers, their wings an emblem of divine communication.

If 38 is significant to your heart, personality, destiny, or spiritual path, then this message is for you: Embodying beauty, compassion, and a generous spirit, you are the essence of emotion. Your affinities lie in the arts, be it jewelry, fashion, or painting, yet these do not overshadow your love for nature and animals, horses in particular. There is a regal air about you, devoid of arrogance. You are fiercely protective, especially within your own home – a sanctuary for all who enter. Creativity is not just a pursuit but a necessity for you. Your talents could manifest in careers like makeup artistry or any artistic field. Emotionally, as a 38 – a master number – you are on a journey of highs and lows until you achieve the equilibrium you crave.

You revere the divine sacred feminine, seeing yourself as a guardian for women, advocating safety for the vulnerable. Fearless in setting boundaries, you create a safe haven within your walls. You champion beauty and self-care, never dismissing them as trivial. Education is a cornerstone for you and your family, driven by the belief that knowledge empowers. You ensure this wisdom, especially that of the sacred feminine, is passed down through generations. You are the bearer and defender of this knowledge, striving for harmony in every aspect of life – from your home's ambiance to your personal style. Disorder and disarray are foreign to your nature. You find solace in the arts, be it poetry, music, or dance, gravitating towards tales of love and romance.

However, there is a shadow side to this – emotional volatility and codependency can surface if not kept in check. You excel in professions where emotions, protection, and artistic expression converge. Your life's trials, particularly emotional ones, are where you test and reveal your true strength, seeking to find balance and sweetness even in sorrow. This mastery over emotional tides not only transforms you but those around you as well, as you strive to see the inherent goodness in everyone.

If 38 marks a pinnacle, year, month, or day: Expect emotions to surge, challenging you to assist others through their emotional landscapes. This period is rich with learning and calls for expression – through art, writing, singing, or speaking. You must channel your emotions constructively. Your heartfelt expressions have the power to heal and inspire. As you navigate through emotional disturbances, remember to let your intuition lead. This is a time for shedding codependent ties and fortifying your emotional fortitude. By asserting strong personal boundaries, you safeguard your well-being. During this time, beauty, home, family, and emotional depth take precedence, with the promise of cultivating beauty, harmony, and fulfilling relationships in their wake.

39: Knight of Cups

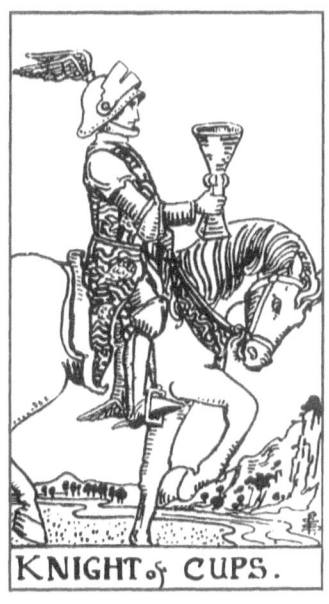

Tarot Symbolism: The Knight, astride his white horse, symbolizes purity. In his hand, he extends a cup, an offering of goodwill and love. Divergent from his counterparts, the Knight of Cups does not charge ahead impetuously; instead, he proceeds with a leisurely pace, savoring the journey. Poised to cross a stream, he epitomizes the act of navigating emotions thoughtfully.

If 39 is a number for your heart, personality, destiny, or spiritual path, then this applies to you: Laughter, joy, celebration, romance, marriage, teaching, generosity, inspiration, storyteller. You are a beacon of upliftment. The world can be a somber place, but like the Knight of Cups, you bring a reminder of our divine nature and our quest for enlightenment. Joy, love, and laughter are the essence of your communication. For you, all paths invariably lead to love. Known as the joy guide in your circle, your sense of humor is a constant, and you naturally disperse the seriousness of life. You are the much-needed comic relief, the embodiment of goodness, reminding us of our worth and the cyclical nature of life with unconditional love as its bedrock. With a heart full of romance, you are a bastion of loyalty and abundance. A future rich with marriage, children, and happiness is envisioned for you. You have a unique ability to dispel the mental and emotional fog that clouds us, allowing enlightenment to filter through. Your spirit craves the beauty of flowers, the tranquility of a garden, the serenity of water. Drawn to nurturing, whether for humans or animals, you find joy in commemorating life's milestones.

Your path may lead you to be the center of attention, perhaps as a model or actor, yet you maintain a humble sense of levity. Laughter is your healing balm, and your humor is infectious. Like your fellow knights, you are brimming with youthful exuberance. However, instead of engaging in battle, you carry a chalice of goodwill, sharing its contents generously. You possess a dynamic allure, becoming a magnet for those who seek peace, joy, and celebration. Sociability is your forte. If negativity creeps in, you risk not engaging fully in life, preferring the comfort of idleness over commitment. Multiple romantic endeavors may pass through your life, with the potential for one to evolve into lasting commitment.

If 39 marks a pinnacle, year, month, or day in your life: A period of festivity awaits – weddings, graduations, birth announcements. Romance permeates the atmosphere, and joyful messages and invitations abound. Now is the time for that dream vacation to a romantic destination. Embrace opportunities for social engagements – accept that invitation and immerse yourself in the joy. This is a wondrous, vivacious chapter of your life meant for full enjoyment. Let your heart lead this joyous dance. In romance, you may find yourself either taking the initiative or being utterly captivated by another. Professionally, auspicious proposals are likely to come your way.

40: Page of Cups

Tarot Symbolism: A young man clasps a cup, his gaze set firmly on his path ahead. The cup, brimming with water, symbolizes emotions – emotions the Page is determined to safeguard and keep steady, come what may. Surrounding him, verdant foliage whispers of success, hinting at the flourishing of any creative venture he embarks upon. With eyes alight with anticipation, he faces the future, confident in his ability to craft and realize the visions that his intuition conjures.

If 40 resonates with your heart, personality, destiny, or spiritual path, heed the following insights: Refer to the section "The History of Zero" for an essential backdrop. You are cocooned in divine safeguarding, where order, systematic approaches, and strategic planning take precedence. Your life is a canvas for the weapons of growth: development, manifestation, politics, law, and structured authority, all infused with compassion. Intuition is your divine shield. Your inner compass inherently knows the boundaries that must stand firm, foreseeing and facilitating the culling of the old to usher in the new. This energy is superb for mapping out long-term goals – be it family life, homeownership, career shifts, or law enforcement pursuits. It's the terrain where structure, discipline, and learning thrive under the Page of Cups' watchful eye.

Many find their calling in justice, perhaps as a bailiff upholding order. With zero as your ally, you confront daunting figures with uncanny protection – never harmed, irrespective of the dangers that lurk. You are drawn to the pillars of justice, law, and order. In the family nucleus, you are the standard-bearer, the unwavering enforcer of respect and peace. Authority is your essence, commanding attention with minimal, carefully weighed words. Your mere presence is a bastion of safety, your strength unmistakable. Military life may beckon, reinforcing your role as a guardian. In matters spiritual, your solidity equips you for confronting darker forces, establishing you as a foundation for safety and stability. In this role, paralleled by Jesus as the Prince of Peace, you are the Keeper of the Peace, the reason for nights embraced in serenity.

If 40 marks a pinnacle, year, month, or day: Prepare for significant strides in your journey. Education, certifications, or missions may loom on your horizon. You might find yourself bound for hazardous territories, driven by service, perhaps in rescue, journalism, or a crusade for justice. Embrace the adventuring spirit when it beckons, for you are destined to forge paths where fear deters others. Your intervention transforms chaos into order, akin to a sheriff restoring peace to a lawless town. Your callings range from liberating the oppressed to more personal milestones like founding a family or acquiring a home. With divine protection and heightened intuition, the groundwork you've laid promises abundant yields. Your readiness and acumen ensure that wherever you plant your feet, prosperity is bound to flourish.

41: Ace of Cups

Tarot Symbolism: The hand of God extends, proffering a chalice of pure love that cascades into five rivulets. This Ace heralds a new dawn. The divine hand is both a benediction and the fountainhead of creation. Symbolizing the Holy Spirit is the white dove. In some tarot decks, the goblet gleams with a golden hue. Poised above it is the third eye, a beacon of pure love and luminescence, forging connections amongst all entities. This celestial light pours through the chalice, suffusing the waters below.

If 41 is a resonant number for your heart, personality, destiny, or spiritual path, then this message is for you: It heralds travel, change, versatility, and love. The world's pleasures await you, offered in copious amounts. You are ensconced in divine protection. Your cleverness, adaptability, and wit shine brightly. Intuition is not just a trait you possess but an art you've honed. You abound in creativity, your life a fertile ground for prosperity, comfort, affection, offspring, and pets. The symbolism of cups is closely tied to emotions, and the Ace of Cups represents an everlasting spring of satisfaction. Every facet of your life is infused with genuine love. Your guiding principles are love, abundance, fertility, and transformation. Your environment is dynamic and exhilarating, perpetually rejuvenating with the thrill and ingenuity that flow from this space. Embrace your identity and sensuality with unabashed confidence. The divine chalice, presented from the heavens, spills its contents through five streams, mirroring the five senses. Beware the temptation to indulge excessively in sensual pleasures. Savor them but remain anchored. This state of grace is fueled by love and intuitive wisdom.

You view the world from the heart's vantage point, your core emotional space, with compassion, equilibrium, and unconditional love. You are a wellspring of energy for your ventures because they are born from what truly inspires you. This serene tranquility stems from the enlightened understanding that love is the pathway through. This is the secret to your vigor. You are eager to communicate your ethos of love, harmony, and equity through your endeavors. Your reservoir of love is limitless, characterized by its empathetic and unconditional nature.

You are remarkably astute and engaging, a source of joy for those around you. Your humor brings lightness to self-perceptions. A catalyst for beginnings, you may not always see things through to the end, but you galvanize us into action. Intuition is your compass; you trust it implicitly. This trust is why you forge remarkable connections globally. You elevate the essence of humanity. Protected and moved by the divine, you convert the splendor witnessed in your travels and contemplations into tangible, purposeful, and inspiring applications. You are a vanguard in your domain, discovering novel approaches to emotional healing and balance.

Your journey through forgiveness, surrender, and release has broadened both your consciousness and your heart, and it is this expansion that you share. Your valor and audacity stem from a place of openness within your heart chakra.

If 41 marks a pinnacle, a year, a month, or a day for you, it denotes beginnings, courage, success, openness, love, compassion, and healing. The element at your behest is the purest emotional essence, stemming from unconditional love and celestial guidance. Your cup overflows. Having glimpsed the light at the end of the tunnel, you disseminate the story of your triumph and affection, magnifying the love, solace, and joy bestowed upon you. This period is steeped in sheer unconditional love. The magic lies in the energy you share, for the love you give is returned manifold. Opportunities for love permeate every aspect of life. Professionally, you are immersed in work that ignites your passion and yields prosperity. This is the advent of new relationships grounded in love, compassion, and understanding.

42: Two of Cups

Tarot Symbolism: A golden goblet brims with love. A man and a woman lock eyes over the chalice, embodying balance and duality – yin and yang. They share a profound sense of pure love and connection that transcends the need for words. Their gazes are not mere glances but soulful explorations. "For where two or three gather in my name, there am I with them," spoke Jesus Christ.

If 42 is a number that resonates with your heart, personality, destiny, or spiritual path, then this message is for you: You are an advocate for peace, adept at cooperation and diplomacy. Your heart isn't just large; it's expansive, bringing people into harmony. Your life is a quest for balance and beauty, both in your surroundings and in your personal connections. In every endeavor, the nurturing energy of the sacred feminine mother is evident. Your creativity, spiritual insight, and empathy set you apart. With loyalty that runs deep, you champion causes that touch your heart. Your ability to articulate your passion has the power to inspire and stir those around you.

You embody devotion, and your connection to the mystical is unfettered, often expressed through music, poetry, and art. Your words have the capacity to move us, resonating with a truth that's both personal and universal. You balance this with a practicality that grounds your optimistic nature. Seeing the divine in others, you aid us in tapping into our own spiritual potential. Your charm, generosity, and forthright nature are only matched by the honesty you expect from others.

Friendship, for you, isn't given lightly. Once bestowed, it's a bond for life. Your open-mindedness allows you to embrace diverse perspectives, maintaining friendships that transcend differences. Your quest for knowledge is unending. For those on this spiritual path, past wounds have led to the quest for unconditional love and self-worth. You pursue emotional challenges that foster deep inner connections, guiding you to recognize the inherent beauty in your life. Your worth is intrinsic, and your heart-centered approach is your greatest gift. Your creative expressions are a reminder of humanity's essence, promoting unity and solidarity.

Throughout life, you might gravitate toward relationships that challenge your integrity, forging your discernment. Through this process, you find forgiveness and clarity, ultimately surrounded by relationships that endure. Solitude is not your preference. Watch out for excess and understand that when not recognized, it can lead to isolation. As wisdom grows, you'll learn to shield yourself from negativity.

You seek not fame or wealth but understanding, to be loved and heard. Be wary of confinement within physical or emotional spaces; stepping out can be refreshing.

If 42 marks a pinnacle, year, month, or day for you, it heralds a time of unfiltered, raw emotion and unconditional love. This period is ripe for commitments, whether matrimonial, familial, or educational. The alignment of time and opportunity is perfect for you now. Harness this surge of emotion, fueled by love and passion, to illuminate your path and inspire others. Maintain your inner balance through prayer and meditation as you embark on this significant venture. You are laying the foundations of your 'church,' in whatever form it may take, drawing others who will aid you in this journey. The keywords for you are love and cooperation, the twin beacons that will guide you through this phase.

43: Three of Cups

Tarot Symbolism: Three women stand together, their celebration centered around a single cup – a symbol of the rewards now manifest from their collective efforts. "Good things come in threes," as the saying goes, and here it holds true. United in friendship, they share not only their achievements but their talents with each other and the wider world.

If the number 43 resonates with your heart, personality, destiny, or spiritual path, then the following insights are for you: You embody the essence of tranquility – quiet, soft-spoken, with an analytical and logical mind. Your intellectual capacity thrives on mental gymnastics, delighting in the challenge of unraveling complexities. Mastery of silence is a skill you've cultivated, allowing you to reflect and formulate solutions, particularly in areas concerning water, agriculture, and farming.

Your proficiency with technology and the human body's mysteries is unparalleled, with astral travel and meditation serving as gateways to the profound wisdom you share. Prosperity in business comes naturally to you, as your innovative and healing solutions stand out. Your curiosity extends beyond the surface, diving into the inner workings of machines and gadgets, driven by an insatiable desire to learn and solve.

Behind the scenes is where you thrive, far from the limelight of fame, intrigued more by the enigmatic than the ordinary. Yet, you find novel ways to handle the mundane through your spiritual practices. Water, a vital element for you, facilitates clarity and creativity, drawing you to travel extensively, whether it's to witness innovative solutions or explore sacred and mystical sites.

Your educational pursuits are unorthodox, favoring practical wisdom over traditional academia, seeking out ancient knowledge and shamanic traditions. Old books hold a special appeal, their worn pages containing secrets that fuel your dignified intellect. Patents and discoveries for environmental betterment are the fruits of your labor, borne from a relentless quest for understanding.

Health for you is a non-conventional journey, finding solace and healing in alternative practices rather than in mainstream medicine. Ancient relics and books captivate you, with studies in sound, frequency, and energy leading to innovations in healing and agriculture. Your prescience is a gift, often perceiving solutions long before they become apparent to others.

If 43 is a number of a pinnacle, year, month or day of yours: Celebration, travel, great news, friendship, support. The wait is over. The conclusion is worthy of celebrating. There is good news. Your past efforts are rewarded. You will travel. There is abundance. You have both the time and the money for traveling. Celebration and travel mark the moments when the number 43 features prominently in your life. Triumphs are met with joyous festivities, signifying the end of waiting and the beginning of rewarding times. Abundance graces your path, allowing for exploration and the sharing of knowledge gained through arduous effort. Professional and personal spheres align, bringing promotion, recognition, and heartfelt connections. Enjoy the equilibrium between rest and revelry; it is well-deserved.

44: Four of Cups

Tarot Symbolism: A young, robust man sits outdoors, his attention wavering. Before him, three cups lie overturned upon the earth, their spillage a testament to his current disinterest. Yet, if he were to turn inward, harnessing the power of meditation and prayer, he might witness a divine spectacle: the hand of the Almighty emerging from a parting cloud, offering him a fourth cup brimming with wisdom and opportunity. His pursuit demands his utmost mental acuity and unwavering focus, for without a noble aim, this chance may slip through his fingers like the contents of the spilled cups.

If 44 is a number for your heart, personality, destiny, or spiritual path, then this applies to you: Authority, justice, karma, forgiveness. You embody focus and methodical precision, thriving on significant projects with seeming ease. This master number beckons you toward greater challenges, propelling you along a path paved with forgiveness – a journey reminiscent of Nelson Mandela's. You possess the energy of The Emperor and the strength of the Strength card, an amalgamation that gifts you with easy access to wealth, influence, and responsibility. The outdoors is essential for you; it provides the backdrop where your clarity of thought sharpens your notable business sense. Leadership comes naturally to you, and you are adept at creating structures that enable vast enterprises to flourish with efficiency.

You find yourself in a continuous cycle of analysis, always strategizing for increased efficiency. Excelling in politics, global leadership, or military endeavors, you wield form, function, and simplicity as your primary instruments. Striving for balance in your emotional and spiritual realms, your rational mind is learning to embrace intuitive insights. Beware of the potential negative expression of your traits, which could manifest as a domineering presence over both yourself and others. It's crucial not to overwork; mental respite is as important as the physical. Drawn to military, law enforcement, or governmental roles, you have a passion for strategic operation. Your ability to maintain composure in high-stress situations makes you the ideal candidate for roles like hostage negotiation or special forces operations, where courage and strategic planning are paramount.

You are methodical in avoiding anything that might cloud your sharp judgment, aiming to remain lucid at all times. Recognition and accolades in your field are not uncommon for you. You take care of your physical well-being, preferring nature as your gym. In dire situations, your expertise is sought to dismantle threats of terror or dictatorship. However, you must remain vigilant not to become the authoritarian you combat. Discipline is your forte, and an orderly life your preference. When you connect with your less dominant intuitive and emotional side, you complete the initiation this master number represents. Achieving mastery over oneself, exemplified by compassion for oneself and others, is your ultimate challenge. You must never forget the humanity within yourself and others, no matter the intensity of the situation, as Nelson Mandela once illustrated with his profound capacity for empathy and forgiveness. His words echo the essence of your path: to inspire cooperation and significance in those around you through authenticity and humility.

If 44 is a number of a pinnacle, year, month, or day of yours: You are walking the path of a master. It's a journey that demands unwavering focus, determination, and forgiveness. You reflect upon your life's worth and deliberate on the future trajectory. Positioned at the center of the lemniscate, you ponder your past decisions, their outcomes, and your ensuing direction. You question the intrinsic value of things, transcending monetary worth. The master within dictates your core values, the causes you champion, and the changes you stand for. In this profound period, you find solidarity, unexpected guidance, and support, setting an exemplary standard of love that inspires on a global scale. As you navigate these transformative times, the support you receive is in direct correlation with your deeds – an immediate karmic response. Transparency improves relationships and financial matters. By tuning into your intuition, you will uncover opportunities that may have otherwise remained hidden.

45: Five of Cups

Tarot Symbolism: A solitary, towering figure cloaked in shadow stands with bowed head, contemplating three toppled cups – a symbol of disillusionment. This moment marks the inception of a release from delusion. Unseen behind him, two cups remain upright, signifying potential that awaits his forgiveness and release. These cups stand patient, ready for when he turns to face the future.

If 45 resonates with you as a number of your heart, personality, destiny, or spiritual path, then the following insights are for you: Your life's quest is the pursuit of balance – anchoring the stability that the number 4 brings, the desire to take root, coupled with the dynamic quest for freedom, evolution, and exploration that the number 5 demands. This liberation often transcends the physical, venturing into spiritual realms. With your heightened empathy, people gravitate towards your blend of intuitive insight and grounded counsel. You're an advocate for liberty, a proponent of nonviolent resistance to uphold human dignity. Your existence is dedicated to a spiritual service – educating and championing the tenets of equality. Your knowledge, sacred and profound, becomes a beacon that instructs and motivates action and self-advocacy. However, vigilance against overexertion is advised; driven by an internal fire, you fight tirelessly against suppression. Strive for harmony between rational thought and emotional intelligence.

Periodic retreats to recharge and center yourself are essential – your path isn't linear, often redirected by the distress you witness in humanity and infringements of rights. These challenges, though daunting, push you to delve deeper, transforming you into a spiritual seeker. Mastery of the esoteric is your pursuit, and you hold others to high standards within their expertise. Beware of isolation or sinking into cynicism during trying times. Use setbacks as stepping stones, merging analytical prowess with your innate intuition, allowing you to advance toward your aims. Embrace change, avoid self-pity or inertia, and know that your greatest transformations often arise from adversity.

If 45 appears as a pinnacle in your life, a year, month, day, or in any significant way – it signals a period marked by loss and relational disappointments. Do not linger in sorrow; this is a phase for learning. Utilize gained wisdom as a foundation for the future. Embrace the quiet; it's an asset during this mystic interval. Abstain from launching new ventures; instead, introspect and release, retaining only the most valuable lessons. This era's gift lies in its wisdom, connecting you to ancient and deep knowledge. The letdowns and closures are necessary, preparing you for emerging opportunities just beginning to dawn on your horizon. Forgiveness is the catalyst for an enlightened viewpoint, allowing mystical awakenings within you, dispelling illusion, and illuminating a newfound path ahead.

46: Six of Cups

Tarot Symbolism: A young child shares a cup brimming with flowers with another, embodying the pure joy and love inherent in sharing and camaraderie. This act represents not only the innocence and delight of childhood but also cooperation and affection. The surrounding buildings and homes of the community underscore a backdrop of safety, fostering a sense of a cherished and supportive upbringing.

If 46 is a number for your heart, personality, destiny, or spiritual path, then this applies to you: Nostalgia, memories, the past, revitalization, harmony, cooperation, leadership. Your dynamic leadership style is compelling; your enthusiasm becomes a beacon, attracting others to your vision. With a profound respect for elders and ancient traditions, you perceive the present as intricately woven with the tapestries of the past, which informs your wisdom and helps you avoid repeating historical errors. A connoisseur of history, you are dedicated to the community's welfare and can sometimes assert your will strongly. Financial success seems to be drawn to you, although it can dissipate just as quickly if not managed with care. By learning from the past, subsequent ventures are undertaken with greater wisdom, yielding financial stability. Your intensity and focus are matched by a strong intuition and a commitment to humanitarian causes. You connect deeply with your inner child, understanding the importance of playfulness in life. As a destiny number, you are the reviver of nostalgic joys – possibly reinventing classic games or operating a vintage-style ice cream parlor. Simplicity and joy are your domain, whereas high-tech ventures may not resonate with you. Should the negative aspects surface, there may be a tendency to be immature, dull, and overly fixated on the past, resistant to the innovations of the present.

If 46 is a number of a pinnacle, year, month, or day of yours: The past is weaving itself back into the fabric of your life, perhaps through the rekindling of old relationships. With time having nurtured growth and self-awareness, these reunions can lead to forgiveness, compassion, and understanding, paving the way for new beginnings. The sum of 4 and 6 equals 10, signaling a positive new direction focused on unconditional love, emphasized by the number 6 in 46. The bonds forming now are not just a stroke of good fortune; they are the result of positive energy and intentions coming full circle. As your environment shifts, sometimes abruptly, it opens doors to long-term opportunities brimming with joy and passion.

Your zest for life is infectious, bringing people together to achieve great things. Embrace the activities that delighted you in childhood – playing, dancing, drawing – as these are the keys to joy. Under this influence, the theme of new life is prominent, with the joyful prospect of children or even twins.

47: Seven of Cups

Tarot Symbolism: A man stands with his back turned, facing a tempting array of seven cups. Each vessel embodies a trial: fame, glamour, vanity, frivolity, illusion, jealousy, and ego. With each achievement, satisfaction eludes him, highlighting the emptiness of such pursuits. Yet, through this realization, he forges his path to mastery. In understanding the hollowness of these superficial victories, he attains the ultimate treasure: self-mastery, which heralds the arrival of true wealth.

If 47 is a number for your heart, personality, destiny, or spiritual path, then this applies to you: Decisions, testing, master number. You are compelled to test your mettle, to trust the intuition you've honed over time. You may even choose to live with a sensory deprivation or a physical challenge to amplify your other senses. Your journey is about self-imposed limitations, discovering the essence of your identity, and manifesting mastery in the realms requiring your discernment. Beware, though – the allure of the aesthetically pleasing can lead you astray. Shiny objects and pursuits may dissolve before you, leaving you in daunting situations; these are but trials on your path to self-realization. Silence is your ally; when you connect with the peace it offers, the grip of temptation weakens. As you shed resentment and embrace growth, your journey mirrors that of an initiate ascending towards enlightenment, conquering temptations and awakening the mystic within. There's scant margin for error in your quest. Missteps have immediate repercussions. Yet, this rigorous discipline is your tool to forge a robust character, becoming a paragon for others.

As you transcend the trappings of money, glamour, and fame, placing them within the correct perspective, your life aligns with divine order, and your true fortune emerges. Stillness invites what you desire; engage with the process, for there are no shortcuts. What you release to the universe will return to you. The pursuit of superficial glamour comes with hidden costs. It's in authenticity, in the serenity of your being, that life arranges itself, revealing a path unexpected yet profoundly right. Your healing journey becomes a shared narrative, connecting you with individuals once beyond your orbit, now integral to your existence. You discover that real value lies beyond the superficial – the true treasure is you, especially in sharing your story. Your intuitive powers are strong, tapping into other dimensions. However, remain grounded; these realms can be captivating but also consuming. Your discoveries in sound frequency healing become your gift to others. Exercise discernment in all relationships; your influence is potent, and vulnerability to manipulation must be guarded against. Once you align emotion with practicality, your success is remarkable, forming a foundation others depend on. You are witty, incisive, and imaginative.

If 47 is a number of a pinnacle, year, month, or day of yours: You will face trials. What once shimmered with promise may end up delivering scant joy until you apply your keen sense of discrimination. When the pursuit of superficial desires ceases, and you balance heart with reason, your aspirations are realized. Life presents unique challenges to test your resolve, and it's in relinquishing specific outcomes, trusting your judgment, and adhering to your principles that healing and serenity are found. Avoid lofty dreams without substance; instead, be methodical and unwavering in your vision. Your practicality attracts the right kind of support, and staying true to yourself is the formula for turning dreams into reality. The tasks you undertake may not radiate glamour – they could be as unassuming as composting or soil engineering – but they are essential and grounded. Let your intuitive wisdom steer you. With discernment, the elimination of the unnecessary, and a steadfast commitment to your values, you navigate toward tranquility, prosperity, and enriching relationships.

48: Eight of Cups

Tarot Symbolism: Eight cups stand upright, brimming with earthly offerings. Yet, a solitary figure turns away, forsaking these material gifts in pursuit of the distant spiritual summit, seeking true fulfillment.

If 48 is a pivotal number in your heart, personality, destiny, or spiritual path, it speaks volumes to you. You've walked the proverbial wheel, completed the necessary work, attained degrees, and amassed wealth, yet you sense an unfulfilled void. Material success flows to you with ease, but you discover tranquility, consolation, and comfort not in the tangible, but in the spiritual realm. The earthly domain can't contain you indefinitely – you find your true place amidst the divine, the angelic, and the celestial.

However, you cannot sever your ties with the ordinary completely. Your life is a continuous quest for equilibrium between the tangible and the spiritual. Your sanctuary lies within states of grace and meditation, where being tethered to the world just doesn't suffice. You walk through life guided by your principles, fearless, accompanied by angels in every step. You possess a blend of romance, loyalty, introspection, wit, and humor. Your intuition and psychic abilities are profound, stirring a sense of responsibility and empathy towards those close to you.

When your earthly duties are fulfilled, you pursue the mountain of spiritual ascension. The journey is demanding, yet inevitable. Only the purest spiritual alignment will suffice. Disillusionment may stem from relationships, be they friendships, romantic involvements, or familial bonds, influencing your timing and decision to forsake the mundane in pursuit of the enlightenment your soul craves. A significant emotional event in which you are a key player will orchestrate unique circumstances, urging us all to unearth the divine within. Your existence straddles two worlds: ensuring the well-being of loved ones here on Earth and, simultaneously, in the ethereal realm, seeking the contentment that evades you on *terra firma*. To encounter you is to be touched by your spirit.

If 48 marks a pinnacle, a year, a month, or a day for you: Abandonment, disillusionment, enlightenment await. In this phase, you'll reach the objectives you've set for yourself only to realize that their achievement brings no lasting contentment. You will renounce the third-dimensional trappings and embark on an unwavering quest toward the peak of enlightenment. Alongside the realization of goals, such as completing academic pursuits and securing financial gains, there comes a striking readiness to leave it all for a quest for life's deeper meaning. The call to move forward, inward, and upward is irresistible, not hindered by shifting circumstances. Your experiences will expand your perspective and pivot you towards humanitarian efforts. In striving to alleviate the burdens of others, you share your wealth, wisdom, and time generously, and in doing so, you connect with the elusive piece within yourself.

49: Nine of Cups

Tarot Symbolism: A solitary man sits, his smile a testament to his accomplishments. Above him, nine cups form an arch, each symbolizing both spiritual and material success. Throughout his lifetimes, he has filled these cups to the brim. The blue hue surrounding him denotes truth, the art of communication, the power of voice, and a serene inner peace.

If 49 is a number for your heart, personality, destiny, or spiritual path, then this is for you: Focused, methodical, loyal. Your achievements have struck a harmonious balance between pragmatism and sentiment. You embody the Emperor's logic and focus (4) alongside the Hermit's wisdom and loyalty (9), adept at discerning when to press forward or when to withdraw. You embody patience and diplomacy, your hard work consistently yielding dividends. You stand by a high personal standard without casting judgment upon others, and your approach to sizable projects is marked by concentration and tranquility. Emotionally charged issues are handled with an enlightening touch rather than criticism, reflecting your strength as a mediator and reporter.

Your responsibilities are many, yet you address each systematically, shining a light on the underlying lessons before progressing to the next. Your reasoned stability is a bulwark against the storms of adversity, and your wealth is accrued through transparent and ethical methods, earning you high regard. Rest is not your preference, as the call to address the next important issue is ever-present. Your belief in justice and karmic law is mirrored in your home, which displays the wealth you've accumulated. Your intellectual curiosity, especially in esoteric fields, is unquenchable, and you generously impart your knowledge. A successful marriage, chosen for love, adds to your contentment and satisfaction, products of your gradual ascent through perseverance, integrity, and an explorative spirit. Your reputation for sartorial elegance precedes you.

Beware of the pitfalls of moodiness, a lack of focus, or an imbalanced pursuit of goals that might leave you feeling unfulfilled despite apparent success. Question whether you've neglected personal relationships or overextended in any life domain. Moderation is key, for while this is a card of wish fulfillment, excess can spoil the fruits of your labor. Celebrate and share your prosperity; your self-esteem and confidence are just rewards for a journey well-traveled. You have charted your course from scarcity to abundance, sometimes even notoriety, embracing life's lows as educational groundings in wisdom and appreciation for the tangible.

If 49 marks a pinnacle, year, month, or day significant to you: Anticipate a period of realized dreams, contentment, and answered wishes. This phase promises emotional equilibrium matched with practical application, bearing the fruits of recognition, success, and esteem. A stable marriage and enhanced wealth are on the horizon, owed to your practicality and accomplished work ethic. Business ventures prosper through your consistent effort, and a tranquil disposition attracts further peace, augmenting a sense of well-being. Your home becomes a testament to what you've strived for. Seize this chance to fulfill your deepest aspirations.

50: Ten of Cups

Tarot Symbolism: A family basks outdoors, their joy manifest beneath a resplendent rainbow signaling the cessation of hardships. Amidst the dance of their children, the parents share an embrace, a tableau of bliss. The ten cups arrayed above brim with the emotional equilibrium earned through conquered challenges. A gentle stream meanders by, a symbol of their serene emotional state, mirroring the idyllic tranquility of the scene – a testament to their elevated consciousness.

If 50 is a number for your heart, personality, destiny, or spiritual path, then this applies to you: The numerology of 50 speaks to liberation, sensuality, and self-assuredness; it is the number of triumph, love, and tranquility, grounding one in both family and self. If this is your spiritual path number, you are destined to break free from the shackles that bind – be it addiction, abuse, family secrets, or negative thought patterns. A definitive end to silence and tolerance, you assert your right to voice and to resist subjugation. Your journey through life's fires has tempered you into a force of courage, catalyzing a positive shift within yourself and your lineage, stirring others to discover their own bravery.

Your celebration of sexuality and sensuality is a reclaiming of divine gifts – no longer subject to theft or shame. Your worth, once obscured, now shines brilliantly, an internal power that cascades into the external, challenging outdated norms and fostering transparency. With your intellect and humor, your presence is sought after; though beware, not all who are drawn to your light harbor noble intentions. Your skills are vast – whether in architecture, music, or craftsmanship, your hands create as much as your mind conceives. Learning is your sustenance, with mental stimulation as necessary as air.

Healing has blossomed within you, yielding a harmony that touches every aspect of life. Marriage, family, fertility, your abode, and career – all thrive in serene alignment. Charismatic and engaging, you thrive in the spotlight, whether in front of a crowd or a camera, quick thinking and a sharp wit at your disposal. Fame and fortune may not be your quest, yet prosperity finds you, accompanied by emotional riches and relationships that endure through time.

As the Hierophant amplified, you employ your charm for noble ends, and with the zero's divine safeguard (see "The History of Zero"), you could guide others through the complexities of intimacy as a consummate sex therapist, aiding them to heal with dignity and love. You excel in communication, with a particular flair for the penning of mysteries.

Should the scale tip too far, you may find yourself estranged from family or overly indulgent in the pursuit of pleasure. Remember, the path back to equilibrium is always within reach.

If 50 marks a pinnacle, year, month, or day of significance for you, it heralds a period of freedom and exploration. Every facet of life aligns in a symphony of peace and satisfaction. Relationships provide a nurturing backdrop as they deepen, potentially blossoming into lifelong commitments. The time is ripe for new encounters, joyous connections, and perhaps a spontaneous journey. Recognition for your endeavors could be forthcoming, making this an especially rewarding and heartening chapter of your life.

Section Four:
The Swords

51: King of Swords

Tarot Symbolism: The seasoned King occupies the throne of justice, sword in hand, a beacon of discernment between the true and the false, the real and the illusionary. His reign is characterized by judiciousness, fairness, and compassion. Behind him, the butterfly symbolizes the perpetual transformation of life, encompassing the cycles of birth, death, and rebirth. The phases of the moon, waxing and waning, underscore the duality of existence, the King's wisdom slicing through opposing views to reveal the core truth of every matter.

If 51 is a number that resonates with your heart, personality, destiny, or spiritual path, then this applies to you: You embody sharpness and focus, along with authoritative discipline. Your approach to life is strategic – you're a lover of games that require forethought, like chess. A staunch believer in justice, your interests naturally gravitate toward law enforcement, the military, or any field where order and responsibility are paramount. As a soldier, lawyer, or judge, you exhibit an astute mind, meticulously analyzing adversaries before engaging in any confrontation. You embody the essence of a warrior.

Should the shadow of your nature prevail, you may verge towards tyranny – overbearing, cold, and insatiable in your quest for power. However, in your more enlightened state, you stand firmly in your power, upholding laws and principles that cultivate peace. You are acutely aware of your values and principles. Your intellectual authority secures you the respect and influence you seek. Despite the pernicious nature of your enemies, your response is invariably composed, detached, and rational. You meld judgment with compassion and remain serene, even under immense pressure – often performing at your best when the stakes are highest. You thrive in high-tension environments where decisions are made rapidly and actions are decisive. Travel is an integral part of your life; work frequently transports you to distant lands, exposing you to diverse cultures and tongues. Your assignments are transient, fulfilling a purpose before moving on. There's an underlying yearning for familial stability, yet the nomadic demands of your career pose a challenge to this desire. In a partner, you value equanimity and intellect over emotional expressiveness, seeking a companion who mirrors your logical disposition. Leadership comes naturally to you, and you ascend to positions of authority with ease, preferring to be the strategist rather than a follower.

If 51 is a number of a pinnacle, year, month, or day for you, legal dealings, justice, and authority will mark the experience. In governance, you often find yourself in a pivotal role, whether on boards, committees, or in legislative bodies, shaping laws and regulations. Your friendships are lifelong, and your protective nature extends vehemently to your kin and close associates. Emotions are kept private, with your actions speaking volumes about your commitment and valor. People seek your counsel and feel safeguarded in your presence. With a posture that commands attention and a voice that demands respect, you serve as an adviser in logic-driven roles – tax, finance, law, strategy. Recognized as an expert, your advice carries weight, backed by extensive knowledge, education, and experience. Decisive and undeterred by emotion, you hold systems, order, and discipline in high regard.

52: Queen of Swords

Tarot Symbolism: The Queen sits regally upon her throne, which is set aloft, disconnected from the earth – this denotes a deliberate separation from the din of the crowds and the banality of everyday life. Elevated, she finds the quietude necessary for thoughts to crystallize with lucidity. The sword in her right hand serves as a symbol of discernment, empowering her to distinguish the authentic from the fallacious. Overhead, clouds hint at sacred knowledge that remains veiled, awaiting revelation. Cherubs surrounding her ensure divine safeguarding, while butterflies flit by, emblematic of reincarnation and the vast tapestry of experiences that have culminated in her profound wisdom. The ever-present wind in this scene speaks to a life of constant evolution and the need for flexibility amidst life's ceaseless transformations.

If 52 resonates with your heart, personality, destiny, or spiritual path, these insights are for you: Your essence is one of contemplation and withdrawal, thriving in silence and nature's embrace. A quiet life away from the clamor suits you best. With an air of dignity and self-assuredness, you are the epitome of grace under fire. Your principles aren't just beliefs; they're the pillars of your life. Science fascinates you, especially when it reveals the mysteries of the natural world, far from human artifice. Esoteric knowledge, meditation, and the tranquility of a garden or the vastness of the ocean and mountains speak to you, connecting you to the primal source energy. Solitude is not mere preference; it's your sanctuary, providing tranquility for deep reflection.

While you might excel in the brainstorming hubs of corporations, you fiercely protect your ideas, insisting they be used ethically. You gather with likeminded peers, exchanging pioneering eco-friendly solutions. Wealth does not ensnare you; you serve the greater good efficiently and affordably. You are altruistic, with an acute perception and the rare ability to hear the guidance of the unseen. You must remain true to your values. Deviating from them could impact your well-being. Your social circle is selective. Avoid those who deplete your energy, as their presence can disturb your peace. You appreciate order and respect nature's symmetry. Artistic expression appeals to you, and you possess an innate understanding of nuances and shades. Being a 7 at heart, the unseen is your realm of certainty, and you seek truths beyond the superficial. You might perceive spirits and entities others overlook. Off-grid living is your aspiration, if not your current reality. Your independence does not equate to misanthropy; your scientific insights and objective studies inadvertently benefit humanity.

As for family life, it isn't your primary pursuit. You thrive in creating a solitary peace, which for you, is compromised by conventional domesticity. Your talents lie in fields that allow introspection and innovation, such as research, psychic phenomena, and the healing arts. Should negativity take root, it can manifest as pettiness or intolerance, traits that repel rather than attract. However, when positive, your attunement with the natural elements is unparalleled. You seek harmony with the environment and strive to improve whatever you touch. Meditation and immersion in water are not mere preferences; they're necessities for your well-being. You resonate with the energy of the living earth, communicating with animals and advocating for environmental harmony.

In times when 52 marks a pinnacle, year, month, or day, it heralds a phase of solitude and introspection. This period might coincide with separation or the need for profound personal space, even if within the context of a loving relationship. It's a time for realignment with the natural order, for healing through the elemental powers that only solitude can facilitate. Distance from others is not a punishment but a path to rejuvenation. Embrace this time alone; it's an initiation into internal healing realms that can only be reached through the quietude of nature. The solitude you experience is a necessary counterbalance, bringing the peace that's been overshadowed by life's constant hum.

53: Knight of Swords

Tarot Symbolism: The Knight charges swiftly and resolutely into the tempest, a testament to the belief that no obstacle is insurmountable when armed with facts, clarity, bravery, strategy, and valor. Brandishing his sword aloft, he declares his conviction and courage. Adorned in armor, he is the epitome of preparedness. He rides the white horse, symbolizing purity, enhancing the nobility of his quest.

If 53 resonates with you as a number of your heart, personality, destiny, or spiritual path, then these qualities may be familiar: Sudden events and an assertive, ambitious spirit are your hallmarks. With formidable will and focus, your energy is as intense as it is abundant. Boundaries for you are not mere suggestions, but ironclad laws. You champion routine, exercise, and uphold authority with the precision of a silent operator completing a mission. Your life is a testament to efficiency, putting logic resolutely before emotion. Emotion exists within you, yet you wield your protective nature to never be found off-guard. Proactive by nature, you're inclined to take immediate action, sometimes leaping before looking. Your passions likely include science fiction, tactical games, and strategic planning. Dangerous sports, martial arts, and contact activities not only excite you but also suit your combative skillset. In hypothetical high-stakes missions, such as a parachute jump for peace or rescue, you'd volunteer without hesitation.

Your potential shines in the military, legal, or law enforcement sectors, where your ability to discern truth under pressure makes you invaluable. However, the sharp edge of your assertiveness can, if unchecked, veer into aggression. You must guard against becoming the bully in the room, ready to ignite at a moment's provocation. Sports are not just a hobby but a necessity to maintain your mental clarity. Exercise caution to engage in competition without destructive force. In your professional life, legalities, enforcement, and military disciplines likely appeal to you, perhaps even detective work. Remember, in your drive for perfection and results, to temper self-critique with self-care. Your talents are exceptional and necessary, but perfection is not always required. Recognize your humanity and allow yourself grace. In times of danger, your instinct is to confront it head-on, often saving others in the process. Remember, your mission is steadfast, but in moments of peace, find purpose and allow yourself the space to recalibrate. If this is your spiritual path number, it's a reminder to advocate for yourself with the same vigor you defend others. Assess before you act, but then proceed with conviction toward your goals.

If 53 marks a pinnacle, year, month, or day: Embrace action, expect upheaval, and be prepared for change and redefined boundaries. This period brims with potent energy, urging you to take control and establish firm limits. Clarity and focus will be your allies as you determine who and what belongs in your life – and what must go. Your decisions will be rapid and resolute. Remain vigilant, gather your intelligence, then act decisively and stand firm. You're not just participating in change; you are the catalyst, setting new precedents and establishing authority. While strength and justice are your guides, caution against haste and imprudence. Your actions are now aimed at restoring order, peace, and respect in your environment.

54: Page of Swords

Tarot Symbolism: A youth stands resolute in the wind, clad in simplicity, devoid of excess. The encircling clouds symbolize truths awaiting revelation. To discern these truths, meticulous investigation and keen discrimination are essential.

If 54 resonates with you as a number of the heart, personality, destiny, or spiritual path, then these attributes apply to you: Determination, evaluation, concentration, education, truth, communication, words. Your intellect is your hallmark, characterized by eloquence and depth of knowledge in areas that capture your interest. You navigate challenges with a sharp mind, using your well-honed ability to articulate as your primary tool, adeptly cutting through opposition. Debates and diplomatic encounters are your arenas of triumph, as you wield words with the finesse of a seasoned swordsman.

However, there is a blade's edge to this skill: Negativity can make your words cut deep, reducing them to mere gossip or insults. Positively, you harness this gift to enlighten, uplift, and inspire. Your brightness, alertness, and innate curiosity are the wellspring of your linguistic prowess. As a courageous reporter, you chase stories across the globe, seeking to shine a light on hidden truths. Your fearlessness is commendable, but caution must be your ally; only reveal your findings from a position of safety to ensure that your words become instruments of change against tyranny and injustice.

Passion burns at the core of your beliefs, allowing you to influence others with your persuasive language. Nonetheless, beware the sharpness of your tongue; let your words soothe as well as sway. Legal matters pull at your convictions, calling you to enact change for the greater good, especially for the disenfranchised. Your integrity is unassailable – you cannot be swayed by wealth or status.

Your passion is a beacon for justice, often championing long-term causes that require your relentless energy. A solitary figure at times, you navigate tense situations with critical communication. You are privy to sensitive information, which, depending on its use, can either topple empires or forge alliances. At your zenith, you embody the valor of truth, standing against ignorance and power with an unwavering sense of justice. Whether you're unmasking secrets as a spy or imparting wisdom in a confessional, your path is one of influence and longevity.

If 54 signifies a pinnacle, year, month, or day of significance for you: Stand resolute and speak your truth. Some may bristle at your stance or message, but this is the hallmark of standing in authenticity, confronting oppressors with unyielding honesty. Now is the time to voice your convictions, to challenge antiquated laws, or to forge new ones that protect and uplift. Resist the snares of gossip and unchecked imagination. You are on the cusp of uncovering secrets that will catalyze the changes only you can enact with your unique talents. By speaking truth, you are a catalyst for an essential awakening, shining a light for those who were once kept in obscurity. Vigilance is crucial as adversaries may seek to undermine you, while allies stand ready to support your cause.

55: Ace of Swords

Tarot Symbolism: In this poignant image, the hand of God upholds the sword of truth, a testament to the divine approval bestowed upon those who wield knowledge and intellect benevolently. The crown that adorns the sword's pinnacle symbolizes the deep honor derived from using one's mental prowess for the greater good. Adorning this crown, rubies shine as emblems of nobility, purity, and passion, each one also a silent witness to the inexorable march of time.

Beneath this potent symbol, mountains rise, their daunting presence emblematic of the rigorous journey ahead. They stand for the unwavering commitment to one's truth and the mental fortitude and clarity needed to illuminate the path to justice. Drawing from the insights of "Numerology and the Divine Triangle," the holly branch draped from the crown whispers of the yuletide season, a celebration of birth and beginnings, while the palm branch evokes the resurrection, a powerful symbol of renewal and triumph inherent in Easter.

If the number 55 resonates with your heart, personality, destiny, or spiritual journey, then the following traits are likely a reflection of you: You possess a formidable mental energy with a natural flair for words and an inclination toward professions in law and religion. You have a talent for revitalizing the old and discarded, breathing new life into them through recycling and reuse. Your discernment is keen, and your judgments are clear, allowing you to profit from your intellectual endeavors. As a logical thinker and a prolific writer, your integrity, morals, and ethical beliefs are strong, anchored in a belief in justice. You are quick to rectify wrongs and thrive on mental stimulation due to your constantly active mind that craves new knowledge.

You pursue equilibrium, education, and understanding of not just our world, but also of the far reaches beyond our galaxy. Your mastery of language, whether written or spoken, might extend to fluency in multiple tongues. You are drawn to diverse cultures, holding deep respect and admiration for them. Your passions include literature, poetry, science, technology, and communication – especially that of ancient knowledge and lore. Your personal and professional interests may lead you to museums, libraries, and archaeological sites. An avid adventurer, you are always ready to embark on quests of discovery.

Your processing speed for information is exceptional, perhaps to the point where traditional learning environments once struggled to keep up with you. Your thirst for knowledge is insatiable, driving you to constantly seek education. Remember, it's equally important to rest as it is to consume knowledge. Your home is likely a hub of activity, filled with your own offspring or those you've welcomed from around the world, like exchange students, foster, or adopted children.

On the flip side, the knowledge you acquire can be a double-edged sword. If used improperly, not for the betterment of humanity, it can lead to your downfall, resulting in a life of isolation. But when channeled positively, your insight can topple tyrannies and empower the powerless. You refuse to be censored or controlled by the oppressive voices of others, standing firm as a beacon of truth and an agent of much-needed change.

When 55 marks a pinnacle, year, month, or day in your life, it signifies a period ripe for success. It's time to engage in writing, speaking, studying, and shedding light on significant ventures. You're poised to tackle projects involving justice and truth, perhaps reforming outdated laws to ensure inclusivity. This is a period of fertile creativity for you, potentially leading to the birth of new ideas and projects. The universe supports you, providing protection and energy. Your victories come through your intellect, wit, and mastery of language, both oral and written. The work you do now, whether it be writing books or crafting speeches, is inspiring and will be honored. Recognized as a powerful influencer, your unwavering commitment to your truth and integrity ensures that you overcome adversaries. There is no going back to the old and outmoded, as the sword cuts away all illusions.

56: Two of Swords

Tarot Symbolism: A woman sits resolutely upon a stone, embodying steadfast beliefs. Blindfolded, she wields a sword in each hand, crossed upright before her – a symbol of being at an impasse with no physical path forward. The blindfold hints at a distrust in appearances, compelling reliance on intuition rather than sight. Each sword demands perfect equilibrium to sustain her current stance. The expanse of water behind her mirrors the flux of emotions, while the moon overhead casts light on her subconscious. To navigate her predicament, she must harmonize intuition, emotional insight, subconscious awareness, and logic to forge her conclusions.

If 56 is a number that resonates with your heart, personality, destiny, or spiritual path, then the following insights are meant for you: You are an advocate for balance in all aspects of life. You possess a diplomatic nature, prioritizing peace above conflict. Your sensitivity and intuition run deep, allowing you to perceive the underlying essence of things and to explore realms beyond the obvious. A love for mental stimulation is in your fabric, coupled with an undercurrent of nervous energy and an inclination to please, which can be a driving force in your life.

This number is considered a master number, demanding an increased effort from you. The pursuit of balance between the desire for freedom and wanderlust, represented by the number 5, and the yearning for family and domesticity, signified by the number 6, is a constant in your life. You oscillate between these poles, sometimes gravitating more towards one than the other. Remember, you're not irrational – these are simply two halves of your nature seeking harmony.

Frills, fame, and fortune hold little allure for you, even though they may come your way. Simplicity defines your ideal lifestyle; envisioning a life on the move in a spacious camper with your loved ones and pets, favoring experiences over material wealth. Solitude and nature are where you find your recharge, and you thrive in their embrace.

Your intuition is a lantern in the dark, revealing truths often concealed from others. This quality draws people to you, finding solace and safety in your presence. Your keen intuition, when melded with your rational mind, can lead to notable achievements. Your thoughts often tread off the beaten path, fascinating you with discoveries, enigmas, and the supernatural.

You tread lightly when it comes to conforming, often finding yourself out of sync with the conventional. You resonate with the unique, brandishing your charm, cunning, and compassion. Trusting your own counsel, especially when at peace, points you towards the right decisions. Your ability to discern justice and comprehend every angle of a situation equips you to face significant choices that blend intellect with compassion.

Even when answers are not black and white, your refined inner guidance is always at hand. If you sway towards the negative, you might feel immobilized and overly influenced by others, leading to stagnation. It's essential to reflect, deliberate, and act autonomously. The symphony of life, especially music, holds a special place for you, offering solace and a means to test your decision-making abilities.

You are encouraged to trust your instincts above all else. Do not be tempted to compromise your beliefs for harmony's sake. Listening to your inner voice will lead you to clarity and peace. Striving to be a peacemaker, you still must honor your own needs and emotions. Tension can lead to anxiety if you're not mindful.

Your perceptiveness allows you to see the dual nature of life, tuning into a unique rhythm that others may not perceive. Through your lens, what might be deemed mundane or frightful by others is transformed into something of beauty, imparting a new perspective that prompts us to appreciate the transformative power in everything.

If 56 marks a pinnacle, year, month, or day – you may feel cornered, poised at a critical juncture. It's essential to understand that not all facts are at your disposal, with possible concealments at play. Trusting yourself is crucial as you stand at this crossroads. Balance in your emotions and finances is necessary, and by blending your analytical mind with your feelings, your intuition will shine a light on what's been missing, guiding your decisions. It's a challenging position, but your inner guidance, paired with clear thinking, is prepared to lead you to judgment and clarity. Your intuition, akin to a bat's sonar, is exquisitely honed to navigate through life's complexities.

57: Three of Swords

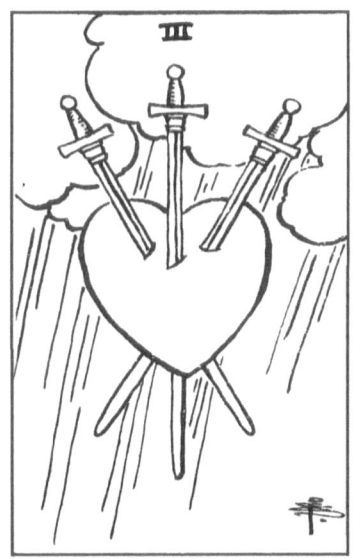

Tarot Symbolism: Three swords pierce and cross a heart, symbolizing the wisdom gained through bearing life's trials with self-compassion and love. Surrounding the heart, clouds depict the turmoil and profound heaviness of emotional strife. Yet, above these clouds stretches a clear sky, a testament that hope, love, and guidance prevail even in our darkest moments.

If 57 resonates with your heart, personality, destiny, or spiritual path, it bears significance for you: You possess a keen intelligence, underscored by a quiet demeanor and a penchant for secrecy. Your creativity flourishes in solitude, with travel and meditation serving as conduits for your artistic expression. A nomadic lifestyle, prompted by professional demands, suits your preference over the monotony of a single setting.

Your values and decisions are deeply informed by personal episodes of heartbreak and detachment. The emotional investment in your charitable endeavors reflects a profound desire to assist others in overcoming their tribulations. With a temperament that can shift like the tides, your accumulated wisdom becomes a beacon for those seeking guidance.

This wisdom, however, is not acquired without cost. Anxiety and depression are familiar adversaries until you discover your unique avenue to healing – a modality you then disseminate in your professional life. To navigate the tumultuous sea of emotions, strive for equilibrium between reason and feeling before arriving at decisions.

Your sensitivity might find you a niche in the cinematic world, preferably away from the limelight, orchestrating the magic from behind the scenes. Your innate understanding of loss propels you towards humanitarian causes, often placing you at the heart of crises, where you tirelessly contribute to the collective healing process.

This understanding isn't a burden of negative karma but a recognition of where your talents are most impactful. In the face of disaster or emotional turmoil, you are instrumental in the healing journey – processing, releasing, and laying the groundwork for new beginnings, all while imparting the wisdom gained through personal hardship.

Your resilience manifests in humor, a transformative tool that reshapes your self-perception and worldview. Each ordeal enhances your heart's capacity for empathy, fostering a talent for comedic, cynical, or critical articulation of truths and insights gleaned from your journey.

You emerge from each ordeal exercising the free will to choose reflection and wit over resentment, thus evolving into the compassionate, enlightened humanitarian the world seeks. Your interests may lead you to advocate for unconventional research, like the therapeutic potential of psychedelics, or to delve into esoteric studies, ancient artifacts, and rituals, all fostering growth and enlightenment. In this cycle of life's lessons, you evolve from a student to a master of forgiveness and hope.

If 57 marks a pinnacle, year, month, or day – it signifies a period marked by disillusionment. Love and trust, once extended without reservation, seem to dissipate without reciprocation. Betrayal may surface, and bonds you counted on may falter. The emotional strain may herald a phase of separation, geographical or emotional, and could potentially culminate in a sense of betrayal or collapse.

This turbulent phase brings to light the true allegiances in your life, prompting a necessary, albeit painful, discernment of who must stay and who must part. Turning to trusted emotional support, you embark on a journey through grief, unearthing gifts hidden within. This marks the beginning of shedding antiquated self-conceptions and destructive patterns, paving the way toward self-love and the rightful demand for respect in all your relationships. Herein lies the genesis of transformation.

58: Four of Swords

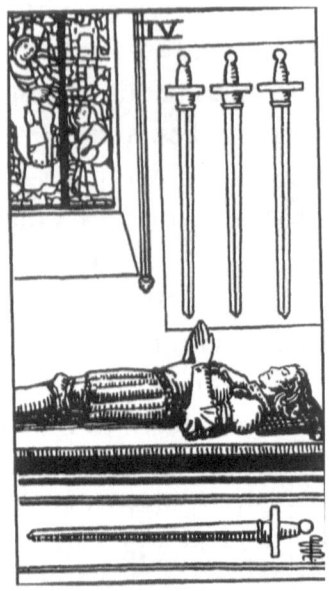

Tarot Symbolism: A soldier lies atop a tomb, his posture one of sleep and respite, not of death. This pose signifies the discernment and wisdom acquired, the catalysts for his current state of healing. Three swords displayed on the wall bear silent testimony to intense suffering endured in the past, suffering from which he now seeks solace and recovery. Beneath him lies a fourth sword, a symbol of preparedness should it be required. Serenity prevails; the lessons of discrimination have been transformed into wisdom, ushering in tranquility and repose.

If 58 resonates with you – whether through your heart, personality, destiny, or spiritual path – this message is meant for you: You are clever, witty, sharp, focused, disciplined. A seeker of peace, rest, and sanctuary, you approach life with honesty and protectiveness. Despite these strengths, you may find yourself frequently overcommitted, enmeshed in tense situations. For those on this spiritual journey, impulsiveness can be your Achilles' heel, propelling you into danger without forethought. The lesson here is one of pacifism: lay down your arms, seek rest, create your haven. While your readiness for battle is admirable, this chapter is about learning the art of repose. You're innately organized, perhaps assertively so, with a restless spirit that does not thrive under constant supervision. Your passion lies with the animal kingdom, especially horses, and your clarity of mind is best found in the great outdoors. Envision a life intertwined with the care of animals, perhaps running a sanctuary, embracing the role of a guardian. However, heed the warning against overexertion; burnout looms if you neglect self-care. Your accomplishments are significant, but they should not come at the expense of your well-being.

Embrace your need for solitude, to be free from the cacophony of daily life. As the sword symbolizes air, your rejuvenation is linked with the wind; activities like paragliding and horseback riding are not just hobbies, they are vital for your mental resurgence. Your acute awareness in post-crisis situations positions you perfectly for roles such as sleep research, emergency response, veterinary fields, and metaphysical studies. You crave order, balance, and harmony, and your introspective nature leads to a profound understanding of these concepts. Your work ethic is commendable, earning respect in your field, particularly for your uncompromising stance on justice and ethics. You possess a bravery that is unflinching. Yet, in facing this vibration's intensity, be mindful of its potential pitfalls: confinement, health challenges, exile. Remember, the tranquility and rest you seek have been hard-won.

If 58 marks a pinnacle, year, month, or day – the themes are of rest, hospitalization, recuperation, separation. It's the calm after storms of unrest, injustice, or illness. This is a period of termination for upheaval, beckoning a time of healing. It calls for respite, for profound and quiet introspection, a mending of emotional fabrics, and a rediscovery of peace. Consider this the prologue to recovery post-crisis or breakdown. Lower your sword, let go of the fight. This interval grants perspective, realigning life's priorities and sharpening your focus. The wisdom harvested through this phase is a precursor to a renewed existence, one that honors the serenity you've earned. The transformation is profound, shifting you from emotional turmoil to a future that promises peace and prosperity.

59: Five of Swords

Tarot Symbolism: The scene unfolds under a dreary, cloud-laden sky – tumultuous and grim. It might resemble the aftermath of a crime or the remnants of a battlefield. The struggle has ceased, yet no victor has emerged. One individual mourns a loss, another walks away with the knowledge that they are not vanquished, aware that their fight will continue. A third person stands apart, cognizant that their role has concluded. This tableau captures the essence of discernment: the wisdom to know when to stand one's ground and when it is prudent to retreat.

If 59 is a number for your heart, personality, destiny, or spiritual path, then this applies to you: Smart, sly, witty, clever. With a penchant for risk and a gambler's spirit, you embody the role of a thrill-seeking, perfectionist humanitarian. Your health hinges on the balance between your energetic pursuits and the serenity you must cultivate. Multifaceted and adept, you juggle numerous endeavors, for idleness is your adversary. Initiating projects is second nature to you, though seeing them through is another matter. Your penchant for risk, whether it's rock climbing or flirting with chance, is undeniable. Your life breathes air and clarity, driven by logic and a zest for intellectual challenges. But caution is warranted – too much indulgence in the thrill can lead to addiction. In finance, your acumen shines when you curb the speculative tendencies. Charismatic in nature, your relationships bloom with ease. Your true talent lies in discerning when to persist and when to yield, advocating for justice without compromise. However, in the heat of competition, remember the significance of a graceful victory and a humble concession. Reflect on your intent: Is it the triumph or the connection that you seek? As an advocate or lawyer, aligned with truth and equity, your force is mighty. Compassion must temper your competitive spirit, lest you lose more than you gain. Through tact and empathy, your humanity and success will emerge, leading to enduring relationships and thriving business ventures. When negativity surfaces – cruelty, pettiness, shirking responsibility – remember that true victory lies in reconciliation and letting go of bitterness.

If 59 marks a pinnacle, year, month, or day for you: The conflict has subsided, yet victory is ambiguous. Perhaps financial resources have dwindled in legal battles, and the advice too late comes – that your cause, though just, was untenable. The aftermath is disordered and recovery will be gradual. Now is the moment for release: to forgive, to make amends, and to progress. Travel and change are afoot, caution against unwarranted risks. Challenges may arise – accidents, disputes, aggression. Keep not to the confines of home, but carry forward with your sense of justice. By fulfilling your duties, triumph awaits. In its most favorable light, this time offers forgiveness, settlement, and a resolution to conflicts. The struggle is past; liberate yourself from its grasp.

60: Six of Swords

Tarot Symbolism: Night has fallen. A woman cradles a child in a boat, while a man steers them across tranquil waters, away from peril and toward sanctuary, toward a new dawn. Six swords lie within the vessel, their tips directed downwards – a silent testament that the conflict has ceased, and safety envelops them now. The still waters mirror the depths of the subconscious, and the trio aboard – the man, the woman, and the child – embody a sacred unity: the Father, the Son, and the Holy Spirit, or the archetypal family of Father, Mother, and Child – cohesive and cooperative.

If 60 is a number that resonates with your heart, personality, destiny, or spiritual path, then this message is meant for you: Refer to the section "The History of Zero" for foundational insight. You are enveloped in divine protection, steeped in matters of love, family, guidance, and assistance. Characterized by fairness, kindness, and justice, your creative and artistic nature makes people feel secure in your presence. As a beacon of safety, you may find your calling in roles like an immigration attorney or paralegal, understanding the harrowing impact of fear, stress, and danger on families. You craft plans ensuring the welfare of others, underpinned by your beliefs in love, commitment, community, safety, and progress. Your daily life is a testament to your deep communication with spiritual guides, aiding others to forge similar connections. It wouldn't be surprising if you operated a sanctuary for transients, be they human or animal, fostering children and aiding individuals in navigating the path to residency.

Bravery in the face of challenges is your hallmark, armed with wisdom that shields you and empowers you to guide others to safety. You adeptly navigate through the threats posed by both people and laws, turning potential weaknesses into protective strengths. Your advocacy for the disenfranchised radiates security to those around you. Having conquered your own struggles, you're committed to aiding those in distress, whether they belong to this realm or the next. Your diligence and application are the roots of your success and garner widespread respect. Travel is woven into the fabric of your existence, as your vocation and passions draw you to distant lands where your skills are most needed. Poised under pressure, you act decisively to maintain harmony, equipped with specialized knowledge and training to perform your noble work. You are independent, accustomed to leadership. Yet, if the negative aspects prevail, and you resist the evolution from outdated patterns, opportunities for growth and resolution may slip away. Your capabilities would shine as a detective, family law judge, or genealogical investigator.

If 60 signifies a pinnacle, year, month, or day significant to you: You're emerging from the depths, ascending towards healing. Having traversed the nadir, the first strides towards freedom and restoration are underway. Support is at hand, accompanied by travel and transformative movement. Legal forces align in your favor, becoming a pivotal part of your journey. This period heralds the prospect of new beginnings – homes, proposals, and the blossoming of love. Legal proceedings are poised to bring closure to bygone conflicts, setting the stage for a resolute conclusion and a renewed chapter.

61: Seven of Swords

Tarot Symbolism: A man stands gripping five swords, his gaze drawn to the two abandoned on the ground. In this moment of decision, he contemplates whether to claim them as well. His demeanor speaks of cunning, his success only partial – a result of his sly deceit. Yet true success, the kind that has thus far slipped through his fingers, awaits when he masters his emotions and aligns with his genuine purpose.

If 61 resonates with your heart, personality, destiny, or spiritual path, take heed: You embody traits of stealth and independence, paired with a sharp intellect and intuitive powers. Your patience and focus become the prelude to calculated action, ensuring success in ventures where you move solo, shunning subordinate roles. Mastery in your field is the fruit of self-discipline and relentless self-improvement. Your affinity for the esoteric and mystical, coupled with a mastery of your emotions and psychic faculties, places you at the fringe of our physical realm, with frequent ventures into higher dimensions. Education, for you, is an unconventional pursuit, richly drawn from the annals of history and ancient texts. Your passion lies in the environmental realm, where you apply your intellect to tackle pressing global challenges with inventive and sustainable solutions.

You thrive in solitude, often opting for a solitary life to concentrate on monumental tasks, such as reversing man-made ecological damage or aiding souls in transition. Your quiet nature is your strength, allowing you to perceive the veiled truth and counteract deceit with ethical tactics. Your life is a journey, with travels that connect you to the ancient world, aligning with your need for constant movement. On the flip side, should negative traits prevail, your cunning could lead to selfish gains. Yet positively, your skills serve to unveil deception, fostering peace and protection for others. Take heart, as the duality in 61 marked by deception, illusion, and trickery is balanced with the name "Holy Spirit," as the destiny number of Holy Spirit is also 61. You are a private enigma, revealing only what you choose, safeguarding your space with invisible barriers. Embrace your unique approach to life and its challenges; what seems unorthodox often yields groundbreaking remedies. Let go of self-criticism; your perfectionism, though admirable, must yield to practicality. Your perceived flaws may well be conduits to remarkable innovation.

If 61 marks a pinnacle year, month, or day for you: Solitude, recovery, and a journey towards authenticity define this period. It's a time for introspection, not socializing, as you seek a sanctuary for healing – be it from physical ailment or emotional deceit. Nature, water, and meditation become your sanctuaries, vital for rejuvenation. The quietude is your gateway to align with your higher self, allowing the puzzle of life to coalesce meaningfully. Seclusion is instrumental for your wellbeing, urging a retreat from toxicity in all forms. Travel, both physical and metaphysical, facilitates the healing and discovery essential for your life's restructuring. Secrets, once burdensome, now surface for resolution with transparency and grace. Toxic entanglements, possibly even a love triangle, are scrutinized for you to realign with your true self, turning this pivotal moment into an opportunity for profound personal realignment and growth.

62: Eight of Swords

Tarot Symbolism: A woman stands blindfolded, her hands seemingly bound, encircled by eight swords. She appears trapped, a figure of vulnerability. Yet, in a moment of revelation, she discovers her bindings are not tight; she can release herself and lift the blindfold to discern a clear path amidst the swords. It is in the embrace of clarity and the release of fear that she finds liberation. She heeds her inner voice, guiding her to freedom. The water lapping at her feet symbolizes the depths of emotion and the undercurrents of the subconscious, hinting at the psychological barriers she is overcoming.

If 62 is a pivotal number for you – in terms of heart, personality, destiny, or spiritual journey – then this message resonates with you: You are driven to orchestrate the minutiae of your existence with meticulous care. Your passion for organization ensures smooth operations at home, within your family, for loved ones, and in business. You're the one who categorizes, labels, and classifies, crafting logical systems to underpin the numerous initiatives you helm. Invariably, leadership and organizational roles find you, no matter the setting. Your home and your family are the cornerstones of your world.

You uphold justice and fairness, finding balance and clarity in outdoor activities. Running clears your mind, and you possess the stamina and focus needed to endure a marathon. While pushing yourself is second nature, beware the fine line between dedication and overexertion. Your expectations for yourself are high, edged with a hint of self-criticism and perfectionism. You are your own harshest critic, and at times, your limiting beliefs can make you feel ensnared or victimized. Yet, your intuition is the key; it's the lever that frees you from the mire of your own thoughts, unlocking the path to emotional self-mastery.

Through inner discipline, you transcend limitations and victimhood, ultimately triumphing in adversity. Every challenge becomes a stepping stone to reclaim your personal power. Your perceptive acumen is astute, capable of noticing the most infinitesimal details – making you well-suited for fields like molecular biology, medicine, or any profession requiring a microscopic gaze. Solitude is your sanctuary; it's where your mind weaves its most profound solutions. Under duress, you exhibit remarkable poise, often producing your finest work amid pressure.

Acknowledging your potency is transformative; it's when you silence the inner critic and conjure focused, pragmatic resolutions. Your history is laced with intense, high-pressure situations that honed your ability to maintain concentration and navigate through storms. When negativity looms, feeling trapped or victimized can lead to vision issues and insomnia. Realizing your heroism within is the ultimate liberation from any shackles that once constrained you. Your dexterity extends to the creative – words, poetry, music, and intricate crafts like needlepoint.

If 62 marks a pinnacle, year, month, or day, you might find yourself amidst overwhelming circumstances that seem uncontrollable and somber. Challenges may arise with friends and family, evoking a sense of entrapment, whether in professional settings or personal relationships. The lesson here is the recognition of your own power. Mastery over your emotions is the bedrock of strength and self-assurance, fostering the changes necessary for emotional liberty.

Setting firm boundaries, eschewing bullies, and releasing materialistic inclinations and toxic connections catalyzes a transition from fear and confinement to a state of empowerment. Embrace meditation, relinquish material attachments, and by doing so, you will unlock your true potential, shifting from fear to empowerment.

63: Nine of Swords

Tarot Symbolism: A woman sits upright in her bed, enveloped by the silence of the night. Sleep eludes her; fear and emotional weariness hold her hostage as nightmares lurk in the shadows. Her coverlet, embroidered with the seven celestial bodies of astrology, is a tapestry of life's lessons learned. On her wall, nine swords point eastward – a herald of hope, the promise of a new day, and the inspiration that comes with the sunrise.

If 63 is a number that resonates with your heart, personality, destiny, or spiritual path, then the following insights are for you: You possess a wealth of wisdom, and your affections extend deeply to children and family, despite the unusual dynamics that may permeate your personal relationships. Establishing firm boundaries has sometimes required legal measures, from which you've learned the significance of asserting your space and the liberation found in moving forward. You are no stranger to patience, and your career likely hinges on your adept handling of words, emotions, and communication. Life's cyclical nature is not lost on you, and in its understanding, you seek to serve truth and alleviate the suffering of others – a calling that ignites your passion. After finding your emotional equilibrium, you embark on mitigating the anguish of others. Be cautious not to absorb their struggles, striving for a balance that allows you to serve without overburdening yourself. It is when you reconcile your personal challenges and align your heart with your intellect that you can genuinely commence your mission to lighten the burdens of others, transforming both yourself and those you aid. Your expansive heart garners immense love from friends, and you embody unselfishness, compassion, and kindness. Frequently, you are drawn to the healing professions, guided by an intuitive sense that operates beyond rational explanation.

Despite personal trials, your resilience shines – a beacon for those grappling with their own emotional chains. Your own path of healing, forgiveness, and release sets you as a quintessential teacher and healer. Rejecting destructive ties and negative spaces, you exemplify love and hope to humanity. Through personal growth and emotional awareness, you attract supportive, loving relationships, positioning you as a luminary for mankind. The spiritual test you face asks, "What if your deepest fears materialize?" Yet, you equip yourself with the power to say, "Even if they do, I will discover pathways to overcome and find serenity." In moments of darkness, your strength becomes evident. However, should the negative aspects prevail, you risk isolating in fear, forfeiting the chance to be a beacon for others.

If 63 marks a significant pinnacle, year, month, or day in your life, it heralds a time of intense transformation – endings and beginnings, emotional turbulence, and eventual healing. Remember, this period is not a punishment but a journey toward emotional moderation and detachment from material and toxic relationships. It's a phase that encourages you to seek support, to look for the silver lining amidst the clouds. With this aid, hope and equilibrium can be restored, preventing fears and anxieties from manifesting into reality. The peace that this time promises will ground you. This era is one for mastering emotional control and embracing a detached, impersonal perspective on life. The distress experienced will dissipate as you learn its lessons, signaling a liberation from emotional confines. As you connect inwardly and assert your intrinsic strength, you celebrate the mastery over your emotional self. Sharing your journey offers profound satisfaction and signifies a notable victory over past afflictions. Now, unshackled from your once greatest fears, nothing can impede your progress.

64: Ten of Swords

Tarot Symbolism: A figure lies prostrate, an embodiment of defeat. Ten swords impale the energy centers along his back, his vitality seeping into the earth beneath him. The red cloak, symbolizing desire, covers his lower half – marking the spiritual awakening birthed from the trials endured. Despite the brooding clouds above, a hopeful gleam reflects off the sword hilts, hinting at nascent starts. Beneath this scene of apparent demise, the tranquil sea whispers of promising journeys yet to come.

If 64 resonates with your heart, personality, destiny, or spiritual path, then the following insights are pertinent to you: You embody strength, tenacity, and determination, with leadership and focus opening new paths. Independence is your strength, and romantic entanglements often take a back seat as you find equilibrium between emotion and intellect. Your capacity for deep concentration positions you as an innovator in medicine, science, or art. Your keen understanding of energy extends to the chakras and the body's electromagnetic fields, offering a holistic approach to health that surpasses traditional methods.

As a pillar of your community, you face challenges head-on, gaining wisdom and insight with each triumph. Your fascination with energy, especially electricity, enhances your proficiency in fields like medicine, where your grasp of the body as an energy system informs your pioneering treatments. Your advanced perspective eventually garners the respect and recognition of your peers, despite the solitude that often accompanies being ahead of your time. Yet, your dedication to humanity's betterment is unwavering, driving you to share your breakthroughs.

Your artistic sensibilities are as sharp as your scientific mind, finding joy in the arts, music, and poetry. A respect for the mystical and spiritual guides you to study the masters of energy, healing, and mysticism. You attract people through your generous spirit, bringing comfort and hope. Fame and fortune are secondary to your quest for knowledge and your alignment with the mind, heart, and intuition which opens the doors to limitless potential and allows for profound, often spiritual, discoveries.

Through trials that would dishearten many, you've honed a unique approach to healing that transcends conventional therapies, directly addressing energy imbalances. Your sensitivity to sound, vibrations, and energies, paired with a steadfast inner guidance, leads to innovative solutions. Although your determination can border on stubbornness, and your focus can be all-consuming, you must remember to pause for self-care.

If 64 marks a significant time for you – a pinnacle, year, month, or day – it signals the end of your darkest hour before dawn, the promise of a new chapter, and the finality of what was once familiar. It may feel as if your vitality has been sapped by betrayal or deceit. Yet, this period tests your resilience, compelling you to embrace change, develop intuition, and meditate. What emerges from these trials are profound spiritual insights, a newfound balance, and powerful positive beginnings, possible only through the necessary process of release and renewal, a time of rejoicing.

Section Five:
The Pentacles

65: King of Pentacles

Tarot Symbolism: The king is seated regally upon a throne adorned with carvings of bulls and grapes, symbols of his dominion. The bulls signify authority, financial strength, and the wealth of tangible assets at his command, while the grapes suggest a state of fruitfulness and abundance. Behind him rise not simple dwellings, but castles and mansions, indicative of his vast holdings and status. Upon his head rests a golden crown, elegantly embellished with roses, emblematic of desires fulfilled to their highest potential, a testament to his wisdom and the self-discipline that secures his achievements. The coin clasped in his left hand highlights his financial acumen and the wisdom with which he manages wealth. In his right hand, the scepter he holds is not just a staff but a tangible representation of his absolute power and authority.

If 65 is a number for your heart, personality, destiny, or spiritual path, then the essence of material wealth, discipline, and abundance is interwoven with your life's tapestry. You tread a path of duality, yearning for the embrace of family and the joys of commitment and progeny, yet equally cherishing your autonomy, craving the liberty to traverse the globe. Adventures are not just dreams but chapters of your existence, and distant lands beckon with their siren calls. Contentment for you is an odyssey, as long as the journey loops back to the warmth of your home and the welcoming arms of loved ones. Your pursuit and accumulation of wealth is not merely a solitary endeavor; you deeply understand and cherish the quality of trustworthy individuals who are pivotal to your prosperity. These comrades, confidants, and collaborators are the bedrock of your success, remaining steadfast because of your genuine acknowledgment and support.

Your professional triumphs stem from the human connections you forge – people are the conduits of business, and their hearts the nexus of these relationships. Maturity, patience, determination, and focus are your guiding stars, and others are drawn to aid you, moved by the benevolence you embody. Your fiscal acumen is matched by a visionary outlook, as you are always a step ahead, safeguarding your future. The tapestry of your life is enriched by the threads of education, respect for boundaries, and the grace of good manners, culminating in a rewarding union and familial bliss. As you ascend in your chosen field, the accolades of honor, fame, and recognition naturally follow. Whether in law, justice, or the stewardship of animals and equestrian pursuits, your illustrious education lays the groundwork for the renown you achieve. At your zenith, you are the epitome of nobility, embodying an aura of aristocracy. Yet, a cautionary note resounds – should the pendulum swing to the negative, an obsession with status and wealth could herald a downfall, marked by loss and disloyalty. Your highest calling is to uplift and encourage, leading by example with diligent work, ethics, and compassion.

If 65 marks a significant pinnacle, year, month, or day for you, it heralds a period ripe with educational opportunities, wealth, and auspicious chances. An era of bounty unfolds, where guidance and support are imparted by a sage benefactor, someone whose life's lessons have prepared them for mentoring you in your current venture or upward trajectory. This alliance, though not of romantic nature, is steeped in mutual respect and a shared passion for your work. Your dedication to your career, characterized by unwavering focus and discipline, has culminated in recognition and reward. You find yourself at the helm of a prosperous journey, backed financially and supported in a manner that allows for continued success. The respect you garner from your contemporaries is a reflection of your merit, and with newfound wealth and influence comes the mantle of greater responsibility. In this phase of abundance, maintaining a grounded disposition is crucial – share the fruits of your success with humility and generosity. Extravagance is the foe that threatens to erode the wealth you've built. Under this vibration, the prospects of marriage, children, and family life are particularly auspicious.

66: Queen of Pentacles

Tarot Symbolism: The queen, garbed in simple elegance, holds court upon her throne. Encircling her seat are carvings of goats, emblematic of Capricorn, alongside depictions of fruit-laden trees and clusters of grapes. Flourishing blooms festoon the space around her, signaling her fecundity and abundance. Celestial guardians in the forms of angels and cherubs encircle her, their presence a testament to divine safeguarding, the serenity of love, and a harmonious accord with the essence of Mother Earth. At her side, a rabbit symbolizes both prosperity and the promise of continual fertility.

If 66 resonates with your heart, personality, destiny, or spiritual path, this speaks directly to you: You embody the essence of domesticity, nurturing, and dignity. Financial stability graces your life, providing for your family, at times as the sole provider. Your affinity for animals and children is reciprocated with deep affection. This master number heralds a journey of mastering unconditional love, forgiveness, and gratitude, which often manifests through your relationships. Wisdom accompanies age, guiding you to a fulfilling partnership. Embracing the maternal archetype, you become a pillar of responsibility, protection, and support. Your role sometimes extends beyond the familial, rescuing the young from dire circumstances and fighting against the atrocities like human trafficking and sexual exploitation. Your home, possibly as a single parent, becomes a sanctuary of love and guidance.

Your spirit thrives on creating a better world, a task to which you are wholeheartedly devoted. Creative gifts abound. Your artistic and musical talents pave the way to prosperity and influence. With an inviting magnetism, your charm, beauty, and genuine nature never leave you in solitude. You attract faithfulness and trust, always seeking to uplift others. Parenthood, whether through birth or adoption, enriches your life, turning your home into a haven of joy, friendship, and comfort. A lover of beauty, you find joy in aesthetics, yet your practicality ensures that you remain grounded and candid.

Your professional path might intersect with the justice system, where your inherent qualities shine as a mediator, family law specialist, or even a judge. You are seen as a guardian, not only of your children but of the environment and its creatures. Intimately understanding the subtle nuances of energy and communication, your nurturing extends beyond the personal to the universal. Your independence is paramount; a restrictive partner finds no place in your life. Financial foresight is a priority, ensuring your family's welfare through robust financial planning.

Teaching and counseling are natural extensions of your being, with many seeking your sound and pragmatic guidance. When negative aspects surface, they bring imbalance, irresponsibility, and upheaval. Yet, at your zenith, you are a beacon of protection and legacy, leaving an indelible mark of wealth, compassion, and love. Nature, balance, and energy resonate with you, drawing you to healing practices that align with the rhythms of the earth.

If 66 marks a pinnacle, year, month, or day: Love, prosperity, and personal growth await. This period heralds a time of financial and social elevation, perhaps through an inheritance or a career advancement. Matters of legality resolve to your benefit, freeing you for leisure and travel. Maintain practicality in your dealings, invest astutely, and you will solidify a prosperous future. Now is an opportune moment to channel resources into your entrepreneurial ventures.

67: Knight of Pentacles

Tarot Symbolism: This knight is a steward of his own land rather than a roving traveler. Atop his steadfast workhorse, he remains within the bounds of his community, surveying his property with an eye for lasting enhancements. His demeanor is marked by a serene patience as he diligently enumerates the tasks ahead. The well-cultivated field, plowed meticulously in neat furrows, stands testament to his commitment to both the present and future prosperity of his lineage. In hand, he holds a gold coin, pondering its prudent investment for enduring benefit. Adorned with grape leaves, his helmet and the horse's bridle symbolize the rich yield of his labors.

If 67 is a resonant number for your heart, personality, destiny, or spiritual path, then this message is for you: You embody the quintessential 'salt of the earth' characteristics – trustworthy, reliable, and methodical. With a meticulous, conservative approach, you are the epitome of moderation. Your patience and hard work are coupled with a robust yet gentle nature, and an artistic, creative streak enhances your intuitive grasp of the world. You are an old soul with a knack for resourcefulness.

You don't chase after ephemeral successes; instead, you are the quintessential planner, focusing on long-term achievements for your family, the land, and your finances. With the foresight to prepare for adversity, you are well-equipped with food and emergency supplies. Your talents likely extend to woodworking, where you craft art and furniture that marries beauty with utility. Conservative yet productive, you shoulder responsibilities gracefully, projecting your vision at least a decade forward, often even laying plans for subsequent generations.

If 67 marks a pinnacle, year, month, or day significant to you, the virtues of patience, dedication, focus, and perseverance become especially pertinent. This period demands a self-reliant approach, relying on your inner resources to navigate a phase rich with planning and practical undertakings. Should your current work feel too tedious, it's a sign to reassess your position or consider a shift in career. This is a time for strategic preparation, budgeting, and prudent planning, ensuring that the necessities of life are secured for the assurance of long-term success. Just as the Knight of Pentacles prepares for winter, so should you with a meticulous eye for detail that promises prosperity.

68: Page of Pentacles

Tarot Symbolism: A young man, attired in unassuming garb, cradles a gold coin, immersed in devising ways to augment his wealth. Surrounded by a field burgeoning with flowers, he contemplates the promise of abundance that awaits – should he sow his seeds with care and diligence. Behind him looms a mountain, a symbol of achievement, suggesting that his aspirations are within reach, provided he begins now and adheres to a practical path.

If 68 is a number close to your heart, personality, destiny, or spiritual path, consider this a reflection of yourself: You embody poise and confidence, projecting a serene exterior. As a student, you excel notably in the earth sciences, driven by an inward critique and a penchant for perfection. Though somewhat reserved, effective communication is crucial in your professional life; expect travel and prioritize organization. Luxury isn't just a desire for you – it's a destination you're determined to reach through meticulous planning and relevant education. You honor the pursuit of knowledge, gravitating towards mentors to ascend within your field.

Detail-oriented, your talents would seamlessly translate to the legal profession, particularly within probate or family law. Outdoor exercise is a necessity for you; it sharpens your focus and clears your mind. You have an intuitive grasp of technology and computational languages, and you excel in synthesizing disparate systems, people, and cultures. Your work bridges gaps, finding common threads in a tapestry of diverse elements. With a mind that thrives on mental gymnastics, your wit is matched by your intellectual agility and expertise.

Prosperity for you is an outcome of dedication to learning and skill refinement. Resist the temptation to indulge excessively in luxuries; moderation is your ally. Embrace patience, adhere to a budget, and remain attentive to detail as you climb. Your career is more cerebral than physical, fueled by a robust energy and ambition to realize your aspirations. Recognizing the value in money, health, and education, you often pioneer new avenues of communication. Stay grounded and practical; your common sense and quick learning will open doors.

Beware, though, of the lure of materialism. Avoid becoming a schemer or falling into procrastination, which leads to inaction.

If 68 marks a pinnacle, year, month, or day, heed this guidance: Embrace travel, business, and further education with a practical and diligent approach. Manage your finances with foresight, and welcome social engagements; they will introduce you to allies in your path. With abundant energy and focus, you are poised to initiate a viable business venture. Don't splurge with your material gains; remain practical, stay focused, steadfast, reliable, and you will create substantial opportunity for work and success. This period is ripe for your entrepreneurial spirit to thrive. Through the fluctuations of this phase, maintain your balance and you shall emerge victorious.

69: Ace of Pentacles

Tarot Symbolism: The hand of God emerges from the clouds, presenting a gold coin – a symbol that prosperity is an innate human entitlement, as accessible as the cosmic consciousness itself.

If the number 69 holds significance for your heart, personality, destiny, or spiritual journey, the following traits resonate with you: Your mastery over the elements is apparent, as you command them with an effortless will. Centered within your own energy, you maintain a harmonious balance between yin and yang, understanding the natural flow of give and take. This intrinsic knowledge aids you in escalating your wealth and wisdom. Moreover, wealth – often accompanied by fame – gravitates toward you with ease, bringing with it material abundance and emotional satisfaction. There is also a sense of divine safeguarding in your journey.

You wield the elements of earth, air, water, and fire with skill, merging them in ways that serve both function and artistry. Your creations, born from this alchemy, bestow upon you both wealth and a sense of security. Your deep appreciation for life in all its manifestations stems from an intimate understanding of the cycles of birth, death, and rebirth. This reverence is what drives you to infuse beauty into the practical aspects of existence, allowing you to relish the luxuries born from simplicity and respect for the elements, and in turn, garnering the admiration of those around you.

Teaching might emerge as a path for you, influenced by the number 9 in 69. The value you place on love, represented by the number 6, is evident in the passion and joy you share through your pedagogic endeavors. Your engagement with the mystical, coupled with an appreciation for esoteric knowledge, marks you as an adept manifester who applies ancient wisdom to yield tangible results.

However, if the shadow side prevails, your creative joy and humanitarian love could be overshadowed by greed, leading to an accumulation of wealth for its own sake. On the positive end of the spectrum, you are seen as a benefactor of the arts, possibly establishing scholarships to support aspiring artists, thus ensuring your legacy enhances the world's beauty and supports future generations.

If 69 occurs during a pinnacle, year, month, or day, this period heralds a significant commencement across various facets of your life. The confluence of opportunity, your adeptness, and prior training, set the stage for wealth, recognition, and perhaps even fame. Relationships begun now hold great promise. Success will not be delivered to you without effort; however, the work you invest promises to be fruitful.

Even if negativity creeps in, failing to tap into your manifesting potential, this period still teems with positivity. Your personal life will experience growth and stability, looking toward a promising horizon. Land and property engagements may prove to be particularly lucrative. Embrace this exhilarating and challenging fresh start; it's a chance to celebrate past efforts, enjoy the esteem of your colleagues, and exercise generosity borne from newfound prosperity.

70: Two of Pentacles

Tarot Symbolism: The individual in question clasps the lemniscate – the horizontal figure 8 – a symbol denoting the realm of commerce and entrepreneurial triumph. The gold coin is poised with precision, signifying the substantial tasks ahead and this person's adeptness at maintaining equilibrium. In the backdrop, vessels ply through the waves, emblems of trade and industrious endeavors. The undulating waters beneath these ships mirror the fluctuating nature of business, amidst which the individual remains steadfastly balanced. Their attire, crafted from leather, signifies a commitment to quality and mastery over baser inclinations.

If 70 is a number for your heart, personality, destiny, or spiritual path, then this applies to you: Refer to the significance of "Zero" for further insight. This number brings forth connotations of divine guardianship, equilibrium, and venerable knowledge. You carry yourself with dignity and assurance, complemented by grace and kindness. Your nature is contemplative, patient, and versatile, with an appreciation for stillness and tranquility. You feel a profound calling to serve, guided by a deep-seated knowledge of your purpose. Gifted in communication, you have a passion for auditory experiences, be it through music, words, or the very frequencies of sound that elude others. Your sensitivity extends to emotions and unseen vibrations, endowing you with the ability to perceive what others might miss.

You play an instrumental role in the deaf community, acting as a conduit between varied dimensions, returning with insights that are both pragmatic and enlightening. Drawn to the scientific realm, you cherish time spent amidst books and study, delving into the esoteric as eagerly as you do into the empirical. Ancient texts and artifacts are not just collectibles to you; they are a mosaic of wisdom spanning eons, which you integrate with contemporary insights to achieve an ideal equilibrium. You often feel anachronistic, more at home in bygone eras, yet your role is clear as a custodian of ageless wisdom, a translator of sacred truths. In your craftsmanship with words and your fair-minded approach, you are esteemed and embraced.

Your creativity is your enterprise; you transform the overlooked into assets, translating the intangible into the substantial. Your potential career paths are as varied as they are specialized, each requiring the quiet focus and equilibrium you naturally possess. In tune with the natural world and the emotions of those around you, your empathy and intuition are profound, necessitating judicious company to protect your own emotional wellbeing. Within the medical field, particularly audiology, your skills contribute to the betterment of others' lives. With the zero adding a layer of divine shielding, you find yourself in a fortuitous position for business partnerships. Amidst life's vicissitudes, your insight and sagacity are your stabilizers, your emotional poise – your superpower.

If 70 marks a pinnacle, year, month, day, or period for you: This phase is characterized by commercial growth, fiscal betterment, collaborative ventures, extensive travel, and the management of manifold responsibilities. Physical health is a priority amidst the whirlwind of activities. Heed your own advice on balance; don't overextend. Allow yourself those precious moments of respite for reflection and breath. Like a superhero of multitasking, your endeavors are not just successful but also lucrative. Potential business partnerships loom on the horizon; integrity will be the keystone of prosperity in such alliances. Promotion and productivity are the buzzwords of your current phase, with ongoing change being a constant companion. Continue to be adaptable, for your novel yet practical ideas are safeguarded by divine favor.

71: Three of Pentacles

Tarot Symbolism: A young stonemason labors on a temple, accompanied by two men: the architects. These seasoned professionals are engrossed in conveying their vision to the stonemason. Despite his youth, the stonemason commands respect from the older architects through his tenacity, determination, and prowess. They are not just superiors but collaborators, recognizing the value he brings to their project. In this triad of mutual respect and collective expertise, they make the seemingly impossible achievable.

If 71 is a number that resonates with your heart, personality, destiny, or spiritual path, then this message is for you: Reserved and contemplative, you possess a quiet wisdom and intense focus, coupled with ambition and patience. Your emotional depth doesn't show on the surface. You approach life analytically, dissecting experiences like a child dismantling toys to understand their construction before rebuilding them, enhanced by your insight. You are the silent observer, transforming your environment quietly through thoughtful action. Your aspirations are kept close to your chest; you prefer to silently forge ahead, turning your ideas into reality without fanfare. You are the master of your domain, whether it be in craftsmanship or therapeutic arts. For you, taking on Herculean tasks comes naturally.

The quintessential master builder, your work ethic is your testament – tirelessly laboring to erect a legacy that may span your entire life. Your dedication knows no bounds, and sometimes it takes the mechanical chime of a timer to pull you away from your work and into the embrace of nature. Your financial prosperity seems an inevitable result of such unyielding determination. Family ties for you may be woven into the fabric of your work, imparting valuable life lessons, or they might know you only through stories and photographs due to your all-consuming vocation. Your craftsmanship is not merely labor; it is a sacred act that leaves onlookers in awe, questioning the origins of your almost celestial talent. Collaboration elevates your work, as teamwork with astute minds births wonders unachievable in isolation.

If 71 signifies a significant period in your life, like a pinnacle, year, month, or day, a steadfast character emerges: reliable, skilled, and enriched with knowledge. Your talents are in high demand for a collaborative venture, one that beckons you to pursue long-term, meaningful objectives. Financial reward, friendships, and professional respect will be the fruits of your labor, borne from an unwavering commitment to your craft. This period is marked not by leisure but by a rewarding endeavor that requires collective effort and individual perseverance. Your projects are destined to be your legacy, their endurance guaranteed by your meticulous approach. As you ascend professionally, remain a beacon of support for others who can flourish with your mentorship. Avoid indolence, as it can derail this fruitful era. Remember that collaboration amplifies your impact – never hesitate to seek assistance.

72: Four of Pentacles

Tarot Symbolism: A penny-pinching miser sits tightly clutching a gold coin, his attire so old and tattered it belies his actual wealth. Beneath his feet lie two more coins, symbols of past financial achievements and savvy investments. Perched atop his head, another coin remains balanced, testament to his dexterity with finances. While money provides him a sense of security, he must come to realize that life's riches also include loving relationships. It's time for him to loosen his grip, if only slightly, to let warmth and companionship into his guarded existence.

If 72 resonates with your heart, personality, destiny, or spiritual path, the following traits are likely familiar to you: a life spent accumulating resources against future uncertainty, amassing considerable wealth through unwavering practicality and frugality. You attend to everyday needs with the utmost patience, conservatism, and a meticulous eye on your finances. Your attire reflects simplicity and function over fashion, and you may be reticent to refresh your wardrobe despite the affordability. A deep-seated fear of poverty guides your strict budgeting and expense tracking, and while this vigilance encompasses not just material possessions but personal relationships as well, it can sometimes lead to a loss of connection.

On your spiritual journey, it's essential to balance your control over finances with the freedom to enjoy life's pleasures, fostering growth in your wealth and personal joy. You embody high moral standards and advocate for the voiceless, serving as a steadfast pillar in your community and family. Your unwavering support is recognized and valued, yet remember that life is not all work; familial happiness and generosity are also critical. If negativity prevails, an obsession with control can turn to hoarding, pushing away the joy, love, and warmth of family. Embrace the more profound values of life, balancing financial acumen with meaningful personal bonds. Indulge occasionally in new experiences or possessions – your budget allows it. Your professional life might lean toward roles like financial advisor or attorney, where your genuine concern for the disenfranchised shines. You might find yourself in less glamorous, bureaucratic roles, yet your compassion and knowledge provide immeasurable help to those with the least.

If 72 marks a significant pinnacle, year, month, or day for you, it's a signal to hone in on the finer details of your life. Focusing on your finances now is the cornerstone of future prosperity. Embrace saving and budgeting; the efforts you begin now have the potential to grow into considerable wealth. Recognize that no detail or task is too minor, as they cumulatively contribute to your value. Success will stem from a consistent approach and adept organization, not from yielding to fears of poverty or the need to dominate every situation. Maintain your path and trust in your capabilities; the stability you've achieved is just the foundation for a fruitful future.

73: Five of Pentacles

Tarot Symbolism: In the biting cold, a man and woman stand outside, their clothes ragged, embodying both physical and emotional destitution. The man, his leg broken, leans on crutches. They are poised just beyond a radiant stained-glass window, through which a welcoming light spills from indoors. This window serves as a poignant metaphor – if only they could realize that the warmth and illumination within is, and always was, intended for them, they might open their minds, accepting the wisdom and abundance that their spirits are capable of possessing.

If 73 is a number that resonates with your heart, personality, destiny, or spiritual path, this description is tailored for you: Adversity, struggle, hardship, along with being creative, intuitive, and introspective, are dynamic elements of your experience. There is a nuanced, delicate balance to your intuition. Your focus on the internal light allows you to externalize love, compassion, and wisdom. This internal radiance sets your path. Wisdom, borne from enduring significant challenges and the profound sense of solitude they bring, has shaped your connection to the divine. It's your ability to transcend ego and fear, concentrating instead on this inner light, that fuels your seemingly boundless energy.

Your perspective on life's challenges not only creates but frequently manifests the miraculous. You simply stay aligned and savor the journey, generously imparting the wisdom you've amassed, which in turn affords you a form of divine protection. Integrity is your cornerstone. The dynamism of your aura exerts a potent influence on those around you, and with every positive exertion of your energy, you enhance your spiritual richness and shine as a beacon for others. Your articulation and grace are evident. Yet, if the negative prevails, you risk overlooking the persistent light within, which signifies your higher self, and remain ensnared in a vicious cycle of emotional, spiritual, and financial want. Your remarkable resilience, indomitable will, and spirited nature elevate humanity.

If the number 73 marks a significant pinnacle, year, month, or day for you, the themes are Loss, bankruptcy, scandal, homelessness, inner wisdom, and a transformation leading to a wealth of spirit. It's through integrity and valuing hard work that each challenge incrementally unveils your internal beacon. Though trials are inevitable, it's through introspection and the realization of your innate wisdom that you reclaim the riches of your spirit. This period calls for meditation, deep reflection, and an exploration of metaphysical truths and the soul. A pursuit of the material may lead to ruin, but in seeking and acknowledging your higher self, you gain the ultimate reward.

74: Six of Pentacles

Tarot Symbolism: A refined, well-dressed man holds a scale, symbolizing balance. His senses are keen, honed to discern even the subtlest of shifts. The scale he grasps is not just any instrument; it represents the delicate equilibrium of karma. Generously, he extends his coins to two individuals. On one side, the image captures the essence of self-mastery – the equilibrium between giving and receiving. The opposing side reveals the starkness of a poverty mindset, a poignant reminder of what might be lost should the opportunity presented by this master number be overlooked. The path forward? The choice remains in your hands.

If 74 holds significance for your heart, personality, destiny, or spiritual path, the following insights are meant for you: Master number 74 (7 + 4 = 11) embodies balance – emotional, spiritual, and karmic. Wealth flows to you, facilitating generosity and support to others on your journey, thereby mitigating karma. The '7' in 74 seeks emotional equilibrium, with '4' taking practical steps to achieve it. Subtlety and emotion are hallmarks of '7', while '4' establishes order, grounding ethereal notions into practical application. You must be ready to capture inspiration at any moment; keep a notepad or iPad handy for your burst of ideas. In your realm, the emotional blends with the unseen and the practical, turning inspired thoughts into tangible enhancements for everyday life. Your grasp on financial affairs can have global repercussions. A lover of science and logic, you are destined for material success, wielding charm and a philanthropic spirit that gravitates towards universally beneficial ideas.

Your mind, scientifically astute and discerning, often leads you to immerse yourself in work, forsaking leisure for the thrill of intellectual or esoteric discovery. You process information rapidly, excel at sleight of hand, and may have a background in magic, health sciences, or earth sciences. Solitude suits you; supervision does not. Your charm and persuasive power draw people and relationships to you, and you're compelled to share your learning with the world. Desk-bound, your work is mental, and you shine in the healing arts, skeptical of conventional medicine in favor of less harmful approaches. Your dexterity is evident in the creation of art or craftsmanship requiring precision. Sleep may elude you, as a restless mind keeps you company alongside a diverse library. Your interests range from poetry to the cosmos, indulged for sheer pleasure. If negativity takes hold, moodiness, condescension, and hypercriticism can isolate you, leaving you in the cold embrace of intellect rather than the warmth of varied human connections. Yet positively, your expansive knowledge in science and healing becomes a beacon of assistance to others, with an ever-eager eye for new modalities and discoveries.

If 74 is a number marking a pinnacle, year, month, or day for you, it denotes a time of giving, receiving, and karmic testing. This master period promises rewards commensurate with your higher self-alignment. Expect financial gains, perhaps an inheritance, but know that your true wealth comes from sharing with others. This reciprocity maintains your balance, ensuring continued prosperity. You are fashioning the world you wish to inhabit, with kindness returning to you exponentially. The lesson is clear: the harmony between giving and receiving is healing. Conversely, if the negative prevails, power imbalances can lead to exploitation, dependency, and emotional or fiscal loss. Balance is not just a concept but a practice for a fulfilling existence.

75: Seven of Pentacles

Tarot Symbolism: A young man attentively nurtures the tree he has planted. Approaching with a blade to harvest fruit, he finds it has yielded only leaves. This scene symbolizes the diligent effort needed to attain 'fruitfulness.' It speaks to the deficiency inherent in pursuing solely material wealth. Nourishing our spirit is equally essential. Additionally, it serves as a prompt to savor both the scenery and the sojourn itself.

If 75 is a number for your heart, personality, destiny, or spiritual path, then this applies to you: You are practical and methodical, honing in on minutiae and consistently putting in the work. Through this approach, you climb to the pinnacle of your chosen field with assuredness. Your passion for enigmas and intellectual pursuits keeps you agile and perennially active. Dedicated to deep exploration, you meticulously gather facts over years, eventually exposing hidden truths with an unyielding courage. You take on the mantle of an investigative reporter or whistleblower, shedding light on secrets and calling out discrepancies with indisputable evidence.

Your commitment to thorough effort means that no task is beyond your willingness to tackle. With perseverance and meticulous work, success – often accompanied by recognition – becomes a common fixture in your life. You invest time in skill development, favoring sustained growth in all facets of your life. For you, there are no shortcuts; every achievement is the result of persistent, gradual effort. You meticulously assess and plan, making decisions that leave no room for second-guessing. In doing so, you enact positive, lasting change, always valuing quality and ascending the ladder of success and status with assured, deliberate steps.

If the negative traits dominate, you may become impatient or prone to procrastination, leading to successive disappointments. A lack of diligence or misdirected efforts could result in engaging with unfruitful ventures. However, when your positive attributes shine, your ambition, focus, patience, and hard work yield remarkable achievements.

If 75 marks a significant time for you – a pinnacle, year, month, or day – embrace dedication, discernment, and the readiness for a journey that might require patience but promises an increase in wealth and status. It's a period to engage deeply with your work, mindful that there are no expedients to excellence. You'll find others who recognize your industrious nature and offer their support for your worthy, long-term objectives. The fruits of your labor may take time to manifest, yet they are assuredly on the horizon. As you ascend in your career, propelled by the backing and respect of your peers, your commitment to your endeavors is reciprocated with promotions and opportunities.

You might find yourself stewarding expansive projects, like nurturing farmland or managing financial investments. In such roles, seeking long-term, secure outcomes is paramount, and expert advice becomes invaluable. Press on, confident of your impending success, and adhere to your high standards of ethics. Remain open to learning and collaboration. If negativity arises, it will manifest as a series of delays and frustrations. However, with patience, integrity, and an unflinching resolve to confront challenges head-on, you are set to effect enduring, positive transformations.

76: Eight of Pentacles

Tarot Symbolism: A workman, garbed in simple attire, dedicates himself with clear focus to the task before him. His demeanor is subdued, absent of loudness or exuberance, yet his expertise in his craft is unmistakable. With meticulous care, he shapes a golden pentacle, attending to each detail with precision. Arrayed behind him are seven additional pentacles, each a testament to his growing prowess. With every piece he completes, his skill sharpens, edging ever closer to mastery. Oblivious to his surroundings, his concentration never wavers from his work. Through such steadfast diligence, he has accumulated wealth. Nonetheless, even he must acknowledge the necessity of respite in his relentless pursuit of excellence.

If 76 resonates with your heart, personality, destiny, or spiritual path, then the following traits may be intrinsic to your character: Your brilliance shines in your chosen field, reflecting a harmonious balance between family, community, and the solitude that rejuvenates you. Drawn to nature's elements, you find your energy replenished by water and the wild. In your work, you embody quietude and simplicity, not given to loud or ostentatious displays. Your commitment is unwavering, fueled by a comprehensive understanding of your domain. The drive to refine your craft is not motivated by financial gain but by a personal quest for excellence and efficiency. You excel in the art of transformation, finding joy in repurposing the disregarded into something of value. Your life is marked by patience, persistence, and acute observation.

If 76 marks a significant time or pinnacle, year, month, or day in your life: Embrace this phase as one of labor and commitment, where your skill and dedication manifest in tangible achievements. While the work may sometimes feel repetitive, the discipline you exercise is paving the way to noteworthy success. The skills you refine and the diligence you exhibit are elevating your status and financial well-being. This is a moment for focused action and continuous learning, laying a foundation for enduring quality. Stay logical and consistent, but remember to incorporate rest. Avoid the pitfalls of overwork which can blur life's broader canvas and jeopardize family ties. Balance, not just work, is the essence of a fulfilled life.

77: Nine of Pentacles

Tarot Symbolism: In a resplendent garden, a woman stands alone, embodying independence. Her attire is elegant, matching the opulence of her surroundings. Grapevines laden with fruit and golden coins signal prosperity. She stands as a figure of achievement, having attained all that she wished for. The falcon perched on her left hand symbolizes her dominion over emotion, spirit, and intellect. This scene is a tapestry of ease, luxury, accomplishment, and abundance.

If 77 is a number for your heart, personality, destiny, or spiritual path, then this applies to you: Achievement, accomplishment, divine guidance, self-mastery are hallmarks of your journey. Your wealth may be self-made or inherited, but the result is complete financial freedom. You enjoy the rewards of your past work without ostentation, and your subtle comprehension of the intangible has been pivotal in your success. Recognizing this master number's potential, you have directed your efforts towards humanitarian causes. Popularity is not sought but has come naturally to you as a result of your genuine efforts. With a sharp acumen and a deep appreciation for nature, you stand atop your achievements, with freedom and a broad perspective as your guiding forces.

Your life's work is dedicated to the guardianship of nature, and with ample resources, you actively combat threats to the global equilibrium. Emotional poise and keen intuition are your allies; they allow you to understand environments and respond with grace. You engage with the world with wit and charm, carrying a heartfelt dedication to leave the Earth richer than you found it. From a young age, you grasped the concepts of energy, manifestation, and your cosmic role, which now enable you to be an agent of protection and change. Material needs are met, allowing you to concentrate on the legacy of your time here. Should the shadow side emerge, it manifests as a lack of self-recognition or the squandering of resources. Your deep connection with nature supports sanctuaries and gardens, and your spiritual resilience – perhaps honed by personal trials – anchors your life's outlook.

If 77 marks a significant time for you – a pinnacle, year, month, or day: Wealth, abundance, and the mastery of self are your themes. Whether by legacy or the fruits of past endeavors, financial liberation has arrived. This newfound freedom opens doors to travel, indulge in luxuries, and pursue dreams unencumbered by economic constraints. The spotlight finds you, celebrating your achievements and dreams realized, like establishing an animal sanctuary or dedicating land to botanical gardens for everyone to enjoy. This period marks a personal renaissance, affirming your worth and spirit.

78: Ten of Pentacles

Tarot Symbolism: An elderly man is depicted alongside his children and grandchildren, symbolizing the enduring legacy transmitted through his lineage. The pentacles are strategically placed to mimic the Tree of Life, suggesting a connection to enduring wisdom and growth. The presence of grey dogs underscores the notion that life is not merely black and white but a harmony of the two. Seated within the courtyard of their expansive residence, the family embodies the culmination of mastery and equilibrium between the material and spiritual domains.

If 78 resonates with your heart, personality, destiny, or spiritual path, it speaks to significant achievements. You have excelled, maintaining focus and discipline. Your use of wisdom and intuition has not only led to financial prosperity but has also preserved your integrity, ensuring that you never lose sight of your true self. This integrity has enriched your spirit and brought you material wealth, and it is your humanity that empowers you to lead.

You have put your resources and energy into humanitarian projects with genuine excitement for innovation and bettering lives. Your indifference to acclaim, coupled with a sincere desire to serve, attract the support you need. Your straightforwardness and passion unite like-minded individuals dedicated to addressing global issues in health, poverty, and education.

If 78 marks a significant time for you, like a pinnacle, year, month, or an important date, it denotes a period ripe with opportunity for communal, familial, and business success. You are poised to achieve substantial growth in wealth and personal development. Your integrity and long-term vision can bring you success on a grand scale, affording you a phase of ease and luxury, allowing you to support the arts and culture, contribute to community enrichment, and create a lasting legacy. Enjoy this prosperous time, and continue to act with integrity, nurturing the beauty and artistry that will outlive your time here.

About the Author

Dyan Starr discovered her passion for numerology at the tender age of ten. By the age of fifteen, she was already conducting charts and readings for others. This marked the start of a lifelong journey with numerology. Dyan has since dedicated herself to creating the Starr System of Numerology, doing Starr charts for her clients, and imparting her unique method through teaching, which remains one of her greatest joys.

Over the years, many clients have asked for and suggested Dyan develop her Starr System into a book. *Hallowed Be Thy Name* marks a significant achievement in her career, encapsulating her extensive experience and passion for numerology. It serves as a testament to her dedication to the field and her desire to share her insights with a wider audience.

Alongside her work as a numerologist, Dyan had a significant career as a Certified Shorthand Reporter with the Los Angeles Superior Court, a role she held for 27 years. Her professional journey showcases a blend of precision and intuition.

Currently, Dyan resides in Hemet, California, where she enjoys a fulfilling family life. She lives with her son, her youngest daughter, and an assortment of animals including three horses, four pigs, and a cat. A recent and notable milestone in her personal life was becoming a grandmother in 2022, a dream she had cherished deeply.

Exact Rush

Discover More with Exact Rush

If you've enjoyed *Hallowed Be Thy Name* by Dyan Starr, we invite you to explore other titles from Exact Rush Multimedia Publishing.

Explore Our Catalog

At Exact Rush, we pride ourselves on a rich selection of titles that focus on spirituality, religion, and identity. From insightful, cerebral non-fiction, to imaginative works that transports you to different realms or teach you something new, our catalog of accurate, informative, and life-affirming titles continues to grow.

Connect with Our Community

Join our community of readers and authors! Participate in engaging discussions, author meet-and-greets, and exclusive book events. Stay updated by following us on social media and subscribing to our newsletter.

Have a Book Idea?

Do you have a story to tell or knowledge to share? Exact Rush is always on the lookout for unique voices and compelling content. If you have a book idea that aligns with our ethos, we would love to hear from you. Our team is dedicated to nurturing and promoting new talent.

Contact Us

To explore our catalog, learn more about our events, or discuss a book idea, please visit exactrush.com or contact us at exactrushllc@gmail.com.

Your journey with Exact Rush doesn't end here. Let's continue to explore, learn, and grow together.

www.ingramcontent.com/pod-product-compliance
Lightning Source LLC
Chambersburg PA
CBHW020322170426
43200CB00006B/242